PSYCHOLOGY IN INDIA

About the Editor

U. Vindhya is presently Associate Professor and Head, Department of Psychology and Parapsychology, Andhra University, Visakhapatnam. Although she had obtained her Ph.D. in Parapsychology, she subsequently shifted to gender issues due to ideological concerns. Her research interests include domestic violence, mental health of women, and the psychology of political activism. She has completed a major research project sponsored by the ICSSR on Domestic Violence in Andhra Pradesh and is currently engaged in a project on the Socio-Demography of Mental Illness. She has published over 40 research papers in national and international journals and edited volumes. She was the recipient of the South Asian Visiting Scholarship at Oxford University, U.K. and Visiting Lecturership at Eotvos Lorand University, Budapest, Hungary. She was the Managing Editor of *Journal of Indian Psychology* from its inception for nearly ten years.

PSYCHOLOGY IN INDIA
Intersecting Crossroads

Edited by

U. VINDHYA
Department of Psychology and Parapsychology
Andhra University, Visakhapatnam

CONCEPT PUBLISHING COMPANY, NEW DELHI-110059

ISBN 81-8069-029-6

First Published 2003

Published and Printed by
Ashok Kumar Mittal
Concept Publishing Company
A/15-16, Commercial Block, Mohan Garden
New Delhi-110059 (India)

Phones: 25351460, 25351794
Fax: 091-(11)-25357103
E-mail: publishing@conceptpub.com

FOREWORD

If change is the only constant in an individual's life, it can be said that diversity is the only reality in the life of a society, a culture or a group. Given the pervasive nature of diversity as a socio-cultural reality, social sciences can hardly ignore it. But the dilemma facing the social sciences to-day is compelling: do we look for diversity in unity or unity in diversity? In the discipline of psychology, this dilemma is manifested in the form of different approaches to the study of psychological phenomena and processes across cultures – cross-cultural and cultural psychology – and also in looking for general/ universal principles as well as context-specificity underlying behaviour.

This dilemma is symptomatic of an age in crisis, an age in flux, an age in which mutually contradicting trends towards divergence and convergence coexist. We are living in a world which appears to be coming together – end of the super-powers-dominated cold war, a more unified global economy, economic communization of the European nations and a sudden change in global cognition with highly sophisticated and efficient information network. It seems, we were never closer to realizing the vision of a global village. And, yet, convergent trends are matched by divergent forces almost everywhere. The end of the cold war came with the disintegration of a giant power nation (USSR) into smaller states resulting in conflict of interests. The global economy brought together the market forces worldwide and, at the same time, widened the economic gap across social classes within the nations and threatened the traditional bases of regional economies bringing in disharmony and conflict. While nations have come closer with politics of a different order – heightened sensitivity to human rights, alternate modes of conflict resolution, track II diplomacy, openness in information flow and liberal intervention etc. – the world is also witnessing increasing parochialism, assertion of regional identities, religious fundamentalism and intergroup conflicts. We are in an age of contradictions. While world comes closer and world trade gets increasingly unified, the very symbol of world trade, the World Trade Centre falls, disintegrates. While the future of political states becomes a point of debate, modern state being viewed as unnecessary and redundant by some and as indispensable by others, smaller entities and subsumed identities clamour for statehood. We talk of citizenship of one world as individualism reaches new heights each day. Caught in the quagmire of contradictions, with opposing forces tending towards universalism as well as individualism, we are left wondering: are we making progress or just going in circles?

Strangely, psychology, like other social sciences, seems to imbibe certain characteristics of the human society which it is supposed to study. Psychologists find it difficult to rise above the very processes under their scientific investigation; they construct reality very much like other individuals do. As a result, it is hard to escape the major dilemma facing the society in general. As we go global, sharing our understanding of near-universal principles of human behaviour, we also become conscious of the irrelevance of our endeavour to the immediate reality. While our pursuits towards understanding human behaviour and experiences lead us to discovering very general principles, we also show signs of self-consciousness, seeking to evolve indigenous perspectives all over the world. In India, psychologists approached the turn towards the twenty-first century by questioning the dominant western framework parading as the universal one. The nineties of the twentieth century, for psychology in India, were characterised by a fervent search for indigenous identity. Socio-cultural relevance, context-specific generalisations and problem orientation in research and development of the discipline became highly acclaimed slogans leading us to zealous debates on the nature and objectives of indigenization, conceptual issues in 'indigenous', 'indigenized', 'Indianized' and 'Indian' psychology. We seemed to have outgrown the alien perspective quite emphatically, to have reached the crossroad, despite the regressive pull of a large bulk of researchers choosing the comfort and safely of the oft trodden path, and, yet, the optimism was sometimes dampened amid the feelings of going nowhere but in circless. One needed the reassurance of definite signs of progress; signs of reaffirmation of our new found status and identity. This volume provides glimpses of such reassurance, of yet another positive departure from the so called main road. Yes, we are at the crosssroad of our own identity or, more aptly, our plural identities. There have been multiplicity of paths, true to our heritage and all leading us to discovering ourselves, our society and our cultures. The dilemma of the universal and the particular persists; so does the sense of progress. The work, research and views in this volume bear ample testimony to many a positive deviation from the hackneyed highway, to the new psychology in India being at intersecting crossroads.

The papers in this volume, ably edited, give us glimpses of new perspectives, new challenges and new ways of looking at reality, at our own reality. They challenge us to have our own network of scholarship, to have different interpretations and perspectives to mental health and counselling. This collection provides new approaches to understanding aspects of our reality – lures us to contextualize our research in diverse areas like linguistic behaviour and collectivism and to challenge our assumptions regarding models of development and organizational culture. As a whole, the volume provides refreshing insights on theory and applications. Perspectives are diverse in that they do not join the bandwagon and at the same time, there is an overarching concern for rooting psychology in our own cultural reality. These papers, selected from the eleventh annual conference of the National Academy of Psychology at Visakhapatnam, do share and project the vision with which NAOP was born. As a founder member and the first convenor of NAOP, I feel privileged and proud to commend this volume to my learned colleagues and young scholars of psychology in India.

February 02, 2002
Bhubaneswar

Ajit K. Mohanty
Professor
Centre of Advanced Study in Psychology
Utkal University

ACKNOWLEDGEMENTS

An endeavour such as organizing a conference and subsequently editing a volume based on the proceedings is not possible without the collaboration and support of a number of people. My grateful thanks to all of them.

To Prof. Anand Prakash and Prof. Janak Pandey, Convener and President, National Academy of Psychology (India), respectively for permission to edit this volume.

To all my colleagues, P.V. Krishna Rao, V.S. Bose, V.S. Pramila, K. Madhu, Shanti Prasad, Nirmala Devi, A. Ashok, M.V.R. Raju, T.V. Anand Rao and V. Harilakshmi for their sustained help throughout the preparation for the conference.

To the research scholars and students for all 'the running around' that is so critical for the smooth conduct of a conference. Thanks are particularly due to my research student, B. Nalini, for her secretarial help.

To the administrative staff, Bangaru Setty, Appa Rao, Janaki, Ramana Reddy, Simhachalam and Pydamma for their involvement in organizing the conference.

To Prof. Ajit Mohanty for writing the Foreword for this volume.

To Sri Ashok Mittal of Concept Publishing Company for promptly agreeing to publish this volume.

To all the contributors to this volume, I owe special thanks. Ultimately, it is the sense of belonging to a peer culture of discussion, debate, collaboration and exchange of ideas that makes efforts such as these worthwhile.

U. VINDHYA

CONTENTS

Introduction

U. VINDHYA

This volume is an outcome of selected papers presented at the Eleventh Annual Conference of the National Academy of Psychology (NAOP) held at Andhra University, Visakhapatnam, from December 14 to 16, 2000.

The Eleventh NAOP, organized at the turn of the new millennium, was meant to be an occasion for critical stock-taking of the development of psychology in the country, particularly in the past half a century, and reflection on the kind of identity and direction envisioned for research in this field in the coming years. The theme of the Conference was therefore titled as "Paradigms of Psychology in India: The Past and the Future" and the call to paper writers was directed towards this focal theme. Despite the call however, contributions poured in (130 papers in all) that were illustrative of two prevailing trends: one, the wide spectrum of research concerns of psychologists in India, and two, the single-track pursuit of research variables that have been by now flogged *ad nauseum*. Assembling these papers together into a volume proved to be both an arduous and exciting task; arduous because of the sifting for papers for thematic relevance and exciting because of the opportunity to sample current psychological research in India, that appears to be committed to diversity in a variety of ways, reflected in the broad range of topics, diverse samples and methods. The volume includes contributions of senior and experienced scholars and those of younger colleagues making their debut in the field. Some of the papers are explicitly critical of prevailing and dominant trends in the discipline, others without being self-consciously critical, have ventured into alternative ways of conceptualizing and doing research.

There has of course been no dearth of critiques of psychology in India. Much of the self-reflection has centred around the need to outgrow the colonial residue of following the alien (western) framework and move closer towards indigenous concepts (Sinha, 1986). Attempts at 'Indianization' of western psychological theories are not new, and have been present from the inception of western knowledge in this country. For instance, the reception of psychoanalysis in early colonial India was marked by an ambivalent relationship with attempts at 'Indianization' of psychoanalytic therapy made by combining psychoanalysis with Hindu philosophical and spiritual principles (Hartnack, 1990). These attempts illustrate how from the beginning, the importance of cultural particularity was suggested, even if not developed further for some time to come.

The beginnings of indigenization marked what has been termed as 'the phase of problem-oriented research' (Sinha, 1986) indicated by a growing acknowledgement of the limitations of the western model and the need to direct research towards concerns relevant to the country. After the initial euphoria of independence from colonial rule, this was also the phase (1960s to mid-70s) characterized by a crisis of governance, with problems of poverty, inequality and deprivation occupying the centrestage of public attention. Called upon to utilize their resources and expertise for dealing with issues of national development, psychologists in the country felt impelled to cast psychological research in a 'sociological mould'. The development of applied social psychology with a shift of focus from individual characteristics to those of social structures and processes was illustrative of this trend during this phase. Nevertheless, addressing themselves to the bulk of research, repeated pleas to address 'the crisis of relevance' (Pareek, 1980), to disengage from borrowed paradigms (Mohanty, 1988) and to contextualize research in local socio-historical and cultural settings continued to be made over the years. The three surveys of psychological research in India commissioned by the ICSSR (Mitra, 1972; Pareek, 1980; Pandey,

1988), while covering the range of research questions addressed during these periods, identified a major gap in the relation between research activities and social concerns of a society in transition. The fourth and latest survey (Pandey, 2000; 2001) once again addresses itself to the substantive array of research concerns emerging in recent years, ranging from animal behaviour and consciousness studies to health psychology and the psychology of gender in the first two volumes published so far. Underpinning most of the reviews contained in the latest survey is the call for cultural sensitivity.

The moves to position psychological research in India on an indigenous basis have not been without their share of confusion about the meaning of indigenization. Uncertainty persisted about the nature of indigenization and how to go about it. Indigenous research came to be understood either as a narrow search for uniquely narrow traits or concepts, or equated with early philosophical or religious (read Hindu) writings, or mere identification of difference with western research findings (Adair, 1996).

While it is beyond the scope of this piece to dwell on the nuances of the debate on indigenization, it may be relevant to call attention to what has been endorsed as indigenization by psychologists in the country. But before doing so, it would be worthwhile to restate two major perspectives on psychological universalism *vis-à-vis* relativism and their relevance for the debate on indigenization. The first viewpoint suggests that there is a powerful relationship between formal psychological theories and the cultural environments in which they are conceived and elaborated. This view is based on a metatheoretical orientation that the cultural context affects the structure and organization of psychological functioning in an essential manner. Taken to its logical conclusion, this would mean conceptualizing a different psychology for each culture (*cf.* Heelas & Lock, 1981, cited in Adair, 1996). The second viewpoint, on the contrary, does not take such a radical position. It assumes that all psychological processes are universal but that the manifestations of these processes can differ between cultures (*cf.* Berry *et al.*, 1992). This view does not argue for a separate psychology for each culture; rather, it proposes that indigenous psychology, developed as a reaction to western-centred psychology, is aimed at reformulation and use of concepts and instruments appropriate to local culture. In line with this perspective of cultural universalism, advocates of this approach argue for a culturally sensitive psychology.

Indigenous psychology as it has been broadly understood in India, has been regarded as a culturally appropriate psychology where it "addresses local behaviours and social issues of importance to national development" (p.56, Adair, 1996). Instead of seeking to develop a new or different discipline from within the culture, it seeks to overcome biases in conceptualizations (in this case the western bias) by recasting concepts in the light of insights derived from local cultural elements.

On an empirical level, the need to make research indigenous has been demonstrated in the choice of topics. The studies on socialization processes and practices; values, beliefs and orientations characteristic of Indian culture, as for instance collectivism and interdependent relational patterns; leadership styles; work culture; attribution; epidemiology of mental disorders are a few representative examples of attempts to make the discipline culturally appropriate in India.

The process of identity formation of psychology in developing countries has been likened to stages in efforts of social minorities to find a positively distinctive identity for themselves. Attempts to assimilate into the mainstream (in this case by replicating western studies) in the first stage are followed by moving to the opposite end of the spectrum characterized by anti-conformity and a search for distinctive cultural attributes. The third and final stage envisages moving beyond both the conformity and anti-conformity of earlier stages and the need for comparison with other cultures, towards a more pluralistic search for 'a psychology that works' (Carr & MacLachlan, 1998).

The crisis of identity is not singular to psychology and going by current reports, confronts several social sciences as well. Declining resource for research and teaching in social sciences as a result of the apathy of the state is only one dimension of the current crisis. Some of the issues identified as of critical importance for social sciences are: (a) relevance and the search for new methodologies, (b) transdisciplinarity and disciplinary grounding, (c) teaching-research nexus, (d) autonomy for the researcher juxtaposed with accountability, and (e) reflective *versus* problem-solving research (*e.g.*, Natraj *et al.*, 2001; UNESCO, 1999). Many of these issues have a bearing on the identity of psychology in India. While the search for relevance for psychologists in this country has largely been based on acknowledgement of the Eurocentric bias and efforts to outgrow the bias, several areas remain uncharted. Once again, it is beyond the scope of this essay to elaborate on these issues, but a few examples should suffice to illustrate my point. A number of studies (*e.g.*, J.B.P. Sinha *et al.*, 1994; D. Sinha, 1988) have called attention to characteristics of 'Indianness' such as hierarchical and status orientation, particularly based on caste and class, maintenance of personalized relationships, and embededness in ingroup. One would expect that the next step would be directed to an examination of entrenched inequalities and hierarchies that exist in India: to an exploration of power relations and their ramifications that form the essential basis of contemporary social life. Going through the annals of psychological literature however, it appears as if there are certain 'blind spots' with regard to exploration and critique of power relations, particularly, in the spheres of caste, gender, and religious grouping. It is almost as if contemporary movements of marginalized sections including women, subaltern classes and minorities, interrogating the premises of knowledge and power, have passed us by, without making any inroads into 'the amiable' psychology of the day. This despite the fact that caste, gender and communal relations and identities govern our everyday lives and our perceptions, values, and prejudices. It is only in recent years that a degree of questioning about the construction of psychological knowledge about women and its implications, and the emergence of a feminist voice are becoming evident (*e.g.*, Bharat, 2001; Davar, 1999, 2001; Vindhya & Kalpana, 1988; Vindhya, 1998). The recently burgeoning dalit literature, challenging the 'intellectual hegemony' of social science discourse, however, hardly finds even a reference in psychological literature. The quest for community in the form of various identity movements based on caste and gender, in fact, highlight the limits of individualistic premises in psychology. Our self-reflection about the nature and status of psychological research in India is centred around questioning the western bias, but perhaps does not extend to questioning the ideological basis of dominant power relations in our society.

Another dimension that impacts on the identity of psychology is the nexus between teaching and research. Ideally of course, there should not be any dichotomy between teaching and research since what is worth teaching is worth researching and vice versa. Over the past half a century or so however, the disjunction between the two is apparent in the call to eschew the predominance of western theories and work towards culturally-appropriate research on the one hand, and such research not finding a place in curriculum content and teaching practices in the class room, on the other. This disjunction has unfortunately, created a situation wherein the identity of contemporary psychology as culturally-appropriate and relevant is not conveyed in the class room. The exogenous hegemony of western ideas and concepts is supplanted by a double hegemony in the classroom: the predominance of western ideas and concepts on the one hand, and the elitist bias in curriculum content and teaching practices. Absence of good text books in regional languages, good translations of classics, further compound the issue.

Psychology in India has therefore progressed, but it can be argued that this has been along a fairly narrow track and central assumptions within the discipline remain essentially unchanged. There is a prescriptiveness and homogeneity at the heart of the mainstream discipline. Whether psychology has transcended the conformity and anti-conformity to borrowed paradigms referred to earlier, and moved towards being pluralistic is arguable. However, expansion of the boundaries of the discipline, a willingness to move away from 'disciplinary security' and cross the boundaries of our own discipline to engage in a meaningful dialogue with other social sciences represent some ongoing efforts that are noteworthy. Already evidence of such transdisciplinarity is emerging from the studies on health, language behaviour, gender, to name a few.

Several contributions to this volume engage with interrogation of the central assumptions of the discipline, the boundaries of the subject, and new ways of conducting research. T.S. Saraswathi's paper voices several concerns about the theoretical and conceptual foundations of psychology in India and the limited epistemology to which it subscribes. She calls attention to the dictates of the dominant positivistic-empiricist tradition which emphasizes context-free psychological knowledge, the hierarchical authority relations between researchers and the 'objects' of their study, among other issues, that continue to be accorded privileged status. More importantly, Saraswathi makes a number of compelling points about our practice and culture of doing research. She emphasizes on the need to transgress disciplinary boundaries, on the use of multiple methods and on the necessity to build networks. She makes the pertinent point that our research culture appears to be characterized by isolation in contrast to the communitarian values and group embeddedness that we claim to uphold as our dominant values. She highlights this isolation by titling her paper "If I have an idea whom do I talk to?" In line with the indigenous tradition, Saraswathi reiterates the importance of cultural context in the understanding of psychological phenomena.

Traditional academic psychology employs reductionist methods that set out to exclude both social context and the structural power relations between individuals as inherent 'bias'. The feminist critique questions these methods and their findings as they fail to identify the relationship between certain kinds of behaviour and the consequences of patriarchy and therefore reinforce what they identify as the 'natural' 'behaviours', for instance, those centred around gender stereotypical roles. There is evidence that psychology, by not problematizing power and context, has actively contributed to the subordination of women under the label 'science'. The feminist critique, by now has reiterated that positivist science, far from being value-free, exhibits a demonstrable bias towards the 'pathologization' of women, particularly in relation to mental and reproductive health. Bhargavi Davar in her paper on feminism, psychology and mental health contrasts the psychology of women tradition as against the feminist psychology perspective. While the former simply adds to the literature on women, riding on the bandwagon of visibility currently being given to issues related to women, the feminist approach is based on critical and oppositional knowledge. What is the basis of this critical knowledge going to be with reference to 'Indian' culture and mental health sciences in India? Bhargavi contends that western mental health professionals have pathologized the behaviours of alien cultures on the one hand, and on the other hand, feminist principles may be considered products of an alien culture, antithetical to 'our culture'. In the context of mental health of women in India, Bhargavi suggests that it would perhaps be more useful to adhere to the universality of women's rights and form linkages with the western feminist critique of mental health sciences rather than accept our traditional cultural values that have been shown to be oppressive and discriminatory to women.

The next set of papers all deal with the importance of cultural contextualization of a number of areas of enquiry ranging from language behaviour, person–other relationship such as the individualism-collectivism dichotomy, issues in psychological counselling to facial expression of emotion. A.K. Mohanty's review paper on psycholinguistic research in India focuses on the socio-cultural factors impacting on language acquisition and socialization, multilingualism, and reading processes. The fact that language is an integral aspect of culture and the fact that India is characterized by an enormous complexity of linguistic diversity, underscore the necessity of adopting a context-sensitive approach and method to study language behaviour. Mohanty notes that Indian studies have shown individual bi-/multilingualism to be a 'positive phenomenon' and the efficacy of mother tongue *vis-à-vis* English as medium of instruction at the primary level. These studies have also indicated that the development of reading skill in Indian languages is a result of literacy in general and alphabetic literacy in particular and not of phonological skills found to be predictive of reading proficiency in

English. Mohanty observes that the interdisciplinary nature of research on language, despite some dissociation between psychological and linguistic studies, has yielded relevant and problem-oriented research.

Individualism and collectivism, defined as alternative conceptions of the person–other relationship, have become increasingly important cultural variables that have been found to have significant effects on people's experiences and behaviour. For the most part, it has become typical to examine individualism and collectivism through comparisons between the cultures of the west, presumed to reflect individualism or sharp person–other boundaries, and those of the east, presumed to reflect collectivism or more porous boundaries between the person and his or her context. In line with earlier studies done in this area by the author as well as others, Jyoti Verma's paper engages with finer nuances of the dimension of individualism-collectivism. Using a student sample, she found vertical collectivism (subsuming of personal goals to in-group goals, and support to competitions of in-groups with out-groups) to be the most preferred orientation among four dimensions of the individualism-collectivism dichotomy. The least preferred was found to be vertical individualism with its emphasis on individual competition with others in order to achieve a distinct status. Obviously, collectivism as an explanatory construct that refers to embeddedness in ascribed and personal relationships cannot stand alone. Delving into its several components provides us with a more nuanced analysis. The adverse implications of vertical collectivism, as Jyoti points out, are that neither freedom nor equality are valued, reflecting the communalism of traditional societies. Although these results have been generated from a student sample, the findings go a long way in explaining our cultural orientation: the entrenched affinities to in-group ranging from kin, caste, region that promote inclusiveness, bigotry and hierarchical distinctions rather than egalitarianism and tolerance.

The universality-culture specificity debate is once again brought to the fore in an area of crucial concern such as facial emotion in

Manas Mandal and Mithilesh Singh's paper. While the universalists search for neurobiological roots of emotion, the proponents of the culture-specific view explain emotion on the basis of social construction. In an experimental study on the assessment of similarities and variations in the recognition of facial expressions of emotion across three cultural groups (Indian, Japanese, North American) Mandal and Singh come up with several interesting results, that recast the debate in favour of an integrated approach instead of setting up the universality hypothesis in opposition to that of culture specificity. The findings that facial expressions of the Indians were best recognized (by Indian observers) are attributed to 'in-group advantage' (when the observer and expressor belong to the same cultural background) thereby supporting the cultural view-point. However, there was no evidence of cultural variation in recognition of certain emotions such as happiness, sadness and disgust, leading to the conclusion that it is the nature of emotion that is crucial in determining recognition of emotional expression.

Sonali Bhatt-Marwaha's paper deals with the 'cultural paradoxes' that hinder the effectiveness of psychological counselling and therapy in India. The cultural collectivism that emphasizes close familial ties and a conception of self that is embedded and relational—of crucial support during crisis—could at the same time block or interfere with individuals' reach for psychological intervention beyond the family/kin ambit. Similarly, the goals of self-assertion and autonomy considered to be the bulwark of western therapies, can be problematic in our situation, particularly for women clients. Such issues draw us back to the question of universality of psychological constructs that may at times conflict with traditional cultural formulations of desirable behaviour. How does one then take a stand and adopt a balance between the interests of the client, the therapist's values, and cultural prescriptions? Taking refuge behind the presumed value-neutrality of psychology in such situations cannot be a justification.

The papers of Mamata Verma, S.K. Upadhyay and R.C. Mishra and of Aparna Vajpayee and R.C. Mishra focus on cognitive performance and socio-economic status. Despite the evidence of age-related unfolding of perceptual functions, the development of these functions was found to be mediated by environmental factors, leading to better performance of socio-economically privileged children (Verma *et al.*'s paper). Since differences in opportunities and experiences of learning account for the variation in the performance of deprived and privileged children, Vajpayee and Mishra examined the effects of intervention through cognitive stimulation and training programmes. The difference in the performance of these two groups of children was found to have levelled off due to exposure to the training programme, underscoring the necessity and value of intervention programmes for children from socio-economically and culturally deprived backgrounds.

Sexuality as a theme of research has been virtually an uncharted terrain in academic psychological research in India. The two papers of George Kurian and of Urmi Nanda Biswas and C.N. Daftuar grapple with this area of inquiry, though on completely different lines. In a wide-ranging and fascinating piece, Kurian focuses on the linkages between sexuality and cognition within a psychoanalytical framework and on the implications of the integration of sexuality with higher order mental functions in racial and ethnic differences. While some of his propositions are provocative, Kurian's discussion linking creative accomplishments of culture including literature, arts, science and technology to a rich and diversified sexuality, and higher forms of cognition to sexual restraint is based on an overarching review of psychobiological researches.

The empirical study of Biswas and Daftuar represents a different research agenda by locating the question of adolescent sexual behaviour within sexuality and health related issues. Combining quantitative and qualitative methodologies, the study attempted to explore both male and female adolescents' understanding and perception of their sexual needs, sexual health and health seeking behaviour. The study is also marked by use of a sample of respondents from a low-income locale, departing from the tradition of psychological research based on student samples.

Abhilasha Srivastava too in her paper on poverty and resilience keeps the lived experience of men and women respondents belonging to urban, low-income neighbourhoods at the centre of inquiry. Despite the well-established link between poverty and mental health, the presence of serious stress and adversity on the one hand, and the manifestation of competent coping or effective functioning, conceptualized as resilience on the other, has been the focus of recent research. Understanding the process of resilience seems to make more meaning particularly in the context of large-scale adversity in our country. Abhilasha's findings on gender differences in resilience and experience of socio-economic stress raise several questions. While her results pointed to higher scores of husbands on resilience and quality of family life, and of wives on experience of socio-economic stress, she does not stop at that point, unlike several studies that mention gender differences either without explaining why or by making misleading inferences that do not take into account the socio-cultural context of women's position in society. The issue of women's psychological health is currently being situated within the social context of their work and roles, a position that challenges traditional intrapsychic, bio-medical approaches in psychology. Abhilasha's findings of increased vulnerability of women to stress therefore need not be traced to the deficit model, but to their life circumstances. She points to factors women have to endure—alcoholism of the husbands and domestic violence—and that her women respondents had voiced, adding to the strain of economic adversity. The finding that the men reported a more favourable quality of family life is in line with earlier studies on marriage found to be more beneficial for men than for women. This finding has to be seen in the context of severe economic adversity, and care-giving functions that are traditionally perceived as that of the wife, combined with additional sources of stress for women such as drunken and violent husbands.

Sadhana Natu's paper on the 'culture of silence' is within the feminist framework of social construction of gender. She examines the ways in which speech and silence are mediated by aspects of social location such as gender. She refers to the socialization and cultural practices that define and delimit the 'appropriate' style and content of speech for women. She highlights the shroud of silence in which experiences such as sexual violence are submerged, to the detriment of women victims. She also makes an important point that while assertive articulation has been an integral part of consciousness raising in feminist therapy, it may not be very helpful with victims of violence for whom verbalizing the traumatic experience may be painful and for whom alternative methods need to be designed.

B. Nalini's paper examines the paradox of development taking the much-acclaimed 'Kerala Model' as a focus of inquiry and outlines the reported adverse social and psychological payoffs such as a high suicide rate, greater prevalence rate of mental illness, increasing violence against women in Kerala. While doing so, she takes care not to posit the two in a cause-and-effect sequence. Based on a select review of the vast literature in this area, she attempts to analyse the paradox in the context of Kerala's development experience.

Rachana Kulkarni and Shagufa Kapadia's paper on the process of marital partner selection in certain caste groups from low and middle-income areas touches upon two institutions that occupy the centre stage in our social lives: marriage and caste. Employing qualitative research methods, Kulkarni and Kapadia come up with interesting results that reflect the process of change and transition in societies such as ours. While factors like the involvement of parents and the kin network in the process of marriage partner selection are apparently common in both the upper and lower caste groups, some amount of flexibility is seen in the former. The flexibility is not however, always in the direction of being progressive, raising the question of flawed modernity that seems to characterize contemporary society. For instance, while education, a higher age at marriage, more involvement of the girl in the process appear to have been incorporated in the rule systems of the upper caste groups, factors like dowry and horoscope matching that continue to be essential requirements in these groups preserve the continuity of the traditional rule systems.

The last two papers focus on the industrial organizational

setting. Based on a review of research, K.S. Rajeswari and R.N. Anantharaman examine the antecedent and process factors of occupational stress among software professionals. Pointing to the gaps in this recently emerging area of research, the authors outline the probable role of psychological dimensions such as self-efficacy, locus of control and exposure to what they term as cross-cultural management (clients for software companies being global in nature) in stress among these professionals. In his study on organizational culture and performance, Kailash Srivastava assesses the impact of the strength of organizational culture, conceptualized in terms of strong leadership and a sense of shared core values, beliefs and qualities on organizational performance and individual effectiveness of a sample of executives drawn from private sector companies. As one would expect, the strength of organizational culture was found to have a positive effect on the financial performance of the organization as well as the performance of the employees.

After this summary of the papers included in the volume, one can perhaps make the (rather bland) statement that the volume provides a sample of the array of diverse topics typical of current psychological research in India. Moving beyond the present volume, some questions that arise with regard to psychology in India are : While diversity is to be welcomed, is there a unifying paradigm? Apart from issuing repeated declarations of dissociation from the western model in its attempts to address the 'crisis of relevance', is the vast corpus of Indian psychological research identified by a distinctive paradigm? What are the underlying ideological premises binding the discipline as it is practiced in India? While this may not be the place to discuss these issues at length, it needs to be mentioned as a tailpiece that this year's NAOP Conference (October, 2001) witnessed the re-surfacing of the debate between the philosophical (or Hindu spiritual) and the social psychological (or psychosocial) view-points, reiterating the point that psychology in India continues to be located within intersecting crossroads.

U. VINDHYA

REFERENCES

Adair, J.G. (1996). The indigenous psychology bandwagon: Cautions and considerations. In J.Pandey, D.Sinha, & D.P.S. Bhawuk (Eds.), *Asian contributions to cross-cultural psychology* (pp. 50-58). New Delhi: Sage.

Berry, J.W., Poortinga, Y.H., Segall, M.H., & Dasen, P.R. (1992). *Cross-cultural psychology: Research and applications*. Cambridge: Cambridge University Press.

Bharat, S. (2001). On the periphery: The psychology of gender. In J.Pandey (Ed.), *Psychology in India revisited—Developments in the discipline, Vol.2* (pp. 300-355). New Delhi: Sage.

Carr, S.C., & MacLachlan, M. (1998). Psychology in developing countries: Reassessing its impact. *Psychology and Developing Societies*, 10, 1, 1-20.

Davar, B.V. (1999). *Mental health of Indian women: A feminist agenda*. New Delhi: Sage.

Davar, B.V. (2001) (Ed.). *Mental health from a gender perspective*. New Delhi: Sage.

Hartnack, C. (1990). Vishnu on Freud's desk: Psychoanalysis in colonial India. *Social Research*, 57, 4, Winter, pp 921-949.

Heelas, P., & Lock, A. (1981) (Eds.). *Indigenous psychology: The anthropology of the self*. London: Academic Press.

Mitra, S. K. (1972) (Ed.). *A survey of research in psychology*. Bombay: Popular Prakashan.

Mohanty, A. (1988). Beyond the horizon of Indian psychology: The Yankee Doodler. In F.M. Sahoo (Ed.), *Psychology in Indian context*. Agra: National Psychological Corporation.

Natraj, V.K., Majumdar, M., Giri, A.K., Naidu, V.C. (2001). Social science: Dialogue for revival. *Economic and Political Weekly*, XXXVI, 33, August 18, pp. 3128-3133.

Pandey, J. (1988) (Ed.). *Psychology in India: The state-of-the-art (Vols. 1-3)*. New Delhi: Sage.

Pandey, J. (2000, 2001) (Ed.). *Psychology in India revisited (Vols. 1-2)*. New Delhi: Sage.

Pareek, U. (1980). (Ed.). *A survey of research in psychology 1971-1976*. Bombay: Popular Prakashan.

Sinha, D. (1986). *Psychology in a third world country: The Indian experience*. New Delhi: Sage.

Sinha, D. (1988). Basic Indian values and behavioural dispositions in the context of national development. In D.Sinha & H.S.R. Kao (Eds.), *Social values and development: Asian perspectives* (pp. 31-55). New Delhi: Sage.

Sinha, J.B.P., Daftuar, C.N., Gupta, R.K., Mishra, R.C., Jayseetha, R., Jha, S.S., Verma, J., Vijaykumar, V.S.R. (1994). Regional similarities and differences in people's beliefs, practices and preferences. *Psychology and Developing Societies*, 6, 131-150.

UNESCO (1999). *World social science report*. Geneva: Author.

Vindhya, U. (1998). Feminist challenge to psychology: Issues and implications. *Psychology and Developing Societies*, 10, 1, pp. 55-74.

Vindhya, U. & Kalpana, V. (1988). Women's dimension in psychological research: A critique. *Economic and Political Weekly*, April 30, WS 20-24.

1

If I have an idea whom do I talk to ? Toward building a sorority/fraternity of Scholars in the Discipline*

T.S. SARASWATHI

It is noteworthy that an invitation to deliver the Inaugural Address to a Human Development professional, a woman at that, for a Conference on Psychology, is in line with the theme of my paper, namely building bridges, networking, and reaching out, both, within and across disciplines.

The ideas I present today are the product of the pooled wisdom generated by colleagues from varied disciplines, who participated in a series of Symposia I had the privilege to organize during my professional tenure. I share the credit for the wisdom and take responsibility for inadequacies in interpretations. I shall focus today on selected issues and concerns, some of which are already part of our shared professional consciousness, and some of which we attend to only in passing. In my opinion, the latter need to be articulated, as they may prove to be crucial for the healthy development of the discipline, perhaps for it's very survival. After presenting a bird's eye view of some of the theoretical and methodological issues that continue to call for attention, I shall focus on three inter-related concerns, namely, communicating knowledge, developing an interdisciplinary frame of mind, and most importantly, networking or building a community of scholars. If time permits I will examine the implications of the above graduate training.

*Inaugural address to the NAOP Conference.

Need for Theory Guided Research

It may appear to be a trite observation to say that much of research in psychology in India, has been almost exclusively driven by an empirical tradition. Absence of a comprehensive and culture sensitive conceptual framework has been and continues to be a glaring lacuna which impedes scientific programmes in the field. One is often aghast, when conducting a literature search on any major topic, to note that nearly eighty percent of the published works are the products of a shot-gun or piece-meal approach that does not contribute to knowledge construction. Strangely enough, applied research seems to contribute more to meaning making than does the so-called basic research conducted in many of our university departments.

Exploration in gender perspective has been another missed opportunity. Theory based research provides rich opportunities for examining and questioning the existing theories in psychology and human development for their adequacy as explanatory frameworks for women's development and behaviour. Such a gender perspective sensitizes us to also explore the facets of the male psyche, left unexplored so far because of the existing belief system regarding how things ought to be. Like in the case of other unpackaged variables, the inquiry leads us to unpackage the process by which individuals and groups in different cultural settings become what they are, leading to the awareness that genetics is not destiny !

Need for Conceptual Refinement

Increasingly, Western scholars in the behavioural sciences, have evinced interest in alternative views of human development, such as the social constructionist view of Russian psychology. I am not sure to what extent the Indian schools of psychology have incorporated a broader repertoire of perspectives in their teaching and learning, compared to the restricted vision seen in earlier curriculum frameworks. Deliberating in this context, Baljit Kaur in her epilogue to our book on New Directions in Human Development and Family Studies (Saraswathi & Kaur, 1993), strongly advocated four aspects of theory construction and refinement. I reiterate them here as they are equally valid today in the soundness of the arguments and their relevance.

Baljit Kaur presents four related arguments (1) Going beyond description; (2) Going beyond outcomes; (3) Going beyond unidirectional relations; and (4) Going beyond singular notions of causality. I shall summarize them briefly here and build on these ideas.

Going beyond description

For reasons that are not hard to understand, we are fixated at the descriptive level, only rarely evincing adequate courage and conviction to move to a level of explanation. The answer to the question **what,** appears easy. But to address the questions **how** and **why,** pose a challenge that the field needs to confront.

Going beyond outcomes

Our second fixation is with independent variables and their perceived outcomes, skipping the vital intermediary of processes that account for why something came to be what it is. Let me illustrate this point with an example of a study that I reviewed in recent years. The study dealt with understanding women in poverty settings, obviously conducted by male psychologists. The major findings of the study were: (a) income, education, debt, and physical quality of life are predictors of perceived poverty; and (b) compared to men, women in poverty settings are more stressed, have more health problems and are more fatalistic !! The study had used one of those standard checklists or schedules, to ask for self reports. My own reaction to this and to several hundred studies of this nature, is why rediscover the wheel ? I could have predicted these outcomes in the absence of formal data. But more important is the possible use of an alternative paradigm that would have yielded richer and more meaningful results. What if the researchers had focused on the qualitative dimensions of how women cope in a male dominated, patriarchal society, and how despite poor nutrition and health care, manage to feed the children and hold the family together ? Even a cursory glance at some of the methodologically sound studies in feminist literature would have led to a stronger conceptual base. Of course that would mean going beyond the narrow confines of a mono-disciplinary boundary and a positivistic paradigm.

Going beyond unidirectional relations

The third point refers to the traditional adherence to the framework that artificially designates some variables as antecedents and others as consequences. A shift in perspective would involve inclusion of proximal as well as distal variables, and provision to examine bi-directional influences in all social interactions. Sandra Scarr (1985) comments as follows in the context of studying the effects of parental management techniques on children's intellectual and emotional development : "The truth about this world cannot be simulated by the isolation of single variables ... (p. 508).

Going beyond singular notions of causality

"(A) related problem is the proclivity to propound singular notions of causation for psychological phenomenon, be it the much debated nature *versus* nurture controversy in development, or a more circumscribed problem such as the perceptual problems hypothesis put forth to account for learning disabilities" (Kaur, 1993; p. 324). Use of multi-variate techniques in analyzing data and adopting an interdisciplinary approach would go a long way in formulating reasonable multi-dimensional causality models. Reality is far too complex to be captured by the limited tools available in a single discipline. And as far as statistical analysis goes, technical assistance is not difficult to obtain with access to sophisticated computer software, provided we have the conceptual clarity regarding the nature of relations we wish to examine. Often it is an extremely depressing experience to read doctoral work with a wealth of valuable data lost in the use of uni-variate analyses.

Communication

Having reviewed some of the theoretical and methodological issues that continue to plague the field, I move on to the next major concern, namely that of *communication.* The significance of effective and appropriate communication cannot be over emphasized. Infact, the conceptual and methodological issues mentioned earlier, can never be confronted and addressed in the absence of effective communication with significant peers. Several levels of communication can be highlighted which include : the subjects of our research; peers from our own and allied disciplines; the lay public as consumers of the knowledge constructed by us; and the policy-makers, regardless of whether they seek us or we seek them.

To begin with, a word about the significance of our communication with the subjects of our research. The idea of the objective researcher, distant and aloof from the subject is antiquated today. Understanding and empathy in the collaborative effort at "meaning making" by the researcher and the subject, calls for a renewed perspective (see Greenfield, 1997; Miller, 1997 and work in the area of situated cognition by Lave & Wenger, 1991 for detailed discussion on this topic). That a 'smart' subject can outwit a sophisticated but trusting researcher, is highlighted by Heath in an interesting example of how her teen-age research assistant and the assistant's peer accomplices managed to make-up near convincing false interviews, representing data from extremely different kinds of subjects (Heath, 1997). The point of Heath's argument is not the shock at the dishonest practice, but how these false interviews make transparent what subjects think the researcher wants from them. Cross cultural psychology is replete with amusing examples on this count.

The second group of significant others in our communication is our peers in the discipline. I shall mention only in passing here to the oft repeated caveat by Prof. Durganand Sinha of the proneness to "reverse ethnocentrism" among Indian psychologists, and to Krishna Kumar's strongly worded criticism that "the West has called for our salute too long". I would however, like to stress that in our communications related to the products of our scientific inquiry, there is a need for a careful articulation of our meta-theoretical assumptions, conceptual framework used, rationale for the method adopted, as well as the appropriateness of the statistical techniques used for analyses and interpretation. The folly of crass empiricism and over-generalization is captured picturesquely by Lawrence (1997) : "Let us be careful about labelling as theory generalizations from findings, about using paradigmatic and measurement constructs as if they were concepts, and about giving investigative procedures autonomy in our work. This will go some way toward stopping the wings from flapping the bird" (p. 292).

The third prime audience for our communication should be peers in allied disciplines as well as practitioners in our own discipline, for whom we must create easily accessible landscapes of disciplinary knowledge without the frills of the usual jargon that often obscures rather than enlightens. At least part of our failure in establishing interdisciplinary networks, a point detailed in the next section, can be accounted for as being due to failure in addressing this critical issue. Insularity instead of openness has only constrained our vision. The problem comes into even sharper focus when the audience for our communication are teachers and parents, who should really be the ultimate consumers of the knowledge that is generated in the field. The practitioner and the lay person can justifiably be a difficult customer, impatient with technical jargon. What is needed in communication in this context is expression in everyday language, minus the frills and pretentious jargon that, I suspect, even the authors cannot decipher. Heath (1997) provides a convincing argument in her paper on "Culture as the contested realm in research on children and youth" for the need for access to contemporary scientific knowledge for educators and counsellors often trained at a different historical time. To quote : "This means that those who see themselves as providing basic research will need to make their studies available in accessible forms. In addition, such researchers must find more ways of working directly with practitioners to produce conceptual tools for rigorous tests of validity than institutional settings offer" (p.115).

Lastly, I refer to communication with policy-makers with whom we need to liaison if we are to translate our "Laboratory" knowledge to the field. The policy-maker and programme planners are often generalists with little patience for discipline specific knowledge, and more receptive to viewer or reader friendly, precise communication. The key question remains "How seriously do we take our responsibility to construct knowledge and then to communicate the same effectively ?"

Towards Interdisciplinary Linkages : Some Reflections

Running through all the earlier sections has been the common thread of my plea for interdisciplinary linkages. In a modest fashion, and limited by my individual constraints, I have struggled to establish interdisciplinary networks and have personally gained immensely from this enriching exchange both, within this country and abroad. Often times, it has been akin to letting in the fragrance of fresh air.

During the recent decades there has been an increasing convergence of disciplinary interfaces among the physical and natural sciences*. Fields like Physics, Chemistry, Biology and Genetics, have facilitated the investigation of problems that are cross or multi-disciplinary by making their boundaries more permeable. Disciplines such as Biotechnology, Genetics and Nutrition, have made great strides in knowledge construction by transcending disciplinary barriers. Unfortunately, the same cannot be said of the social and behavioural sciences such as Psychology, Economics and Sociology which have remained predominantly insular. In fact, especially in India, there has been increasing specialization and compartmentalization even within social science disciplines.

The rationale for advocating an interdisciplinary perspective in teaching, research and application is not difficult to seek. Path-breaking contributions to the field have been made, both historically and on the contemporary scene, by scholars who themselves had

---

*The following section is reproduced with permission from a document prepared for the festschrift volume in honour of Dr. Wig, edited by Prof. Sreenivasa Murthy.

specialized training in more than one discipline, for example, Piaget, Lewin, Bruner and Cole, to name only a few. Understandably, such scholarship is hard to come by in a single individual. However, there exists a grossly under utilized potential for converging the expertise of several individuals who have specialized in allied disciplines and would stand to gain by establishing a network.

Conceptually, the arguments that support an interdisciplinary perspective in thinking or problem solving find favour with most scholars. Operationally, however, the ground reality is studded with hurdles. The factors that constrain an interdisciplinary perspective and exchange of ideas across disciplines, range from the limited nature of our specialized training to deep seated personal insecurities and ego hassles that come in the way of team work. I have often wondered why scholars from collectivistic and relational oriented cultures, such as in India, find it difficult to work as a team respecting each other's expertise, whereas those from highly individualistic and autonomy oriented cultures, as in the West, excel at team work (Saraswathi, 1998).

Having been associated with several interdisciplinary projects in the capacity of a participant (Barooah *et al*, 1994; Magrabi & Verma, 1987), a consultant or a co-ordinator (Saraswathi, 1993; Saraswathi, 1999; Saraswathi & Kaur, 1993), I have noted with interest the factors that seem to contribute to successful team work, when the team consists of experts from varied (allied or disparate) fields. These include : (1) charismatic and/or nurturant authoritative (not authoritarian !) leadership; (2) careful selection of team members, both in terms of their expert knowledge as well as their social compatibility or ability to work as a team member; (3) adequate funding to provide support services especially communication links and networking; and (4) clear goals and commitment to the same (even though at times, except in the case of the one wearing the leader's mantle, this may emerge in the course of the team's work). It is often interesting and heartening to watch the group dynamics that is coloured by skepticism at the initial stages, to a clear recognition of the strength of networking and gains accrued from mutual support, when it is time to part ways, having accomplished the task on hand.

The positive outcomes of concerted efforts by inter-disciplinary teams are many : For one thing it broadens the perspective of all participants. There is a convergence of expertise leading to meaningful problem solving. Moreover, there is a conscious avoidance of redundancy (the ritualistic re-discovering the wheel) with acceptance of the necessary know-how that is already available in another discipline. From the perspective of landscape making (Kumar, 1995, Round Table Discussion) of the required knowledge base, the inputs from allied disciplines definitely makes the landscape richer in quality. Another noteworthy gain from an inter-disciplinary partnership is the reduction in idiosyncratic, discipline specific jargon in order to facilitate cross disciplinary communication.

Towards Indigenization

One of the least explored, yet intriguing facets of the inter-disciplinary approach, is the promise it holds for strengthening indigenization or cultural relevance of knowledge construction*. I foresee this possibility because some of the social science disciplines are more grounded in their cultural roots (Anthropology and Sociology), compared to others that have a history of heavy leaning on Western theory and empiricism (Psychology, Education and Psychiatry). A good mix of the two can lead to a healthy exchange by which the latter is enriched with an infusion of cultural meaning, and the former by methodological rigor and alternatives. To quote Enriquez (1977), the Filipino psychologist : "the development of such a psychology represents endogenous indigenization, wherein culture is treated as a source for theoretical constructions, rather than exogenous indigenization, wherein culture is treated as a target of investigation" (p. 240).

In listing the gains that can accrue from an inter-disciplinary

---

*It is noteworthy that in Ongel & Smith's (1994) analyses of 721 articles in the 96 issues of JCCP published between 1970-1993, indigenization as a theoretical basis of studies, was noticeable by its absence. Of course, this could also be a reflection of JCCP's editorial policies.

perspective and endeavour, one cannot gloss over the problems and constraints. As mentioned earlier, successful inter-disciplinary programmes have been characterized by strong leadership, commitment to a cause, respect for others' disciplinary expertise, and funding, none of which are easy to come by. Nevertheless, it is a worthwhile endeavour to provide a forum for exchange of ideas, be it on a focussed problem solution or a broader canvas of landscape making in a relevant area of knowledge.

A Plea for Building a Network of Scholars in the Discipline

During the past three decades in this profession as a teacher, a researcher, a consultant, there is one single chorus I have heard, cutting across gender, region and languages: "Whom do I talk to when I have an idea". In conferences, seminars, workshops, and in letters penned by young men and women in remote corners of this country, the voices are different but the despair is shared, namely, the absence of a fraternity of scholars who can provide peer support for sounding ideas, critiquing, challenging, and providing an impetus to establish a strong indigenous knowledge-base. It appears paradoxical that in a culture that is supposed to be collectivistic and relational, among people who are not known for their reticence in expressing their view on everything ranging from personal problems to politics, we are unable to build teams that will support and grow together. Knowledge construction is a collective exercise and it is a matter of great concern that we are unable to bring together in a sustained manner, a group of committed scholars, to reflect on ideas based on inquiry and contemplate on a shared social reality.

In a Round Table meeting, organized by me in 1995, Krishna Kumar mused over whether the problem was related to our perception of how knowledge is constructed. He argued that the Indian scholar, at least in some of the social sciences, tends to treat knowledge as a pre-constructed product, with little attention to the process of production, because we see ourselves not as theory builders and creators, but sonly as consumers of knowledge generated abroad (read West). At the most, we may see ourselves as producers of scholarship with which others may choose to formulate theories and construct knowledge (see Introduction in Sarawathi, 1999). It is said that a good scientist must be at one and the same time confident and an iconoclast (Connolly, 1997). What is our problem ? Confidence or conviction ? It would be too glib to attribute it merely to our colonial legacy.

Discussions with Western scholars on this issue, highlight the fact that, when the Western scholar is using a concept, he/she is in dialogue with his own tradition – he is an integral part of the cultural milieu, its language, its metaphors, and its history (Kumar, 1995 at the Round Table Discussion). Such an embeddedness, if at all it exists in the case of the Indian scholar, is blurred. Hence we seem to fall back on letting the West have the standard setting role. It is only when we reach the turning point of dealing with some of the issues articulated above, and are willing to debate, dialogue, or at least converse about them, can we hope to attain salvation from what Prof. Sinha used to call the "immortality of irrelevance" and steer the discipline in its rightful trajectory. If this argument is seen as relevant, a forum like the National Academy of Psychologists can deliberate on ways and means of promoting and sustaining networking at various levels.

Heath (1997) offers a few suggestions that may be useful in this endeavour, "scholars of different radically different epistemologies can join together to push for more long-term follow through studies to benefit findings from several fields and areas of policy interest" (p.119). This implies the coming together of anthropologists, sociologists, historians, psychologists, educators and other specialists, depending on the topics of common interest (language development; psycho-social intervention, etc.). This coming together is also likely to break the false dichotomy between qualitative and quantitative methodologies. "Collaborative research partnerships ... will open a rethinking of categories, instruments, and discursive practices that have heretofore gone unquestioned. These integrated approaches offer a high goal for scholarship and a considerable challenge for clinical practice and education, as well as hold promise for understanding much about socio-cultural processes we have not yet begun to imagine" (p.122).

As of now, I shall conclude with a few implications that can be drawn for graduate training as the students are torch bearers of tomorrow.

Implications for Graduate Training

Marsella (1998) presents some useful and interesting arguments in favour of training students in what he terms as global – community psychology. He recommends that such a programme could include areas such as cross-cultural psychology, cultural psychology, indigenous psychologies, international relations, cultural anthropology, urban sociology, public health etc. While it sounds Utopian at present, it is appealing in its practical wisdom and could help make the study of psychology more relevant, especially for the non-western world. In order to meet the new challenges of globalization and market economy, "The training must involve multi-cultural, multi-disciplinary and multi-sectoral premises, methods and interventions. This will ultimately promote inter-cultural, inter-disciplinary and inter-sectoral thinking" (p. 1289). Plenty of food for thought there, for psychology in India. At a less ambitious level, the following recommendations may contribute toward building a curriculum in psychology that will move in the direction of the grand plan offered by Marsella.

1. Provide a sound grounding in Theory and Research Methodology with emphasis on the need for flexibility and imagination as well as cultural sensitivity in theory building and research design.

2. Make a conscious effort to contextualize in an indigenous as well as a cross-cultural perspective, developing an attitude of critical inquiry.

3. Build a network of Indian scholars through graduate colloquia, workshops and seminars, along with a regularly updated bibliography of Indian publications in Psychology and Allied disciplines.

4. Develop a sound programme of internship of adequate duration in socially relevant settings.

5. Encourage applied and policy oriented research. Gear basic research also toward the ultimate criterion of understanding real people behaving in the real world !!

REFERENCES

Barooah, R. *et al* (1994) (Eds.). *Capturing complexity : Women, Households & Development.* New Delhi : Sage.

Connolly, K. (1997). Foreword. In J. Valsiner, *Culture and the development of children's action : A theory of human development* (2nd ed.). (pp. iii-v). New York : Wiley.

Enriquez, V.G. (1977). Filipine psychology in the Third World. Philippine Journal of Psychology, 10, 3-18. Cited in Ho, D.Y.F. (1993). Relational orientation in Asian social psychology. In U. Kim & J.W. Berry (Eds.)(1993) *Indigenous psychologies : Research and experience in cultural context.* (pp. 240-258). Newbury Park : Sage.

Greenfield, P. M. (1997). Culture as process : Empirical methods for cultural psychology. In J.W. Berry, Y.H. Poortinga & J. Pandey (Eds). *Handbook of cross-cultural psychology.* Vol. 1 (pp. 301-346) (Second edition). Boston : Allyn & Bacon.

Heath, S.B. (1997). Culture : Contested realm in research on children and youth. *Applied Developmental Science,* 1(3), pp. 113-123.

Kaur, B. (1993). An agenda for future theory building research and action. In T.S. Saraswathi & B. Kaur. *Human development and family studies in India : An agenda for research and policy.* (pp. 317-335). New Delhi : Sage.

Kumar, K. (1995). Round Table Discussion. *Symposium on Socialization in the Indian Setting.* Baroda, December 13-18, 1995.

Lave, J. & Wenger, E. (1991). *Situated learning : Legitimate peripheral participation.* Cambridge : Cambridge University Press.

Lawrence, J.A. (1997). Developmental science : A case of the bird flapping its wings or the wings flapping the bird. In J. Tudge, M.J. Shanhan & J. Valsiner (Eds.), *Comparisons in human development : Understanding time and context.* Cambridge, MA : Cambridge University Press.

Magrabi, M. & Verma, A. (1987). *Household resources and their changing relationships.* International Agriculture Publication. General Series Number 3. University of Illinois at Urbana – Champaign.

Marsella, A.J. (1998). Toward a "Global – Community Psychology". Meeting the needs of a changing world. *American Psychologist,* 53 (12), pp. 1282-1291.

Miller, J. G. (1997). Theoretical issues in cultural psychology. In J.W. Berry, Y.H. Poortinga & J. Pandey (Eds). *Handbook of cross-cultural psychology.* Vol. 1 (pp. 85-128) (Second edition). Boston : Allyn & Bacon.

Ongel, U. & Smith, P.B. (1994). Who are we and where are we going ? JCCP approaches its 100th issue. *Journal of Cross-Cultural Psychology,* 21 (1), 25-53.

Round Table Meeting Proceedings (1995). *Symposium on socialization in the Indian context.* Unpublished manuscript. M.S. University of Baroda, Baroda.

Saraswathi, T.S. (1993). *Reaching out : IDRC-HDFS research network (India).* Final report (unpublished). Department of Human Development & Family Studies, M.S. University of Baroda, Baroda.

Saraswathi, T.S. (1998). Many deities, one God : Convergence of cultural and cross-cultural psychology. *Culture & Psychology, 4 (2),* 147-160.

Saraswathi, T.S. (Ed.) (1999). *Culture, socialization, and human development.* New Delhi : Sage.

Saraswathi, T.S. & Kaur, B. (Eds.) (1993). *Human development and family studies : An agenda for research, policy and action.* New Delhi : Sage.

Scarr, S. (1985). Constructing psychology ; Making facts and fables for our times. *American Psychologist,* 40 (5), 499-512.

Srinivasa Murthy, R. (in press). Mental health in India.

2

Feminism, Psychology and Mental Health*

BHARGAVI V. DAVAR

Psychology and Feminism : The Question of Exchange

The contemporary question of the relevance of psychology in a 'developing' society and in a multi-cultural context is being addressed in the mainstream. However 'gender' as an important area of thinking, research or curriculum has so far been resisted by the University Departments. On the erroneous assumption that feminist psychology is about 'women's issues' having no larger place within the mainstream discipline, it is left solely to Women's Studies Centres, to the Certificate or Refresher courses. Over the years there has been a steady increase in the number of women teaching Psychology. This has not necessarily entailed a woman-centred or woman-powered view within the discipline. Unless there is an overall change within the University system, just the presence of women can hardly matter. Perspectival, attitudinal and curricular changes have not happened, as, the structural and decision-making processes within the Universities have remained patriarchal. The 'modernisation' of Psychology has meant selective growth in some areas such as Health, Behavioural, Occupational or Organisational and Cross-cultural or 'Asian' Psychology, which promise direct consequences for 'national development'.

* Revised version of the Millennium Lectures given at the NAOP Conference.

Feminists, often working outside the mainstream, have been substantially contributing to theoretical and methodological issues within Psychology. However focus on the discipline itself, its institutionalisation, the growth of pedagogy and the professions, and how feminism must intervene there, if at all, have not been given the same importance. The question of teaching and doing feminist research in Psychology within oppressive institutions that have doggedly retained their colonial paint is yet to be contended with. So these concerns have mainly remained within the subjective realm, as the experiential reality of feminists having to conduct academic work within a patriarchal institution resistant to social change.

The recalcitrance of Psychology to feminism deserves a studied explanation as movement of thought and critique of the gendered nature of discourse have happened to some extent in other social sciences. Vindhya (2001) has suggested that feminism and psychology are founded on ideologically opposite principles about human beings: *collectivism* versus *individualism.* Feminism is a radical movement theorised into a discipline of thought about men and women in communities. It is based on the axiom that the 'personal is political' which has been repeatedly substantiated in using 'gender' as an analytical category while examining the private sphere (such as family and domesticity). So, notions of 'rationality', 'personality', 'self', 'autonomy', 'privacy', 'consent' etc., which form the technical and ethical backbone of psychology have been questioned as often serving patriarchy and the presiding cultural imperatives. Attempts have been made to re-script these notions with 'gender' as the site of understanding. In doing so, it was evident that the *individual* can no longer be the unit of conceptualising mentality and a structural approach had to be utilised. Therefore, personal space had to be recast in political terms, against considerations of hierarchy and power in society, and their impact on a collective, *viz.*, women.

The attempt to create *both* a 'feminist psychology' *and* 'a psychology in feminism' is experienced to be sometimes difficult for individual feminists. The tensions between the two fields of thought and praxis may be reconciled in interesting ways but may possibly never go away. Therefore, straddling Psychology and Feminism together may result in a feeling of double bind. We find ourselves being told *both*, that in bringing gender into psychology, we are dealing with 'soft' issues, and that, in accepting scientific epistemology, we are not critical enough as feminists! Feminism in India, because of its strong roots in left ideology has always questioned scientific epistemology and any focus on the individual, as an expression of knowledge/power. Feminist psychologists have the double burden of persuading *both* the patriarchy of the discipline as well as the relevance of science and method. They have to deny *both* the mainstream view of a value-neutral, a political science as well as the sceptical position that science is *only* about power. In practical terms, this double bind induces a sense of rejection and isolation from *both* psychology and feminism.

One way of reconciliation (Davar, 1999a, 2001; Natu, 1999; Shah, 2001; Vindhya, 2001) is to question available theories in Psychology from the point of view of restoring women's subjectivity and life-world. The feminist theories of psychology from the West have inspired these efforts. They have showed how social power rules mentalities, and regulates women's individual behaviour. In this sense, a shift in the analytical framework of psychology from the individual to the socio-political has been adopted. Feminist questions of science and scientific method 'cast doubt on the positivistic view that science discovers pre-existing facts and that the scientific method can effectively safeguard against the intrusion of values and biases into the production of knowledge. An alternative view is emerging which sees science as embedded in the history, politics, and culture of society. In this view, psychology, like all science, is a cultural institution and a social activity subject to external influences as well as internal regulation' (Marecek, 1989, p. 369).

The feminist critical view is in line with other efforts in addressing disciplinary issues in psychology and its accountability to social equality. Kahn and Yoder (1989), Prilleltensky (1989) and Garrett and Graham (1990) write about the purist view in mainstream psychology on mind, mental states and about individual behaviour, devoid of history, culture and social power. It is the view that enchanted psychologists like Fodor who imagined psychology to fall within a 'methodological solipsism', where we can isolate, name and manipulate, like a crystal of salt, purely logical entities called 'mental states'. In this view, the individual is chosen as the site of change and as the basis of social welfare and service activities. There is the nearly *karmic* or deterministic assumption that outcomes of these activities are due to an individual's own (psychological) action and that people (should) get what they only deserve (*e.g.*, the common assumption underlying AIDS policy / law / interventions in India). Macro-level social processes are not taken into the account here, and when individuals fail to fit this model, as they invariably will, they get blamed for it as having certain 'immutable' personality traits or 'life style' problems. This is how psychology, and in general, the mental and behavioural sciences, maintain the *status quo* and assist the state by regulation of individual behaviour, quelling dissent and in maintaining the social order.

There is an overall lack of a critical perspective in the mental and behavioural sciences in India and academic Psychology has never addressed issues of power, inequality and social change directly. It has never addressed *oppression* and *resistance*, and the mentalities of marginalized peoples who survive, cope with and overcome oppressive life contexts. This lack within the discipline in itself is symptomatic and may need more studied historical and cultural explanations. It has however sustained the ideological basis of psychology within the cosily situated spiritual, upper caste, affluent or middle class, patriarchal worldviews, leaving the gendered and structural basis of Indian society unquestioned. This has limited the growth of the discipline precluding relevant debates about post-modernity. Here, I refer to issues pertaining to cultural revivalism and the contestations about cultural and national identity; the question of religious minorities, *dalits*, and other oppressed groups and what psychology can offer them; and other important issues that psychology must address in a post-colonial nation-state where subjectivities are contested on multiple fronts.

Gender in Psychology

Why do we need a special analytical concept like 'gender' within psychology? Feminism is the theorisation of the women's movement at one level, and at another, it is a critical radical discipline which studies the way 'gender' (masculinity/femininity) is constructed within discursive practices (*i.e.*, knowledge systems and other representations of thought). It is a critical, cultural and historical study of the worldviews of both men and women, of communities and of society in general, about their construction of gender and how they use it to regulate the intellectual as well as the daily life. With respect to the mental and behavioural sciences, feminism is about "how certain social perceptions and attributions of anatomy, physiology, behaviour, personality, cognition and social roles have defined and delimited *masculinity* and *femininity* in cultures, thereby regulating the lives of men and women, their subjective experiences about self, body and emotion" (Lohokare & Davar, 2001, p. 367). 'Gender' in its analytical scope and implications for practice is inclusive of both femininity and masculinity.

For instance, it is of interest to feminism that some men, especially of the lower classes or castes, or men, who suffer from a psychiatric diagnosis such as psychosis, are often portrayed in the human science literature and the popular media as being overly aggressive to the point of violence. Regular newspaper reporting of violent and 'deranged' men 'vandalising', 'disrupting', 'attacking', etc., has elicited our critical response. Such irresponsible reporting often shows scant regard for individual dignity or the imperative of confidentiality. Similarly, upper caste solidarity pan-gender is expressed in showing *dalit* boys to be sexually aggressive and abnormally, savagely masculine (Tharu & Niranjana, 1994). We may recall racist psychology favoured the view that blacks were sexually promiscuous, hyperactive, aggressive, violent etc. In these examples, the masculinity of the men is played up and exaggerated in order to impose certain social and other punitive sanctions. These perceptions then work against the community as a whole, where for example, the *collective of men with psychosis* or *dalit men* are seen as violent *as a whole*, and a naturalised, causal connection is proposed between savage or 'uncultured' minds, mental illness and violence. This putative connection in the social consciousness tightens the nexus between marginalisation (race, class and caste), masculinity, criminalisation and insanity.

In the case of women, similar kinds of gender politics in inter-personal negotiations are forwarded. Women's emotional lives are undervalued, misinterpreted or used for societal goals serving a regulatory function. Aggressive women, for example, (as Dimple Kapadia of *Zakme Aurat* or Rekha of *Khoon Bari Mang*) are seen to be heroic women whose masculine heroism is often justified within the context of marriage, heterosexuality and a morality of conjugality. They are not seen to be acting on behalf of all women, on behalf of all *wronged* women, nor for that matter, is there any possible justification from the point of other types of sexual moralities. Certain types of emotion, *e.g.,* aggression, seem to be acceptable in men but in women, it seems to need a special culture-accommodating understanding. Some aggressive women are also labelled as 'witches' and burnt or killed even today in India. Women who cry all the time, or who have lived a life of suffering in their marital homes, are given symbolic powers, again in an individual way, for *e.g.,* the proverbial Tamil heroine, *Kannagi*. In Tamil Nadu, in the South of India, *'Kannagi'* signifies the chaste wife who not only endures her husband's abandonment, neglect and infidelity, but also upon his wrongful execution by the king, avenges his death. In a fit of depressive rage she burns the city down by tearing off her breast and tossing it into the city. In a highly interesting collection of essays, Lutz and Abu-Lughod (1990) have theorised the diverse cultural contexts wherein 'outlawed' emotions of women are situated within the rules of patriarchy. This continues the line of critical thought set forth by writers such as Bailey (1983), Hochschild (1983), Heller (1982), Schweder and Levine (1984) and others who have written about the politics of emotion in communities. Other examples of how gender, and women's psychological lives, get constructed and regulated by socio-cultural worldviews have been discussed in the Indian literature.

Gender and Methodology in Psychology

Two main trends may be seen among feminists considering the sciences, as discussed by Peplau and Conrad (1989). One is what Sandra Harding calls the 'Successor Science' which envisages a day of reckoning and redemption following the Feminist Revolution when all scientific concepts will be replaced by an entity which will not in anyway resemble modern science in its assumptions of objectivity, universality and rationality. The second trend, which I am more inclined to agree with, is feminist realism[1] (Davar, 1995, 1999, 2001). This view sees (1) science as a type of *acceptable* human behaviour, (2) accepts rationality as an important condition of the construction of science, and (3) while not aiming to discard scientific ideas entirely, questions and rescripts them from the location of 'gender' (and other marginalisations) making the discipline answerable to social change[2]. While there is no *essential or logical* contradiction between science and social change, the *value* interest of knowledge may be questionable, problematising praxis.

Arguments have been made that there is a special methodology called 'feminist' methodology and that only certain types of methods are valid from a feminist point of view. Thus the emphasis on 'ethnographies', 'experiences', 'narratives', 'qualitative methods', 'documentation', etc. and the scepticism about data, statistics or quantification. However, Peplau and Conrad (1989) have argued against the claim that certain types of method are *essentially* feminist, or that there is a unique or particular type of feminist method. The issue of scientific method is a general issue in the philosophy of science, whether natural or social, and radical concerns we can articulate about *any* method (such as universalism, reductionism, and culture relevance) are one and the same. Sexism in Method is not about *which* method is to be used, qualitative or quantitative. When used with a vested interest in patriarchy or cultural domination, both these methods may be sexist. Methods are tools to be used for specific purposes and have no ontological status. Only an *ontological* assumption that *qualitative methods describe (women's) reality better* can entail the feminist preference for this method and their scepticism of other methods. But ontological assumptions are anathema from a feminist point of view. We would therefore want to shelve the question of preferences in Method, keep criticism alive regarding *all* methods, and simply question the worldview, theory, intention and purpose to which a particular tool, *any* tool of science, is put.

Peplau and Conrad (1989) further argue that sexism is not about who are the subjects (men, women or both), or who does the research, man or woman. In India, too, there has been the twin concerns (Natu, 1999) expressed about (1) not creating spaces within feminism for feminist men, and (2) contending with the phenomenal growth of a 'Women's tradition' in Psychology where no *feminist* perspective is forwarded. Indian Psychological Abstracts, reviews and bibliographies over the years have showed an enormous growth in the 'women's tradition' paradigm, not necessarily contributing to the growth of a feminist psychology[3]. To talk in terms of 'gender', as against 'women', is to have a *political* view about knowledge/power.

In reiterating the theme that it is the perspective which marks a research study as 'feminist' and not the type of method used, Sheilds and Dervin (1993) list the following as what they believe to be core assumptions of feminist research :

1. The phenomenological value of women's experience of their social and personal worlds.
2. The recognition of gender and gender relations as learned or constructed.
3. Awareness of self-reflexivity, inter-subjectivity and gender-reflexivity in the research situation.
4. A belief that research is for social equality, emancipation and social change.

The psychological research interest in the area of women and work has existed for some decades. I give an example to illustrate the difference between the 'psychology of womens' traditions and feminist research in psychology. In explaining why there seems to be a tendency for women to have comparative levels of achievement at work, the 'psychology of women' tradition has 'found' the following: low achievement motivation, a fear of success, 'the mommy track' (women choosing care giving or maternal roles as avenues of satisfaction), or the 'impostor phenomenon' (not internalising a feeling of success and therefore always feeling like an impostor). As is evident, these are proposed as deficiencies that 'inhibit' a woman from equal achievement in the work sphere.

A feminist view of the same phenomenon would focus on: job discriminations; serving only in support or housekeeping functions; lack of support at home for work and lack of appreciation of a woman's success; overload of caring functions at home; ineffective birth control; lack of reproductive choice; sexual harassment at work; the devaluation of women's performance at work; and the lack of role models. The feminist framework has looked at the entire social context within which the 'psychology of women' and her low achievement levels are played out.

Shah (2001) has given an extensive review and suggestions for making clinical psychology free from gender bias. Among her suggestions I mention only: avoiding gender stereotypes in question formulation; generating new, woman-friendly explanations where only biased views exist (*e.g.,* in victimisation by violence); re-formulating gender warped research priorities (*e.g.,* in defining 'basic' research *vs.* 'specialised'); inclusion of both men and women in research studies; avoiding ad hoc decisions about dropping one sex, or sex differences because of contingent or even analytical reasons; avoiding the use of negative connotations or biological explanations in attributions or labels of sex roles; accurate reporting of non-hypothesised gender differences; adequate controls and appropriate significance tests, multiple validation to rule out competing explanations to that of sex differences; use of both quantitative and qualitative techniques to bring out contextual variety across sexes and heterogeneity within sexes; and avoiding definitely sexist approaches [*e.g.,* 'Women performing roles appropriate to their sex are mentally healthy'] or theories. Woman related subjects (reproductive experiences, experiences of body and sexuality, friendships, community, work and domesticity) need to be more extensively studied in the context of psychology and mental health, using woman-friendly methodologies.

Mental Health and Women

Normative ideas on mental health have been constructed on the 'male as normal' [or 'male/healthy, female/insane'] model. By implication, women, their cognitive and emotional lives, their 'life-worlds', and femininity in general has been seen as definitively psycho-pathological. Repeatedly, feminists in India have objected to the pathologisation of women's lives, behaviours and mentality, and the normalisation, legitimation or condonement of oppressive social circumstances of domesticity or the public sphere. Feminists in the West notably Phyllis Chesler, Elaine Showalter, Barbara Ehrenreich, Carol Gilligan, Juliet Mitchell, and more recently, Joan Busfield, Ussher, Annemiek Richters, Nancy, Felipe, Russo and others, have kept up a critical tradition *vis-à-vis* the mental and behavioural sciences. They have seen the proliferation of diagnoses within the DSM ('Diagnostic and Statistical Manual' of the American Psychiatric Association) as a means of bringing more and more of women's psychological and sexual behaviours within the highly controlled regime of psychopathology. Of special interest has been the 'mother-bashing' literature explaining psycho-pathological development, pathologisation of natural sexual and reproductive processes and victim blaming in the context of 'treating' marital violence (Vindhya, 2001). The diagnoses of 'hysteria' [which, incidentally, one still found in the Indian literature until the 1990s] has proved to be a sexist museum piece in diagnostic history. 'PMS' [Pre-menstrual syndrome], 'depression', 'post-partum depression', etc., have been recast by including women's 'voices' and critical ideas about women's experiences of sexuality and emotions (Davar, 1999c). Feminists have argued that diagnoses such as 'Masochistic Personality Disorder' which was later changed to 'Self-Defeating Personality Disorder', as a 'category requiring more study', are disempowering for women, as they characterise feminine traits as pathological (Richters, 1999). Richters wonders about the gender warp in psychiatry which sees 'Extreme Dependency' as an abnormality, which is a definitively feminine trait, and not, for example, 'Extreme Independency', a masculine trait. Also, why is it that women, who often have to care for an old and ailing or a substance abusing husband, a few children at different levels of development, ailing parents or other elders, are called '*dependent*'? The women operating in the domestic sphere have to juggle a few hundred household chores, budget their time and resources, plan in advance, procure, clean and stock, and put away for a rainy day. Why is it that they have been denied an *instrumental* rationality in the psychological literature?

Kahn and Yoder (1989) in discussing alpha bias (the bias that men and women are *naturally* different) and beta bias (the bias that men and women are the same) in psychological and feminist theories, say that they would prefer to assume a beta bias position and stand by the 'men and women are equal' feminist position but with the caveat that *social* factors, rather than natural or biological ones, have led to any noted gender differences in mentality. Valid differences in cognitive and other dimensions of mental life are small and most claims of 'cognitive deficits' in women have been shown to be a deficit of understanding of the wishfully thinking male scientist!

Practising mental health professionals often use concepts in order to explain or understand clinical aspects. In the context of women, such concepts include 'dependency', 'affiliative drive', 'high emotionality', 'sensitivity to rejection', 'hysterical personality', 'neurotic suggestibility', 'weak ego', etc. Such clinical concepts are often validated in a circular way, by making reference to 'clinical experience' or 'clinical research'. They are rarely validated through extra-clinical studies. When used in understanding marital situations, for example, these concepts only forward disempowering views for a woman, who is now left with having to work that much harder at perfecting her female role, improving domesticity, caring functions and relationships. She has to do this with the now added 'knowledge' that there is some inherent deficiency in her anyway, and so, however hard she works, she is never going to succeed. Such constructs forward *values* through the clinic, and not science! Attitudinal research has shown that counsellors, social workers, clinical psychologists and psychiatrists do respond to gender within the clinic in multiple value laden ways, though the impact of this on treatment outcome is unknown (Shah, 2001).

Questions can be raised about the sexual morality of clinical practise especially about :

1. The use of sexual stereotypes, social expectations and cultural imperatives as pre-given, and not clinically negotiated values for clinical work.
2. Exclusive and vicarious focus only on issues of sex, sexuality, sexual preferences and sexual relationships even when sexuality is not an area of personal conflict.
3. Disregard of sexual boundaries, unresolved transference/ counter-transference and sexual exploitation of clients.
4. The use of non-validated sexist theories or clinical concepts.
5. Use of culturally accepted systems and values and counselling against woman's self-interest.

Clinicians have been urged to explore the sexual morality of their clinical practice using their own casework narratives. Certain ethical principles of practice have been demanded from the point of view of women patients, gender and sexual morality (Davar, 1999a).

Conclusion

Various aspects of women's lives (domesticity, work sphere, motherhood are some examples) are culturally endowed with significances, not always in the woman's interest. Cross-cultural paradigms and 'cultural' understandings of human behaviour have addressed the issues of modernity without at the same time compromising on the cultural imperative of conformity for women to stipulated social roles (Davar, 1999). In bringing together a list of concerns about 'culture' in psychology, Pedersen, Carter and

Ponterotto (1996) ask: 'Should culture be preserved at the expense of women who 'carry culture on their backs?' They question whether 'cultural sensitivity' could be a way of condoning injustices and preserving the *status quo* (also see Prilleltensky, 1989). The authors point out how culture mediates gender and wonder what would the end product of a discipline, which aims at equality among culture, gender and life style, look like. These concerns have been expressed in the context of women in India and their mental health, particularly in examining psychological and counselling practices on victimisation by domestic violence. Mental health professionals, even those of Indian origin working with migrant Asian populations in the West have argued for middle-line views that do not upset traditionally held values. Feminists who have critiqued cross-cultural ideas in mental health opine that claiming a universality to the 'women's rights' issue and making linkages with western feminist criticism of mental health sciences, is at the moment more consequential to a discourse on Indian women's mental health than an acceptance of patriarchal values brought in by 'culture'. We await the articulation of woman-validating views in cross-cultural psychology and psychiatry.

The cultural paradigm is based on the valid judgement that western mental health professionals have pathologised the behaviours of alien cultures. For example, non-westerners who are possessed or go into trance have been given various diagnostic labels, reviewed by Barthalomew (1990), including 'hysteria', 'psychosis', 'multiple personality', 'schizophrenia', etc. Women, more prone to possession than men, are said to be 'neurotic', 'suggestible', having a weak personality/ego structure, etc. Psychoanalytic interpreters such as Gyananath Obeyesekere have seen the women as infantile and as not having grown out of a certain type of hysterical sexuality.

But traditional understandings of possession are equally problematic. *e.g.*, the community within which the women play out these behaviours may see the women who does not get possessed as failing their cultural expectations (Skultans, 1991)! On a scientific definition, such women are mad, on a communiutarian definition, the women are bad! Kalpana Ram (1992) has extensively documented a women centred understanding of such phenomena, which tries to escape the double bind that both science and tradition seem to wrap them in.

Psychoanalysts make linkages between 'Hinduism' and 'Indian psychology' to make that discipline 'culturally' relevant (Kakar, 1981; Vaidyanathan, 1999). However, this effort has been full of disempowering and blame-building claims and assumptions about women, women's bodies, sexuality, motherhood, and understanding women's 'depression' (Davar, 1999b). Some of the most insidious claims made repeatedly in this literature have been the following: that in the Indian culture, 'the hegemonic mother' is the 'master narrative' against which the developmental lives of sons are built. This mother, who is supposed to be the typical Indian mother, is characterised to be suffering from sexual repression, unresolved oedipus conflict, and a consequent depressive rage. She then neurotically and obsessively turns towards her son and finds attachment in a covert (or overt) sexual manner. The Indian male's psyche is said to develop with a central focus on this sexual monster who is Mother!

Kakar's (1997) extensive documentation of casework 'validating' these themes may be read as background to this summary presentation. The feminist interrogation of this text alone would run into several tens of pages. Among the criticisms raised, we may make a note of atleast the following :

1. The fathers, and their problem behaviours, especially their neglect, physical or sexual abuse of their sons is rarely addressed. It could be argued that the 'symbiotic' bonding between mothers and sons, and the 'effeminacy' of Indian men has more to do with protesting the authority of the father, either his symbolic power or his actual power (as in violence/abuse).
2. Lack of data. So little is known about Indian women's sexuality, and about sexuality in motherhood, that these claims do not seem to be based on valid information.

3. The patriarchal context of motherhood and parenting in general, in India, and the complexity of marital relationships within patriarchy, are rarely addressed.

'Cultural' interpretations have to appreciate the reality that women (and other marginalised groups) often experience tradition, domesticity and community as coercive. They may 'adjust', 'accommodate', 'comply', 'internalise' or 'cope', but in the final analysis we need to recognise oppression as the appropriate analytical concept. Their seeming 'consent' to this oppression is to be viewed against the patriarchal context of domestic and social life. The mental health professional practising in whatever cultural context need not assume, as a first assumption, that 'cultural' worldviews have no experience of oppression.Ideas such as "sati" is a type of suicide ", " Child sexual abuse has a ' cultural ' basis," commonly found in the literature, need to be treated with extreme caution. Whenever a "cultural" explanation is forwarded, in a hierarchical and diverse cultural context such as India, it is always significant to ask, '*whose* culture?' as also ' who is speaking for whom? '

In the context of writing about 'culture' in psychology, often only the elite Hindu views are forwarded. Views from other religions, castes and communities from India are significantly omitted. For example, Sinha and Kao (1997) note the absence of an Islamic perspective in their book. This book makes an appeal for 'indigenous' psychologies and makes interesting disciplinary linkages between diverse 'Asian' philosophies and religions. The authors justify their neglect of the Islamic perspective thus :

> "One reason for not incorporating a piece on the Islamic perspective is that our selection has focused primarily on the South and East Asian regions. It is not that we accord less significance to the traditions, perspectives and developments of other regions of Asia" (p.19).

The authors seem to suggest that the Islamic perspective in

psychology cannot come from India and that Muslim psychologists are only in other countries, perhaps Pakistan or the Gulf! At best, this is professional naivete, at worst, it is cultural sophistry facilitating exclusion. Just as we cannot take the Indian 'community' for granted, in the proposal for 'indigenous' psychologies, some thought and caution must be exercised as to who constitutes and constructs 'indigeneity'. 'Indian' psychology and psychiatry have been peopled by Hindu gods and icons, even that, mostly Sanskritic: Ganesha, Kartikeya, Devi, Rama, etc. The elitist assumptions of the mental and behavioural sciences have worked against the psychological experiences of women. The following example highlights the expectations of early psychologists from upper caste women. De (1946) in Bengal 'closely observed' the 'symptomatology' of 'Married Spinsters' to include the following :

> "Some women cannot tolerate the idea conveyed in the words wife and mother.
>
> "Signs of married state which are prevalent in different societies are not accepted by these women.
>
> "The vermilion mark on the forehead of Hindu women, which is the most important and essential distinctive mark of the married state is objected on various grounds.
>
> "The veil is often discarded.
>
> "The iron bangle worn by Hindu married women is interpreted by them as an 'irony' of fate" (De, 1946, pp. 84-85).

Such women who could not adjust to their caste status or their marital status were said to be suffering from unresolved oedipal conflicts. It was said that psychoanalysis could cure them of this disease!

In contemporary India, the mental and behavioural sciences have a responsibility to respond to the issue of communalism and marginalised mentalities and belief systems, in the context of the vast increase in ethnic dynamics and violence. The very contestation of peoples to a 'subject' status within the nation - state and the linkages with the colonial process need to be addressed. The cultural revivalism, 'saffronisation' of India and its linkages with socio-economic processes of neo-colonialism is to be addressed along with the development agendas of psychology.

Labelling of women's behaviour, especially through the proliferation of 'neurotic' disorders where women are supposed to predominate brings more and more of situational behavioural responses of women within the 'illness' paradigm. A socio-political understanding of how power regulates knowledge and human behaviour is a much-required foundation for the mental and behavioural sciences. Women's bodies, the linkages with their emotional lives, the contextualisation of these within the larger socio-political processes, and the linkages with a patriarchal worldview should be necessarily addressed by psychologists. In forwarding 'cultural' ideas there is the need to always foreground the question, *whose* culture. Deprived groups often experience cultural articulations of scientific ideas as doubly oppressive. The rationalism of science and the morality of culture often complement each other in producing a doubly hegemonic totalising narrative. Women especially have to suffer this double hegemony. The foundational linkages between colonialism, communalism and psychology and the implications for women are yet to be more fully treated and can enable rich future research. I urge a re-appraisal of pedagogy and curricula in Psychology against these concerns. Someone has to ring the wake up alarm within the University as in the outside world, more and more of us express concern about creating empowering women's spaces within a globally accepted 'development' and 'human rights' scenario that seems to have nurtured a violent cultural revivalism. Psychology and the other mental and behavioural sciences, need to refurbish their foundations in order to meaningfully address the gender question in the context of a politically transforming Indian society.

NOTES

---

[1] As elaborated in these texts, science for me is about having consensually arrived at worldviews and techniques for keeping the planet peaceful, habitable and caring

for all of humanity. Realism, for me, is a habit of language that human beings in general, and scientists in particular, speak, in order to negotiate their lifeworlds in a *meaningful* way. 'Meaning', like 'rationality', 'truth', 'objectivity' and 'reality' itself, is a myth, but, a myth that we seem to necessarily need.

[2] Unlike disciplines such as sociology and anthropology, the health and behavioural sciences, based in medicine, chemistry and neuro-science, do have strong components of the natural sciences which cannot be completely dismissed. In partaking of a social science leaning in mental health, I have often found myself helplessly holding the question, "What to do with the genes, the brain, and the neurotransmitters?"! The social constructionist paradigm is very much strained when a person with a diagnosis of manic-depression is *relieved* to know that his or her disorder may be inherited or that drugs have *helped.*

[3] Some supposedly progressive 'women's ' universities ' have included subjects on Women and Psychology where the texts and materials provided will hardly be described as being of contemporary relevance. They only serve to reinforce existing social, gender stereotypes and social inequality. While not encouraging the women students to think critically, they only contribute to teaching a patriarchal morality.

REFERENCES

Bailey, F.G. (1983). *The tactical uses of passion: An essay on power, reason and reality.* Cornell: University Press.

Bartholomew, R.E. (1990). Ethnocentricity and the social construction of 'mass hysteria'. *Culture, Medicine and Psychiatry, 14(4),* 455-494.

Davar, B.V. (1999a). *Mental health of Indian women: A feminist agenda.* New Delhi: Sage Publications.

Davar, B.V. (1999b) Indian psychoanalysis, patriarchy and Hinduism. *Anthropology and Medicine, 6(2),* 173-193.

Davar, B.V. (1999c). *Gender, depression and emotion.* Unpublished manuscript.

Davar, B.V. (2001) (Ed.). *Mental health from a gender perspective.* New Delhi : Sage Publications.

De, N. (1946). Married spinsters. *Indian Journal of Psychology, 21 (1-4),* 84-85.

Garrett, R. & Graham, G. (1990). Why not naturalistic psychology? *Philosophia, 20 (1-4),*pp. 377-385.

Heller, A. (1982). The power of shame. *Dialectical Anthropology,* 6 (3), 215-228.

Hochschild, A.R. (1983). *The managed heart.* California: University of California Press.

Kahn, A.S. & Yoder, J.D. (1989). The psychology of women and conservatism.

Rediscovering social change. *Psychology of Women Quarterly, 13,* 417-432.

Kakar, S. (1981). *The inner world: A psycho-analytic study of childhood and society in India.* 2nd ed. New Delhi: Oxford University Press.

Kakar, S. (1997). *Culture and psyche. Selected essays.* New Delhi: Oxford University Press.

Lohokare, M. & Davar, B.V. (2000). Women in disasters and mental health: Special issue on Disasters. *Indian Journal of Social Work,* TISS, Mumbai

Lutz, C.A. & Abu-Lughod, L. (Eds.). (1990) *Language and the politics of emotion.* Cambridge: Cambridge University Press.

Marecek, J. (1989). Introduction. *Psychology of Women Quarterly, 13,* 367-377.

Natu, S. (1999). Psychology and the need for feminist interventions. Paper presented at '*Women and mental health: Planning gender sensitive community interventions.* Organised by Bapu Trust for Research on Mind and Discourse, Pune, September 17-18 at YMCA, Pune. Bapu Archive, Pune, No. 1999/bapu/wk-1/1. Pune : Bapu Trust.

Pedersen, P.B., Carter, R.T. & Ponterotto, J.G. (1996). The cultural context of psychology: Questions for accurate research and appropriate practice. *Cultural diversity and mental health,* Vol. *2(3),* 205-216.

Peplau, L.A. & Conrad, E. (1989). Beyond non-sexist research : The perils of feminist methods in psychology. *Psychology of Women Quarterly, 13,* 379-400.

Prilleltensky, I. (1989). Psychology and the *status quo. American Psychologist, 44,* 795-802.

Ram, K. (1992). *Mukkuvar women: Gender, hegemony and capitalist transformation in a south Indian fishing community.* New Delhi: Kali for Women.

Richters, A. (1999). Trauma as a permanent indictment of injustice: A socio-cultural critique of DSM-III and DSM-IV. *Curare, 22(1),* 13-20.

Schweder, R.A. & LeVine, R.A. (Eds.). (1984). *Culture theory: Essays on mind, self and emotion.* Cambridge: Cambridge University Press, pp. 215-237.

Shah, A. (2001). Gender issues in mental health: A clinical psychology perspective. In B.V. Davar (Ed.) *Mental health from a gender perspective* New Delhi: Sage Publications.

Sheilds, V.R. & Dervin, B. (1993). Sense making in feminist social science research : A call to enlarge the methodological options of feminist studies. *Women's Studies-International Forum, 16(1),* 65-81.

Sinha, D. & Kao, H.S.R. (1997). The journey to the East: An introduction. *Asian perspectives on psychology* (pp. 9-22). New Delhi: Sage Publications.

Skultans, V. (1991). Women and affliction in Maharashtra: A hydraulic model of health and illness. *Culture, Medicine and Psychiatry, 15 (3),* 321-359.

Tharu, S. & Niranjana, T. (1994). Problems for a contemporary theory of gender. *Social Scientist,* 22(3-4), March-April, 93-117.

Vaidyanathan, T.G. (1999). *Vishnu on Freud's desk.* New Delhi: Oxford University Press.

Vindhya, U. (2001). From the personal to the collective. Psychological / feminist issues of women's mental health. In B.V. Davar (Ed.), *Mental health from a gender perspective* (pp. 82-98). New Delhi: Sage Publications.

3

Multilingualism and Multiculturalism:
The Context of Psycholinguistic Research in India*

AJIT K. MOHANTY

Psychologists all over the world are pleading for development of indigenous framework reflecting a concern that psychology must be culturally embedded and contextualized in order to be relevant (Mohanty & Prakash, 1993; Sinha, 1984, 1986, 1996; etc). In India, the growing literature on indigenous psychology (*e.g.*, Adair, Puhan & Vohra, 1993; Misra & Mohanty, in press; Sinha, 1986, 1989, 1993, 1996) shows the concern over western dominance (Mohanty, 1988), and rejection of such dominance (Sinha, 1981) characterised as a "movement" (Sinha, 1996, p. 135). While rejection of western dominance is not an end itself, it underscores a necessity for understanding psychological processes in the context of immediate socio-cultural reality. Theory, problems and methodology of psychological research must be contextualized. In respect of psycholinguistic research, this is quite obvious since language is an integral aspect of culture and the processes of acquisition of language and enculturation are inseparable. "The acquisition of language is culturally conditioned and language is the most potent device through which cultural knowledge is transmitted. Children develop competence in their language, communication and other socio-cultural

*Revised version of Millennium Lecture given at the NAOP Conference.

functions through participation in social interactions (Gardner, 1984; Ochs, 1986; Vygotsky, 1978). Such interactions provide the contextual framework for language which acts both as a transmitter of socio-cultural knowledge and as a powerful medium of socialization" (Mohanty, 2000a, pp. 208-209). The literature on language socialization has emphasized the mutual role of language and cultural processes. Mohanty (2000a) has shown that the formal code and functions of language are embedded in the cultural context which sets communicative norms and priorities. The ethos of language in society — the dominant monolingual or multilingual norms, the degree of pluralism, sociolinguistic conditions of language use, linguistic policies and planning — influence the goals and social priorities in communication. These influences are reflected through a variety of forces operating at the individual and societal levels such as assimilation/ integration and shift/maintenance orientations in respect of culture and language, degree of monolingualism, bi-/ multilingualism, relative social emphasis on orality or literacy etc., which are associated, in turn, with major social issues in respect if official language, medium of instruction, vitality of minor and minority languages. In a review of social psychological aspects of multilingualism in India, Mohanty (1990) has shown how the processes underlying language contact and maintenance can be understood in terms of sociolinguistic features of Indian society. It has been shown, for example, that the complementarity of languages in various domains of language use in India and similar other patterns of language use ensure a non-competitive relationship between them leading to maintenance rather than shift of languages in language contact situations. Understanding of psychological processes underlying linguistic behaviour is incomplete without an appreciation of the socio-cultural context as well as the formal and structural features of language. In view of the enormous complexity of Indian multilingualism, the sociolinguistic diversity and the dynamics of the relationship between various languages and their user, any theoretical and conceptual framework for language behaviour in Indian must take note of the context conditions as well as characteristics of languages. Mohanty (2000a) has represented this relationship in a model which is shown in Fig. 3.1

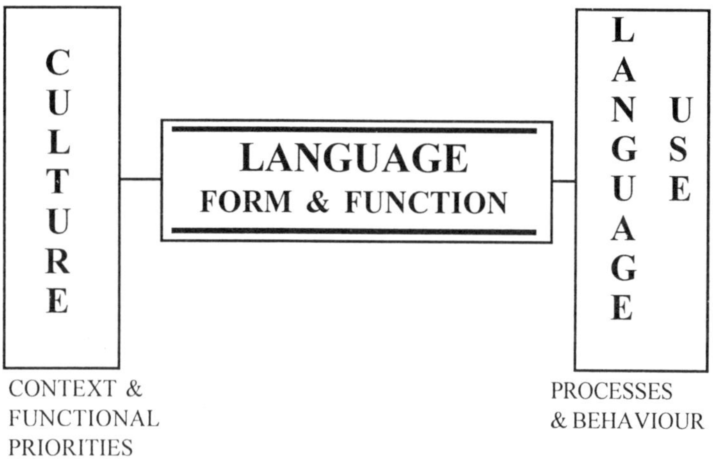

Fig.3.1 : Relationship between Culture, Language, and Language Use (after Mohanty, 2000a)

According to this model, a host of socio-cultural functions such as the prevalent social norms regarding pluralism, multilingualism, official language policy and planning, norms of language use and other sociolinguistic factors affect communicative goals and functional priorities which are necessary parameters in the process of acquisition of languages, language socialization, individual and societal bi-/multilingualism, linguistic identities and preferred modes of language use in various domains of communication etc. Thus, psycholinguistics in India must adopt an indigenous framework based on sensitivity to and due appreciation of the sociolinguistic and cultural context. In this review, I have sought to examine the major trends in Indian psycholinguistic research to analyse the extent to which developments in some major areas of study have been sensitive to the need for contextual and indigenous framework. Research in three major areas *viz.* (i) language acquisition and socialization, (ii) multilingualism, and (iii) reading processes, are reviewed in this paper since these are important and representative areas constituting the bulk of Indian psycholinguistic studies.

Language Acquisition and Socialisation

Studies on language acquisition across various cultures and languages have generally combined the shifting theoretical paradigms in linguistics with cross-linguistic methodology (Mohanty & Perregaux, 1997). Data from different languages have called for a re-examination of earlier assumptions based on studies from English language and at the same time, they have also drawn our attention to the necessary relationship between unique features of specific languages and the strategies in their acquisition. For example, Slobin (1982) has pointed out, the strategies for acquisition of subject subject-verb-object (S-V-O) languages like English are different from those of S-V-O (subject-object-verb) languages like Turkish and Indian languages. In the former, word order serves as a reliable marker for grammatical and semantic relationships, whereas in the latter object inflections play a major role. Thus, it is quite evident that the underlying processes of acquisition are better understood by an appreciation of formal features of language making an inter-disciplinary approach quite imperative. Unfortunately, Indian research lacking in such inter-disciplinary and cross-linguistic perspectives have generally failed to capitalise on the Indian linguistic diversity. Review of Indian research (Mohanty, 2000a) shows that psychological studies have focused on environmental conditions of acquisition in typically cross-sectional analyses whereas the form and structure of language have been focused in linguistic studies using longitudinal data. Thus, while psychologists have been global in their approach in an individual difference paradigm, linguists have studies phonological and syntactic development with little emphasis on psychological processes. Major trends in various Indian studies on language acquisition can be summarized as follows :

(a) Studies on phonological development have primarily focused on formal aspects of the sound system of language. Despite studies in various languages such as Hindi (Sharma, 1969), Tamil (Thirumalai, 1972), Kannada (Kumudavalli, 1973; Sridevi, 1976), Telugu (Nirmala, 1981a, b) etc. cross-linguistic comparison fails to go beyond looking at the sequence of acquisition of specific sound features of such languages. As Vasanta (1992) has noted the approach is purely linguistic rather than psycholinguistic.

(b) In respect of morphological development, Indian studies show broad cross-linguistic similarities (Devaki, 1987, 1992) in order of acquisition as well as the process of inflections and derivations. Indian researchers seem to be satisfied in demonstrating similarity with studies of English speaking children (*e.g.,* Brown, 1973) without considering the possibility that such similarities may be artifacts due to use of common and borrowed grammatical categories (Mohanty, 2000).

(c) Acquisition of a broad range of syntactic and semantic features has been analysed in several Indian languages. Such features include case relations (Lakshmi Bai, 1983/1984, 1984; Nirmala 1981a; Sailaja, 1989), negation (Lakshmi Bai, 1986; Usha Devi, 1990; Vaidyanathan, 1984), and interrogation (Vaidyanathan, 1988). These studies mainly focus on the order of acquisition and although such orders are different from that reported in respect of English speaking children, there is little effort at conceptual level analysis.

(d) However, some features of Indian languages, such as flexible word ordering, have been exploited in understanding the processes underlying language acquisition. In respect of word order, two issues have been addressed - preference for and developmental priority of certain orders over others, and the basis of choice of word order in language use. Studies with Oriya locative sentences (Mohanty & Mohanty, 1981) and grammaticality judgement of Telugu sentences (Vasanta, Sastry & Ravi Maruth, 1994) have shown a preference for subject-object-verb (S-O-V) word order over other possible ones. Word order preferences in case of bitransitive sentences are not consistent. Some studies (Mishra, 1994, Vasanta & Sailaja, 1993) show a preference for subject (S)—indirect object (IO)— direct object (DO)— verb (V) word order whereas others (*e.g.,* Mohanty & Mishra, 1985) show a preference for S-DO-IO-V order. It must be noted, however, that, in case of Indian languages, case markers and object inflections seem to be reliable indicators of syntactic and semantic relations in sentences. Studies on production of Hindi locative propositions (Mohanty & Mishra, 1982; Mishra & Dubey, 1987) show that children follow a pragmatic topic-comment strategy. When two objects (nouns) are pictured in a certain locative relationship, in describing the picture children followed a word order in which the noun topicalized by prior context occurred earlier in the utterances. Thus, when the prior context cards focused on a 'cat', for example, the main picture card showing a cat sitting under a table was described as ***billi mej ke niche baithi hai***, whereas the same was described as ***mej ke niche billi baithi hai*** when the context cards focused on a 'table'. These studies show a clear inter-disciplinary approach focusing on typical linguistic features of Indian languages in understanding the process of language use.

(e) Indian studies on factors affecting language development hardly go beyond showing a relationship between several characteristic variables such as SES, deprivation and disadvantage, caste, and home environment etc., and measures of language development. The processes through which such relationship is mediated in case of Indian children are least understood. However, there are some exceptions. Anjali Singh (1987) studied the development of some linguistic skills of 2 to 3 year olds growing up in Indian joint families of different levels of social class and in orphanages. She analysed the nature of interaction in children's environment and noted that language development is not affected by social class as such but by the quality of linguistic environment to which members of the joint families (mother, father, grand parents, siblings) contribute. The study showed a significant positive contribution of grand mothers to language development of children. There are also some intervention studies (*e.g.* Mohite, 1983; Sahu & Swain, 1985) which add to our understanding of the role of cultural variables in language acquisition besides showing an application orientation.

Analysis of the trends in acquisition research (Mohanty, 2000a) leads to the following general observations :

(i) Despite a rich tradition of scholarly study of language and grammar and the challenging linguistic diversity in our multilingual set up, Indian research on language development lacks an indigenous orientation and conceptual framework. Methodology and problem of Indian studies remain confined to disciplinary boundaries creating a cleavage in the focus of linguistic and psychological studies.

(ii) Formal characteristics of Indian languages as well as processes of influence of environmental cultural conditions need to be emphasized in cross-linguistic studies in India.

Studies on Language Socialization

Social interactions provide for a child the context of language and also act as transmitters of socio-cultural knowledge. Through repeated participation in such interactions children are socialised to develop culturally appropriate communicative competence. The process of language socialization is defined as "socialization through language and socialization to use language" (Ochs, 1986, p. 2). Through the process of language socialization, children learn the linguistic codes as well as socio-cultural conventions for their appropriate use. Mohanty and Perregaux (1997) have analysed some specific cultural devices in language socialization which has some common goals such as transmitting affect and values in communication, orienting towards status and role appropriate language use, developing stylistic preferences and functional priorities in social communication. In addition, when a child grows up in a multilingual society goals of language socialization are also somewhat different and special. For example, a language user must learn to communicate in multiple languages by developing awareness of language variations and develop strategies to deal with such variations and functional separation of languages into different domains of social communication resulting in situation and interlocutor specific differentiation of languages in use as well as hierarchy of preferences. The task of language socialization in multilingual context is further complicated by the requirement of code switching and code mixing in routine social interactions. Mohanty (1994c) has listed some specific goals of language socialization in the context of Indian multilingualism. In a recent study, Mohanty, Panda and Mishra (1999) have analysed the developmental pattern in multilingual socialization into three periods each further differentiated into two stages as follows:

(i) ***Period of Language Differentiation***
   (a) *Emergence of language differentiation*
   (b) *Knowledge of language differentiation*

(ii) ***Period of Awareness of Languages***
   (a) *Emergence of social awareness of languages in use*
   (b) *Development of social understanding of the role of languages*

(iii) ***Period of Multilingual Functioning***
   (a) *Assignment of functional roles to languages*
   (b) *Multilingual functioning in communication*

The language socialization studies are necessarily embedded in the sociolinguistic context of Indian multilingualism. These studies draw our attention to the special adaptive strategies which Indian children seem to develop through the process of multilingual socialization early in development. Although the specific mechanisms of such socialization is not fully understood it seems to be leading to appreciation of diversity and pluralistic norms which make individual bi-/ multilingualism a positive phenomenon in India. In this respect, Indian studies on bilingualism bring a refreshingly distinct conceptual and methodological perspective.

Studies on Bilingualism

The field of blingualism research in India seems to have developed a multidisciplinary perspective with meaningful contributions from linguists, psychologists and speech pathologists. The focus has been on conceptual issues, cognitive and social consequences of bilingualism and applied pedagogical issues in respect of medium of instruction and mother tongue education. Some studies have also been addressed to development of bilingualism, nature of speech pathology among bilinguals and and development of reading and writing skills of bilinguals.

Defining bilingual persons or communities as "those with an ability to meet the communicative demands of the self and the society in their normal functioning in two or more languages in their interaction with other speakers of any or all of these languages" (p. 8), Mohanty (1994a) offers a classificatory system for different types of bilingualism. In his work individual and community level bilingualism in India has been conceptualized as the first incremental step towards societal multilingualism linking grassroots level bilingualism to non-competitive and maintenance oriented relationship among languages in the Indian society.

Contrasted with the western studies in which bilingualism is usually confounded with cultural differences (between the monolinguals and bilinguals), the Indian studies in general and Mohanty's Kond studies in particular (see Mohanty, 1994a, for details) have drawn comparison samples of bilinguals and monolinguals from the same culture. The findings of these studies as well as other Indian ones (*e.g.*, Southworth, 1980) have been conceptualized in a model (Fig.3.2) of the relationship between bilingualism, metacognitive process and cognitive skills in the context of Indian multilingualism (Mohanty, 1994a, b).

In their review of cross-cultural studies, Mohanty and Perregaux (1997) have pointed out that when cultural pluralism and multilingualism are accepted norms of a society, individual and community level bilingualism exerts positive influences. In such societies, "the social norm influences the individual in favour of

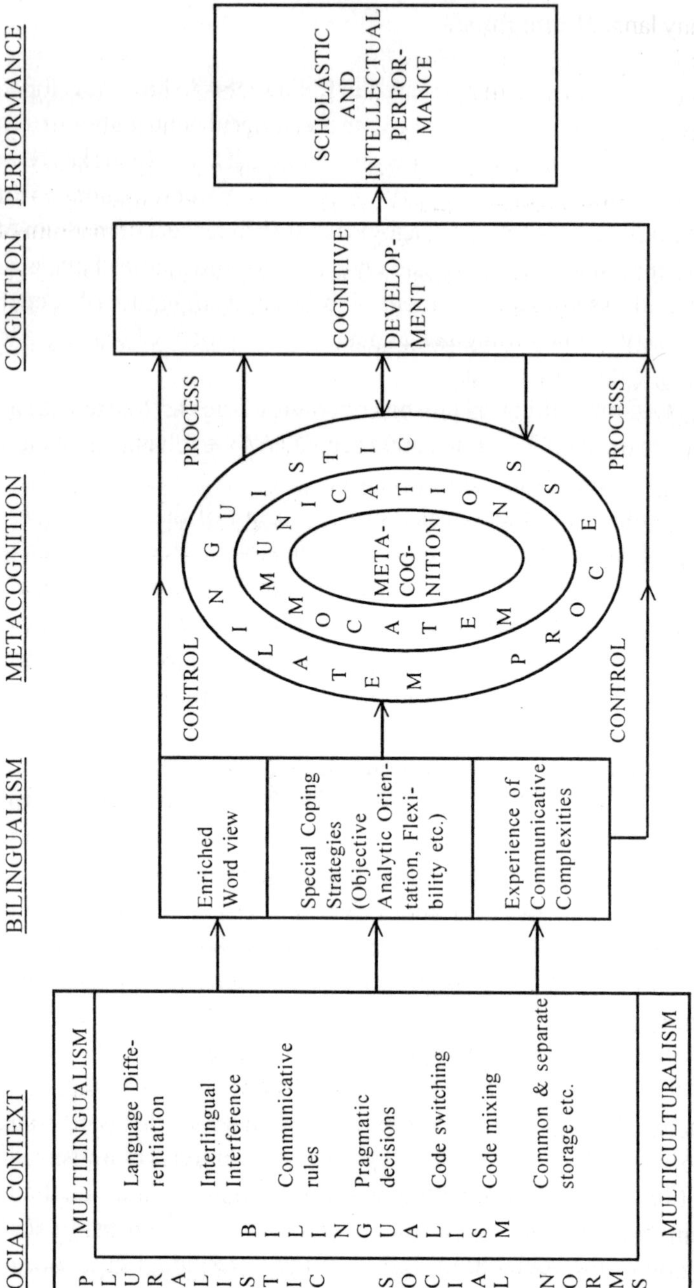

Fig. 3.2 : A model of the relationship between Bilingualism, Metacognitive Processes and Cognitive Development

many languages and not one, making bilingualism a positive force in his or her life. Thus, when other factors are controlled, social psychological and cognitive consequences of bilingualism can be expected to be positive in pluralistic and multilingual cultures" (Mohanty & Perreguax, 1997, p. 236). Using cross-cultural models of intergroup relations in plural societies (*e.g.* Berry, 1990), Mohanty (1994a) has related language contact outcomes to different types of intercultural relationship. Accordingly, stable bilingualism and language maintenance orientation in situations of language contact can be characterised as integration, language shift and transitional bilingualism as assimilation and linguistic divergence as separation. Analysis of attitude towards maintenance of language and culture of the in-group and the contact group in tribal non-tribal contact situations in Phulbani District of Orissa (Mohanty, 1990, 1994a) has shown that bilingualism of the individual and community levels promotes social integration.

Bilingualism studies in India have also addressed the issues relating to medium of instruction and bilingual education. In a series of studies, Srivastava and his colleagues (Srivastava, 1990; Srivastava & Khatoon, 1980; Srivastava & Ramaswamy, 1987) compared pupils from mother tongue medium schools with those from English and other language medium schools on school achievement and other psychological measures such as self-concept. With the effect of intelligence partialled out, there was no difference between different instructional medium groups. School climate related variables like selection and admission criteria, teaching methods, use of teaching aids and materials etc. accounted for the advantage of English medium pupils. Based on such findings and conceptual analysis of the issues, a number of researchers and scholars in India (Krishnamurti, 1990; Mohanty, 1994a; Srivastava, 1990; Srivastava & Gupta, 1990) have pleaded for the use of mother tongues as instructional media in schools with provisions for teaching English and other languages at a later stage. In a recent study Patra (2000) compared IQ and SES controlled pupils of grades 6 and 8 from Oriya mother tongue (MT) medium and English medium schools on measures of language (reading, writing and metalanguage in Oriya and English), mathematics and science achievement measures. The Oriya medium children performed better than their English medium counterparts on all tasks and at both the grade levels (except the reading task showing no difference at grade 8 level). In a second part of the study, Patra (2000) compared Oriya medium grade 6 and 8 students from schools with either early (Grade 1) or late (Grade 4) introduction of English as a school subject. The findings showed no difference in English proficiency measures by grade 8. Thus, time spent on English by an early start in the same did not make any difference and the two groups reached similar levels of English proficiency by grade 8. Thus, available evidence points to the efficacy of mother tongue medium schools over English or L_2 medium ones. Further, early exposure to English (L_2) does not seem to enhance L_2 proficiency in the long run. Based on these findings and a theoretical review, Mohanty (2000b) has analysed the issue of mother tongue education in India from a psycholinguistic framework which "justifies bilingual education with the mother tongue as the sole medium of instruction at least upto the primary level after which use of L_2 as another medium can be gradually introduced and increased until the use of both the media of instruction are approximately equal. Introduction of other languages can be planned depending on the level of proficiency sought to be developed within a time frame" (p. 13). Mohanty (2000b) goes on to conclude that, "bilingual education must be a policy for all children in their psychoeducational development from mother tongue to multilingualism in India where mother tongues, regional languages, national language and English as a language of wider communication must all be promoted through carefully selected programmes" (p.14).

On the whole, Indian studies on bilingualism have been rooted in the sociolinguistic context of our multilingualism with a clear interdisciplinary approach. Pedagogical applications of these findings have also been addressed particularly in respect of the mother tongue education. The linguistic diversity in India and the variety in sociolinguistic contexts have enabled the Indian researchers to offer some unique database and to enhance our understanding besides addressing to some relevant issues. Bilingualism as a psychosocial process has been examined from an indigenous perspective relatively unaffected by the dominant monolingual view of the west.

Factors in Development of Reading

Development of reading skill is fundamental to educational achievement. Review of Indian research on reading (Mohanty, 2000a) shows shifting of emphasis from English to other Indian languages. Mohanty (2000a) also notes an emergence of indigenous approaches in focusing on the role of contrastive features of our languages and cultural conditions in reading acquisition. This is evident from the analysis of processes and problems in reading acquisition in the context of Indian orthographic system. It may be pointed out here that most of the western studies are based on alphabetic scripts such as English in which phonological coding plays a significant role. In contrast, Indian writing system is semi-syllabic in nature combining syllabic and alphabetic principles. Writing systems are broadly classified as ideographic, syllabic and alphabetic depending on the level of representation. In ideographic system of writing spoken language is represented at the level of morphemes as in case of Chinese writing system. In syllabic writing, such as Japanese *Kana*, spoken language is represented at the level of syllables and in alphabetic system like the Roman scripts language is represented at the level of phonemes or morphophonemes. In Indian orthography, letters are expressed in syllabic units called syllabic alphabets (or alphabetic syllabary) which can be analysed into consonant and vowel components. Thus, the Indian writing system is semi-syllabic with a high degree of grapheme-phoneme correspondence resulting in very few irregular spellings and homonyms.

In the context of such a writing system, Indian research on reading acquisition generally show a lack of relationship between phonological awareness, phonological segmentation skills and level of reading skill (Mohanty, 2000a; Prakash, 1987; Prakash, Rekha, Nigam & Karanth, 1993 etc.). These findings are at variance with the studies on acquisition of English which show that phonological skills are good predictors of the level of reading proficiency. Indian studies show that phonemic skills did not develop spontaneously but only as a result of literacy in general and alphabetic literacy in particular. Thus, it has been suggested that western models of reading acquisition may not be applicable in the Indian context (Prakash, 1990). Prakash (1990) further argues that western methods of teaching reading (with their emphasis on developing phonological skills) may not be effective in case of Indian writing system in which letter identification may be the most crucial factor in learning to read.

A host of other Indian studies on reading (see Mohanty, 2000a, for a review) shows the role of information processing and metalinguistic skills as well as reading awareness in learning to read. Mohanty's (2000a) review of research in the area leads to the following conclusion.

> On the whole, Indian contribution to the field of reading development has been quite substantive as well as responsive to the contextual conditions of reading in Indian languages with their semi-syllabic orthography. While these studies have generally supported western findings in respect of the dominant impact of metalinguistic and reading awareness as facilitators of reading development, they have been distinct in showing that, because of the nature of Indian writing systems, phonological segmentation skills and phonological awareness do not play as significant a role in learning to read in Indian languages as has been projected on the basis of western studies particularly with the alphabetic scripts (p. 235).

However, despite this, there is a lack of applied orientation and lack of understanding of the current practices in teaching reading. As a result, there is little effort to utilize the available knowledge in remediation of reading problems and dyslexia.

Conclusion

Finally, to answer the question regarding the extent to which Indian psycholinguistics has been responsive to the contextual characteristics of the multilingual, multicultural society, it is necessary to reflect back on the proposed framework of the relationship between the cultural context, the form and function of language and language behaviour. The field of psycholinguistic research is necessarily interdisciplinary. As such, the formal linguistic features of Indian languages such as flexible word ordering, morphosyntactic rules and orthographic nature etc. are inevitably drawn as important variables. Further, Indian psycholinguistic research in general emphasizes the role of socio-cultural factors, such as social class, basic multilingual character of Indian society, family pattern of interaction, community level relationship between language etc., in shaping the process of language development and use. In some specific areas, however, the influence of western studies and approaches is still quite visible. Further, except in some areas, there is an absence of inter-disciplinary approach resulting in some dissociation between psychological and linguistic studies. Inter-disciplinary orientation is necessary to bring to focus the psychological as well as sociolinguistic features of language use in society. Psycholinguistic research in India has a good beginning contextualized in the Indian multilingual and multicultural reality but the true inter-disciplinary character of the discipline and its applications potentials remain to be fully realized.

REFERENCES

Adair, J.G., Puhan, B.N. & Vohra, N. (1993). Indigenization of psychology: Empirical assessment of progress in Indian research. *International Journal of Psychology*, 28, 149-169.

Berry, J.W. (1990). Psychology of acculturation: Understanding individuals moving between cultures. In R.W. Brislin (Ed.), *Applied Cross-Cultural Psychology*. London: Sage.

Brown, R. (1973). *A first language: The early stages.* Cambridge, MA: Harvard University Press.

Devaki, L. (1987). Learning of morphological rules in children: A comparative study of two cognate languages — Tamil and Kannda. Unpublished doctoral dissertation, Mysore University, Mysore.

Devaki, L. (1992). *Development of morphological rules in children.* Mysore: Central Institute of Indian Languages.

Gardner, H. (1984). The development of competence in culturally defined domains. In R.A. Schweder & R.A. LeVine (Eds.), *Culture theory: Essays on mind, self and emotion.* Cambridge; Cambridge University Press.

Krishnamurti, B.H. (1990). The regional language *vis-a-vis* English as the medium of instruction in higher education: The Indian dilemma. In D.P. Pattanayak (Ed.), *Multilingualism in India.* Clevedon: Multilingual Matters.

Kumudavallia, S. (1973). The relationship between articulation and discrimination in Kannada speech sounds in terms of distinctive features. Unpublished Masters' Dissertation, Mysore University, Mysore.

Lakshim Bai, B. (1983/1984). Case relations and case forms in child language. Osmania Papers in *Linguistics,* 9 & 10, 73-101.

Lakshmi Bai, B. (1984). Dative in Dravidian: a perspective from child language. *Psycho-lingua,* XIV (2), 135-144.

Lakshmi Bai, B. (1986). Development of negation in Tamil-Telugu bilingual children. In J.A. Fishman (Ed.), *The Fergusonian impact,* Vol. 1: *From phonology to society.* New York: Mouton de Gruyter.

Mishra, B. (1994 December). Word order in expression of bitransitive verbs in Hindi: Impact of deprivation. Paper presented in the International Conference on Early Childhood Communication, Utkal University, Bhubaneswar.

Misra, B. & Dube, J. (1987). Pragmatic strategy in word order of children's expression of locative preposition on in Hindi. *Indian Journal of Current Psychological Research,* 2 (2), 93-97.

Misra, G. & Mohanty, A.K. (Ed.) (in press). *Perspectives on indigenous psychology.* New Delhi: Concept.

Mohanty, A.K. (1988). Beyond the horizon of Indian psychology: The Yankee doodler. In F.M. Sahoo (Ed.), *Psychology in Indian Context.* Agra: National Psychological Corporation.

Mohanty, A.K. (1990). Social psychological aspects of languages in contact in multilingual societies. In G. Misra (Ed.), *Applied social psychology in India.* New Delhi: Sage.

Mohanty, A.K. (1994b, July). *Bilingualism in a multilingual society: Implications for cultural integration and education.* Keynote address of the International Congress of Applied Psychology, Madrid.

Mohanty, A.K. (1994c, December). Language socialization in a multilingual sociejty. Paper presented at the International Conference on Early Childhood Communication. Utkal University, Bhubaneswar.

Mohanty, A.K. (2000a). Language behaviour and processes. In J. Pandey (Ed.), *Psychology in India Revisited — Developments in the discipline,* Vol. 1: *Physiological foundation and human cognition.* New Delhi: Sage.

Mohanty, A.K. (2000b, August). From mother-tongue to multilingualism in education: A psycholinguistic perspective. Paper presented in the seminar on Regional Languages as Medium of Instruction, Department of Linguistics, University of Kerala, Trivandrum.

Mohanty, A.K. (in press). Psychology of language acquisition and bilingualism in India: The cultural input. In J.W. Berry, R.C. Tripathi *et.al.* (Eds.) untitled volume in honour of professor D. Sinha. New Delhi: Sage.

Mohanty, A.K., & Mishra, B. (1982). Effect of context on word order in children's expression of locative propositions *Psychological Reports,* 50, 1163-1166.

Mohanty, A.K. & Mohanty, M. (1985). Expression and comprehension of Oriya bitransitive sentences: Effect of word order. Psycho-lingua, XV (1), 7-18.

Mohanty, A.K. & Mohanty, N. (1981). Effect of word order and reversibility on comprehensive of Oriya locative sentences. *Indian Journal of Psychology,* 56, 59-66.

Mohanty, A.K., Panda, S. & Mishra, B. (1999). Language socialization in a multilingual society. In T.S. Saraswathi (Ed.), *Culture, socialization and human development.* New Delhi: Sage.

Mohanty, A.K. & Pereguax, C. (1997). Language acquisition and bilingualism. In J.W. Berry, P.R. Desen, & T.S. Saraswathi (Eds.)*Handbook of cross-cultural psychology,* Vol. 2: *Basic processes and human development* (2nd ed.). Boston: Allyn & Bacon.

Mohite, P. (1983). Development of language curriculum for pre-school children. *Child Psychiatry Quarterly, 16* (4), 168-184.

Nirmala, C. (1981a). First language (Telugu) development: a short descriptive study. Unpublished doctoral dissertation, Osmania University, Hyderabad.

Nirmala, C. (1981b). Medial consonant cluster acquisition by Telugu children. *Journal of Child Language,* 8, 63-73.

Ochs, E. (1986). Introduction. In B.B. Schieffelin & E. Ochs (Eds.), *Language socialization across-cultures.* Cambridge, Mass: Camhridge University Press.

Patra, S. (2000). Role of language of instruction in the multilingual school system of India. Unpublished doctoral dissertation, Utkal University, Bhubaneswar.

Prakash, P. (1987). Development of reading proficiency: Relationship with metalinguistic awareness and cognitive processing skills. Unpublished doctoral dissertation, Utkal University, Bhubaneswar.

Prakash, P. (1990). Orality-literacy transition and instructional process in India orthographic context. *Indian Journal of Adult Education,* 51 (4), 100-102.

Prakash, P., Rekha, D., Nigam, R. & Karanth, P. (1993). Phonological awareness, orthography and literacy. In R. Scholes and B. Willis (Eds.), *Literacy: Linguistic and Cognitive Perspectives.* New York: Lawrence Erlbaum.

Sharma, V. (1969). A linguistic study of speech development in early childhood. Unpublished doctoral dissertation, Agra University, Agra.

Singh, A. (1987). Certain deprivational factors in language development in children. Unpublished doctoral dissertation, University of Allahabad, Allahabad.

Sinha, D. (1981). Social psychology in India: A historical perspective. In J. Pandey (Ed.), *Perspectives on experimental social psychology in India.* New Delhi: Concept.

Singh, D. (1984). Psychology in the context of third world development. *International Journal of Psychology,* 19, 17-29.

Sinha, D. (1986). *Psychology in a third world country: The Indian experience.* New Delhi: Sage.

Sinha, D. (1989). Cross-cultural psychology and the process of indigenization: A second view from the third world. In D.M Keats, D. Munroe & L. Mann (Eds.), *Heterogeneity in cross-cultural psychology.* Lisse: Swets & Zeitlinger.

Sinha, D. (1993). Indigenization of psychology in India and its relevance. In U. Kim & J.W. Berry (Eds.), *Indigenous psychologies: Research and experience in cultural context.* Newburry Park, CA: Sage.

Sinha, D. (1996). Indigenizing psychology. In J.W. Berry, Y.H. Poortinga & J. Pandey (Eds.), *Handbook of cross-cultural psychology,* Vol. 1. (2nd ed.). Boston: Allyn & Bacon.

Slobin, D.I. (1982). Universal and particular in the acquisition of language. In E. Wanner & L.R. Gleitman (Eds.), *Language Acquisition: The state of the art.* Cambridge, Mass: Cambridge University Press.

Southworth, F.C. (1980). Functional aspects of bilingualism. *International Journal of Dravidian Linguistics,* IX (1), 74-108.

Sridevi, S.V. (1976). The aspects of acquisition of Kannada by 2 + year-old children. Unpublished Masters' dissertation, All India Institute of Speech and Hearing, Mysore.

Srivastava, A.K. (1990). Multilingualism and school education in India: Special features, problems and prospects. In D.P. Pattanayak (Ed.), *Multilingualism in India.* Clevedon: Multilingual Matters.

Srivastava, A.K. & Khatoon, P. (1980). Effect of difference between mother tongue and another language as medium of instruction on mental ability, achievement and creativity of VII standard children. In E. Annamalai (Ed.), *Bilingualism and achievement in schools.* Mysore: Central Institute of Indian

Languages.

Srivastava, A.K & Ramaswamy, K. (1987). Bilingualism, sex and personality development of school going students. *Scholar Critic,* 5 (9), 75-90.

Srivastava, R.N. & Gupta, R.S. (1990). Literacy in a multilingual context. In D.P. Pattanayak (Ed.), *Multilingualism in India.* Clevedon: Multilingual Matters.

Thirumalai, M.S. (1972). Some aspects of 4 year plus old stage in the acquisition of Tamil phonology. *Journal of AIISH,* 3, 7-12.

Usha Devi, A. (1990). *Acquisition of syntax: A case study of Telugu.* New Delhi: Bahri.

Vaidyanathan, R. (1984). Verbal environment and early language acquisition: A pragmatic approach. Unpublished doctoral dissertation, Bombay University, Bombay.

Vaidyanathan, R. (1988). Developmenht of form and functions of interrogatives in children: A longitudinal study in Tamil. *Journal of Child Language,* 15, 533-551.

Vasanta, D. (1992). Phonological development and phonological disorders: A review article. In T. Balasubramaniam & V. Prakasam (Eds.), *Sound patterns for the phoneticians: Studies in phonetics and phonology in honour of J.C. Catford.* Madras: T.R. Publications.

Vasanta, D. & Sailaja. V. (1993 February). Psycholinguistic evidence for word order variation within dative constructions in Telugu. Paper presented in the National Seminar on World Order in Indian Languages, Osmania University, Hyderabad.

Vasanta, D., Sastry, J.V. & Ravi Maruth, P. (1994 February). Grammaticality judgement of Telugu speaking elementary school children. Paper presented in the National Seminar on Language Development and Language Disorders, Osmania University, Hyderabad.

Vygotsky, L. (1978). *Mind in Society.* Cambridge, Mass: Harvard University Press.

4

Situational Preferences for Different Types of Individualism-Collectivism

JYOTI VERMA

Introduction

Triandis (1995) contends that individualism and collectivism can be identified by examining the tendencies: (a) to define the self which can emphasize personal or collective aspects or can be independent or interdependent (Triandis, 1989; Markus & Kitayama, 1991), (b) to have priority of in-group goals over personal goals or *vice versa* (Triandis, 1990; Yamaguchi, 1994), (c) to emphasize on exchange rather than communal relationships (Mills & Clark, 1982), or rationality rather than relatedness (Kim, Triandis, Kagitcibasi, Choi & Yoon, 1994), and (d) to give importance to attitude and norms as determinants of social behaviour (Davidson, Jaccard, Triandis, Morales & Diaz-Guerrero, 1976; Bontempo & Rivero, 1992).

The Different Types of Individualism-Collectivism

It has been suggested that the most important attributes that distinguish among the different kinds of individualism-collectivism, refers to the emphases on horizontal and vertical social relationships (Triandis, 1990; 1995). Societies that accept horizontal patterns, assume that one self is more or less like every other self. On the

Thanks are acknowledged to Prof. J.B.P. Sinha for his valuable comments and suggestions on the draft of this paper. The author also wishes to thank Dr. R.B.N. Sinha for his help in statistical analysis.

other hand, vertical societies believe in maintaining hierarchwy between selves on certain grounds. Further, in Horizontal Individualism (HI), people want to be unique, and do their own thing, but they are not especially interested in becoming distinguished for high status; in Vertical Individualism (VI) people often want to become distinguished and acquire status, and they do this in individual competitions with others. In Horizontal Collectivism (HC), people want to be as similar as possible, and they emphasize common goals with others. In Vertical Collectivism (VC) people sacrifice their personal goals for the sake of in-group goals, and support competitions of their in-groups with out-groups.

There are also some costs associated with each cultural pattern. The horizontal individualist pattern can result in social isolation. The vertical individualist pattern can result in extreme stress. The horizontal collectivist pattern could absorb much of the individual's energy in social relationships, costing task accomplishment, while the vertical collectivist pattern could result in authoritarian regimes and ethnic cleansing. Rokeach (1973) has discussed political systems that value especially both "equality and freedom" highly, and correspond to Horizontal Individualism (social democracy, *e.g.*, Australia, Sweden), "equality" but not "freedom" highly and correspond to Horizontal Collectivism *e.g.*, the Israeli Kibbutz), " freedom" but not "equality" and correspond to Vertical Individualism (*e.g.*, competitive capitalism such as in the US), and neither "equality" nor "freedom" and correspond to Vertical Collectivism (*e.g.*, the communalism of traditional societies with strong leaders, including India).

While there are a number of ways to measure collectivism and individualism, there is correlation (Triandis, McCusker & Hui, 1990) among the measurements suggesting the presence of a "cultural syndrome" (Triandis, 1993). Cultural syndrome is defined as shared attitudes, beliefs, norms, role and self definition and values, centered around a theme found among those who speak a language dialect, and live in the same historical period and geographic region. The theme for collectivism is the centrality of the in-group. The theme for individulaism is the importance of the individual.

Measurement of the Individualism-Collectivism Construct

The literature includes many measures of the individualist-collectivist tendencies. Triandis (1995) reports that tendency 'a' that is, to define the self with an emphasis on personal or collective aspects or in terms of independent self *versus* interdependent self, can be measured with contents anlayses of the responses to 20 statements that begin with " I am....." (Triandis, McCusker & Hui, 1990), or scales that measure an independent *versus* interdependent self, developed by Singelis (1994) and Gudykunst, Matsumoto, Ting-Toomey, Nishida & Karimi (1994).

The tendencies described under category 'b' that is, giving priority to in-group goals over personal goals or *vice versa,* can be measured with a scale developed by Yamaguchi (1994) or by examining individual preferences for individualist or collectivist goals and/or values (Schwartz, 1994; Triandis, McCusker & Hui, 1990), Tendencies that refer to emphasis on exchange rather than communal relationship described under 'c', can be measured by scales developed by Clark, Ouellette, Powell and Milberg (1987), and those that reflect the tendencies to give importance to attitude and norms das determinants of social behaviour (d), by using the Fishbein and Ajzen (1975) model of attitudes and behaviour.

Nevertheless, measurement of individualism and collectivism has been difficult. The appendix in Triandis (1995) describes several relevant methods, but none are able to capture the very broad constructs satisfactorily. Singelis *et al.* (1995) developed 32 attitude items, 8 for each of the four kinds of collectivism and individualism (*i.e.,* HI, VI, HC, and VC). While these items do have alphas in the range of .69 to .75, they seem to be quite susceptible to the social desirability factor.

Triandis and Gelfand (in press) developed a series of scenarios that are less susceptible to social desirability. Since the participants are confronted with the social desirability of four aspects which they have to rank order, they are forced to choose among four socially desirable responses and thus, this reduces the influence of social desirability. These researchers also reported that the responses to the scenarios were correlated with the responses to the attitude items, thus suggesting that they have convergent validity. Verma and Triandis (1999) used these scenarios for studying whether Indians were high on Vertical Collectivism dimension.

Since literature suggests that Indians are context sensitive and prefer to give situational explanation to their decisions and behaviour (Sinha & Tripathi, 1994), the present author wanted to study the circumstances under which Indian students decide to choose a particular cultural dimension reasoning that this might be the most suitable option for meeting the demands of the given situations.

Some Implications of the Study

Researches interested in studying the different dimensions of otherwise broadly classified cultures as individualist or collectivist, are likely to give way to appropriate characterization of the said cultures. Further, an understandings of the cultural dimensions is likely to help speculate and perhaps predict the costs and highlights of endorsing to a particular cultural patterns For example, some costs associated with each cultural pattern may be as follows: The horizontal individualist pattern can result in social isolation. The vertical individualist pattern can result in extreme stress. The horizontal collectivist pattern could absorb much of the individual's energy in social relationships, costing task accomplishment, while the vertical collectivist pattern could result in authoritarian regimes and ethic cleansing. Rokeach (1973) has discussed political systems that value especially both "equality and freedom" highly, and correspond to Horizontal Individualism (social democracy, *e.g.*, Australia, Sweden), "equality" but not "freedom" and correspond to Horizontal Collectivism (*e.g.*, the Israeli Kibbutz), "freedom" but not "equality" and correspond to Vertical Individualism *(e.g.,* competitive capitalism such as in the US), and neither "equality" nor "freedom" and correspond to Vertical Collectivism (*e.g.,* the communalism of traditional societies with strong leaders, including India).

Furthermore, attempts to study the different cultural dimensions could promote efforts for developing appropriate methodologies for measuring them aptly. Second, there is the need for understanding the attitude, preferences and practices of people of India origin in India or elsewhere in the world in their respective contexts more articulately and arriving at a position to predict and suggest necessary changes in their social, political and inter-cultural domains of life for better interpersonal, political and international relations.

Objectives of the Study

In Verma and Triandis' (1999) cross-cultural study on Indian and American college students, the situations described in the scenarios were quite familiar for the American students but the scenarios did not assure hundred percent familiarity with the content for the Indian respondents. In the present study, the Indian researcher wished to see whether making appropriate changes in the content of the situations for making them appear more familiar to the Indian respondents, was likely to have any significant effect on their choices of the different cultural dimensions.

Secondly, since the present study followed the earlier cross-cultural study soon after it was reported, the Indian researcher wished to observe whether scenarios were reliable means for measuring dominant cultural dimensions likely to be preferred by a particular cultural group (in this case Indians). Finally, the study aimed at finding out which situations elicited predominantly collectivist responses and which predominantly individualist choices.

Sample

A total of 150 students (80 males and 70 females) from the Post Graduate departments of Patna University, belonging to both science and social sciences faculties, responded to the 16 scenarios.

Measure

The measure comprised sixteen scenarios describing familiar situations/themes in the day-to-day life of a student. For example, the situations referred to setling of a restaurant bill among a group of friends (# 1), purchase of an expensive set of furniture for studying (# 2), choosing one word for describing oneself (# 3), suggesting how happiness is acquired (# 4), consulting others for accepting a good job far away from home (# 5), selecting the most interesting book (# 6), pointing out towards the most important thing for promotion in a job (# 7), suggesting important considerations behind making a new dress for an important social function (# 8), expressing one's view on the concerns of an ideal national budget (# 9), choosing the most preferred attribute for describing one self (# 10), dealing with a younger sibling who behaves according to his/her sweet will (# 11), deciding how to distribute award money among a group of five team members (# 12), arranging a band for the college sports day (# 13), choosing a vocational paper (# 14), ordering snacks for friends when eating out (#15), and voting for the President of Student Council (#16) (see Appendix).

Each scenario was followed by four alternatives comprising four possible ways of handling the given situation (or considerations to be taken into account for making a decisions in the described circumstances). Each alternative represented one of the four cultural dimensions, namely, either HC, HI, VC or VI. The respondent was required to choose the alternative that he/she considered the best for dealing with the respective situations. The respondent's willingness to choose a particular alternative indicated his/her preference for a particular cultural dimension in the given context.

Procedure

The students were approached individually or in small groups of three to four in their leisure time. They were requested to go through the scenarios carefully and select the most preferred option out of the four provided to them following each scenario.

Treatment of the Data

1. For each scenario, the percentage of the total sample that selected each of the four responses was derived from the frequency count of the responses in the four alternative categories. Further, means were computed for the percentages of the choices falling into each category (*i.e.*, HC, HI, VC, and VI) across the 16 scenarios. The scores for HC and VC dimensions were added individually to arrive at a composite 'C' or Collectivism score for each scenario. Similarly, composite 'I' or Individualism scores were derived by adding up scores on VI and HI dimensions.

2. A comparison of percentage of choices in the different cultural dimensions was made between the observations from the Verma & Triandis' (1999) study and that of the present study by applying Chi Square.

3. One way Analysis of Variance was applied to examine whether the four cultural dimensions were significantly different from each other.

4. Scheffe's test (1957) was applied to observe whether the mean scores of the four cultural dimensions were significantly different from each other.

Results

Table 4.1 contains a couple of important observations. First, highest mean was observed for the Collectivist choices while the lowest was for the Individualist ones. A comparison between C and I dimensions showed that situations that were likely to elicit collectivist responses were those described in scenarios 1, 3, 4, 6, 7, 9, 11, 12, 13, 15 and 16. On the other hand, the situations that appeared

Table 4.1 : Percentage of Collectivist, Individualist Horizontal and Vertical Choices in the 16 Scenarios

Scenarios	Collectivist Choice	Individualist Choice	Horizontal Choice	Vertical Choice
1. Settling of a restaurant bill among group of friends	61.99	38.00	80.66	19.33
2. Purchase of an expensive set of furniture for studying	19.32	80.66	63.32	36.66
3. Choosing one word for describing oneself	83.32	16.66	35.99	63.99
4. Suggesting how happiness is acquired	66.66	33.33	20.66	79.33
5. Consulting others for accepting a job far from home	48.66	51.33	51.33	48.66
6. Selecting the most interesting book	84.66	15.33	9.33	90.66
7. Telling what is most important for promotion in job	56.66	43.33	58.00	41.99
8. Consideration behind making dress for a special occasion	39.99	59.99	59.99	39.99
9. View on the concerns of an ideal national budget	63.99	36.00	78.66	21.33
10. Preferred attributes for self description	21.32	78.66	25.99	73.99
11. Dealing with a younger sibling	92.66	7.33	19.33	80.66
12. Distribution of award money among team members	83.99	15.99	59.99	39.99
13. Arranging a band for the college sports day	78.00	21.99	59.33	40.66
14. Choosing a vocational paper	1.99	97.99	78.66	21.32
15. Ordering snacks for friends when eating out	57.99	42.00	90.66	9.33
16. Voting for the President of the Student's Council	72.66	27.33	20.66	79.33
Mean	58.37	41.62	50.78	49.20

Note : Collectivist Choice = HC+VC, Individualist Choice = HI+VI, Horizontal Choice = HC+HV, Vertical Choice = VC+ VI.

promising for individualist choices, were confined to the situations described in scenarios 2, 8 (with a tie with H dimension), 10 and 14.

Secondly, the present study also gave some information about the significance of the VC dimension. Triandis (1995) contends that Indians are vertical collectivists, in this connection. In our cross-cultural study (Verma & Triandis, 1999) we had observed that Indian students showed their preference for the VC dimension students showed their preference for the VC dimension especially when they had to make a second choice (that is, if they were required to make a second best choice as well for dealing with the given situation). However, when comparing the Indian students' percentages of VC choices with the American students, we observed that Indian students, always showed higher percentages of VC scores over other cultural dimensions across scenarios.

Observations from the present study suggested that the highest percentage of preference for V and C dimensions were made for dealing with at least five situations, namely, choosing one word for describing oneself (#3), suggesting how happiness is acquired(# 4) selecting the most interesting book (# 6), dealing with a younger sibling who behaves according to his/her sweet will (# 11) and voting for the President of Student Council (#16). The mean score for the VC dimension was also the largest among the four cultural dimensions.

In our previous study (Verma & Triandis, 1999) we observed 29 per cent, 24 per cent, 25 per cent, and 23 per cent of the Indian respondents choosing HC, HI, VC and VI dimensions respectively. The Indian profile appeared well balanced (as the most balanced possible profile would give 25 per cent to each cultural pattern) and the Indian students appeared high on horizontal and vertical collectivism while low on horizontal and vertical individualism. Furthermore, we found that the male and the female students did not differ in any significant manner in showing their preference for the four cultural dimensions (*i.e.,* HI, HC, VC and VI).

Coming to the findings of the present study, it was observed that 25.08%, 25.70%, 33.29% and 15.91% of the respondents selected HC, HI, VC and VI dimensions respectively. Furthermore, greater number of respondents chose VC and HI dimensions this time. It may be recalled that slight changes were made in the content of the scenarios for making them appear more familiar to the Indian respondents. Chi Square was computed to ascertain if significant difference was evident due to these changes in the percentage difference was eviddent due to these changes in the percentage of choices made by the respondents in the different categories of the two studies. However, the Chi Square was not significant (Chi Square = 2.97, *df* = 3) and taken in totality, the observations suggested that there was consistency in the choices made by the respondents in the two studies.

It may be recalled that the Means for the HC, HI, VC and VI dimensions were 37.62, 38.56, 49.93 and 23.87 respectively. The percentages recorded in the different cultural dimensions were based on 16 times 150 responses, and even a small difference in the percentages is statistically significant. One way ANOVA was applied to see whether the means of the different cultural dimensions differed significantly from each other. This resulted into a highly significant F ratio ($F = 33.78$, $df = 3, 596$, $p < .001$), suggesting that the four cultural dimensions were significantly different from each other.

Table 4.2 presents a comparison of mean scores among the HC, HI, VC, and VI dimensions. It was observed that Scheffe's was significantly different for at least four pairs of means out of the six. Accordingly, significantly more percentage of respondents preferred VC options than the HC choices (means = 49.93 and 37.62 respectively), and VC choices also had a significant edge over the preference for HI choices across the scenarios (means = 49. 93 and 38.56 respectively). The findings supported the contention that Indians were likely to be high on Vertical Collectivism (Triandis, 1995).

At the other instance, significantly more percentage of the total sample preferred to choose HI, and VC dimensions in comparison to VI (means = 38.56, 49.93 and 23.87 respectively). In sum, Vertical Individualism was found to be the least often preferred dimensions out of the four. This dimension comprised items suggesting strong

Table 4.2 : Scheffe's Test (1957) for the Comparison of Mean Scores of HC, HI, VC, and VI Dimensions

Dimensions	Mean	Mean	N1 + N2 / N1 × N2	Within Variance	Scheffe's F ratio
HC vs HI	3.63	4.08	.0133	2.90	5.25
HC vs VC	3.63	5.10	.0133	2.90	56.12**
HC vs VI	3.63	3.22	.0133	2.90	4.36
HI vs VC	4.08	5.10	.0133	2.90	26.95**
HI vs VI	4.08	3.22	.0133	2.90	19.16**
VC vs VI	5.10	3.22	.0133	2.90	91.56**

Note: HC = Horizontal Collectivism, HI = Horizontal Individualism, VC = Vertical Collectivism and VI = Vertical Individualism, ** = < p.01, N = 150.

preference for individualist orientation. It seems that the present respondents did not show strong preference for such items.

Finally, preference for HC and HI dimensions was not significantly different. It is likely that the respondents were showing their general preference for the common horizontal character of the said dimensions. If one looks at table 1, it will be evident that the students preferred to endorse highest percentages of HC and HI choices in at least 9 scenarios all together (HC in 5 and HI in 4 scenarios respectively). However, not finding any significant difference between the choice of HC and VI dimensions is some what confusing. In this case the mean for HC dimension is larger though not significantly different than the VI dimension.

Discussion

What needs to be specified for addressing to certain issues that might emanate from individualistic and collectivistic situations, is that Indian collectivism need to be understood in its complexities and any interpretation of the seemingly inconsistent behaviour of the Indian people specially in the cross-cultural context, should be made in the light of the fact that Indians prefer to have a set of *cherished values* which rarely become the guiding principles of their lives. They also have a set of *core social values* that they try to protect and retain unless tempted by situations that overshadow their importance and utility. They have a third set of *instrumental or functional* values that are the real guiding principles of their lives and are commonly reflected in what they decide and practice.

Therefore, it is the situation which determines the selection of a specific cultural pattern (i.e., HC, HI, VC or VI) backed by the set of values which is considered most appropriate and beneficial for the person concerned in that particular situation. Empirical studies that try to incorporate this cultural context while talking about Indians, offer scope for a better understanding of issues that might emerge from individualistic and collectivistic situations. It has been said that the present study aimed at having a convincing impression regarding which situations elicited predominantly collectivist responses and which predominantly individualist choices. Further, the study intended to examine whether scenarios were reliable means for measuring dominant cultural dimensions that were likely to be preferred by a particular cultural group. In view of the objectives of the study, and an intention to specify the results of the study to understand issues emanating from individualistic and collectivistic situations it was decided to discuss the findings under the following headings: 1.Collectivism *vs.* individualism, 2. The collectivist profile, 3. The individualist preferences 4. The vertical collectivist profile

Collectivism *vs.* Individualism

Across the scenarios the students endorsed Collectivism dimension 58% of time while their preference for the individualist choices added up to 40.89%. These scores presented an interesting comparison with the findings of our earlier study (Verma & Triandis, 1999), where we found 53% and 47% preference for collectivism and individualism dimensions respectively. In the present study preference for C dimension got a small boost and preference for individualist choices got somewhat subdued. The trend however was consistent with the earlier trend.

Out of the sixteen scenarios, in seven situations the respondents clearly preferred to endorse collectivist items. Looking at the observations in a totality, it appeared that the students preferred to *describe* them selves as co-operative and dutiful (# 3), *were happy* making lots of friends and by getting status and respect in the society (# 4), *were interested* in a book which guided them regarding how to make friends and how to fulfill one's duties (# 6), *believed* in *strengthening family ties* and respecting one's parents (# 11), showed preference for the value of *equality* on the one hand, and handing over the *decision making power to the group leader* on the other (#12). Furthermore, the students took care that the entertainment band they arranged for an official function, *pleased their friends and seniors* (# 13) and preferred to choose the student council's leader who was *influential* and was the *choice of their friends*.

It was only in three situations that the students preferred to endorse the individualist choices. For example, in case they had to buy a set of expensive furniture for personal use, they preferred to give importance to their own *liking* for the furniture and wanted to ascertain whether it was a *good investment* (# 2). Secondly, when asked to tell about them selves the students preferred to mention about their *achievements* and why they were *different from others,* (# 10), and lastly, in choosing a vocational paper they preferred to choose the one that was *interesting* for them, and helped them *excel* while competing with others. It was quite clear that the young students took an individualist stance in situations that had implications for their personal and individual causes.

However, it may be noted that when a comparison was made for percentage of choices among the Collectivist, Individualist, Horizontal and Vertical dimensions, across the 16 scenarios the collectivist responses appeared highest only for *one fourth* of the situations (4 out of 16). For example, when asked to describe one self in one word only (# 3), when asked to deal with an younger sibling who behaved according to his/her own wish (# 11), when asked to tell how a reward had to be distributed among team members (# 12) and when given the responsibility to arrange a musical band for an official function (# 13).

Interestingly, equal number of scenarios (4 out of 16), encouraged the respondents to decide in favour of individualist choices. In this context, one of the scenarios was about buying an expensive set of furniture for personal use, (# 2), another one was about letting others know about one self with the help of four given attributes (# 10), the third was about choosing a vocational paper (# 14) and the last about suggesting what could be the most important concern while deciding to make a dress for an important social function (# 8). Scenario 8 however, had a tie with the Horizontal dimension in this case (as the frequency count showed same numbers in both the categories). Evidence for choosing both individualist and collectivist orientations for an equal number of times, supported the claim of Indian social scientists (e.g., Sinha & Tripathi, 1994) that Indians are not predominantly collectivists but prefer to switch on to either of the orientations depending upon the demands of the situation (that is, depending upon *desh* or place, *kal* or time, and *patra* or person).

The Collectivist Profile

The students thought that the best way to handle a bill among a group of friends was to distribute the cost equally among all or let the person who proposed to eat out take care of the bill (# 1), they preferred to choose the words 'cooperative' or ' dutiful' if they must give one word description of the self (# 3), happiness was suggested to be acquired by getting lots of status and prestige in the society and by making lots of friends (# 4), and the most interesting book seemed to be the one which suggested how to fulfill ones duties and obligations and how to make friends (# 6).

Furthermore, the most important thing regarding getting promotion in a job was being loyal towards the company and obeying the people in authority position (# 7), an ideal national budget ought to be able to fulfill the basic requirements of all irrespective of their economic status (# 9), and a younger sibling who behaved according to his/her sweet will, need to be reminded that all efforts should be made to behave in accordance to the wishes of the family members (# 11). Responses from the remaining scenarios suggested that reward money won by a team ought to be distributed equally among all the team members or the team leader could decide how to go about this (# 12), taste and liking of friends and authority figures should be taken into account while arranging a band for the college sports day (# 13), ordering snacks for friends (# 15), and while deciding whom to vote for the President of students' council (# 16).

It appeared that in all the above situations, the students either chose to think in terms of their group (i.e., HC), or felt that the best resolution of an issue was possible through giving due importance to the liking and wishes of senior and capable persons (i.e., VC). Accordingly, HC dimension got prominently sampled in scenarios 1, 7, 9, 12, 13 and 15 while the vertical collectivist preferences were predominantly evident in scenarios 3, 4, 6, 11, and 16.

The Individualist Preferences

The individualist preferences got prominence in the following four situations. First, when a decision had to be made regarding buying expensive furniture for personal use (# 2), getting a dressed stitched or purchased for attending a marriage (# 8), while deciding what one would like to tell others about oneself (# 10), and when choosing a vocational paper (# 14). It was quite obvious that all the four instances that lead to individualist preferences referred to very personal matters in the young student's life. Therefore, their choices appeared to be guided by concern for personal liking and good investment (# 2), individual liking and having scope for being praised by others (# 8), 'achievement' and 'uniqueness' as the preferred attributes to be associated with the self (# 10), and a future oriented decision making in the light of what was personally beneficial for the person, or with an aim of getting ahead of others (# 14).

Sinha and Tripathi (1994) observed that the situations in which individualist alternatives were endorsed by Indians most often pertained to solving personal problems, attaining personal achievement, deciding about the vital matters of life, and voting a person for a public position. Besides, individualistic choices were made more often than collectivist choices in situations relating to respondents' career, medical care, and skills and ability of coworkers.

In sum, the bottom line seemed to be that the college students were individualist in their choice of personal items, decisions about their career, and concern for achievement. They chose to be collectivist in the matters of family integration, friendship and giving due respect to hierarchy, when asked to be known as cooperative and dutiful persons, and at the question of loyalty towards the organization, etc. It appeared that the present sample of Bihari students preferred to be collectivist in social interactions and individualist in personal matters.

The Vertical Collectivism Profile

It was observed that the most likely events that stimulated the present respondents to appear vertical collectivists were (a) when asked to give an one word self description, (b) suggest how happiness is acquired, (c) tell about the most interesting book for themselves, (d) imagine a situation where they have to deal with a younger sibling who behaved on his/her own sweet will, and (e) vote for the President of the Students' Council.

In the above situations the preferred options respectively were, opting to choose 'cooperative' as the one word for self description (# 3), suggesting that happiness was acquired through getting lots of status, prestige and respect in the society (# 4); selecting a book which was about how to fulfill one's duties and obligations (# 6); reminding the younger sibling that parents were important and he or she should behave in accordance to their (parents) wishes (# 11) and voting for a person who was impressive and could influence others (# 16).

It may be noted, that the chosen responses in the above mentioned contexts mirrored the respondents' concern for their close in-group members towards whom they acknowledged having certain duties and responsibilities. This was evident in the preferred theme of an interesting book, or what a younger sibling was to be told. So was the word 'cooperative' that the students chose as self-description. Furthermore, according to the present respondents, 'happiness' went beyond being a personal experience and was acquired when the society bestowed status and respect to the person concerned, while a person who had to be voted for an important position, should be impressive and capable of influencing others. The last two choices had something to say about the other components of VC dimension that is, preference for hierarchy and distinction and were pointers to the vertical dimension of collectivism.

Scenarios as a Reliable Measure for Cultural Patterns

Since no significant difference was found between the percentage of respondents who chose different types of the cultural dimensions, in the present study and the one by Verma and Triandis (1999), it may be said that the scenarios may be seen as a reliable measure for measuring the cultural orientation of a particular cultural group. Minor changes in the content of the situations, did not bring about any significant difference in the observations of the two studies.

Summary and Conclusion

The present study was a follow up of the Verma and Triandis' (1999) cross-cultural study in which 16 scenarios describing familiar situations/themes in the day-to-day life of a student were used for measuring collectivism and its different dimensions. The researcher made some appropriate changes in the content of the scenarios for making them more familiar for the present respondents and wished to examine whether scenarios were a reliable means for measuring the dominant cultural themes of a cultural group. The objective was to study preference for different types of collectivism under variant situations.

150 Post Graduate students of Patna University responded to sixteen scenarios. Each scenario offered four alternatives indicating dominant preference for either Horizontal Collectivism, Horizontal Individualism, Vertical Collectivism or Horizontal Individualism. The results revealed that the four cultural dimensions were significantly different but there was no significant difference in the percentage of choices made in each category by the students in the two studies.

Vertical Collectivism had the largest mean followed by Horizontal Individualism, and Horizontal Collectivism. The smallest mean was observed for the dimension Vertical Individualism. A comparison among the dimensions suggested HI, and VC responses were chosen significantly more often than the VI responses while Horizontal Collectivism did not differ significantly from HI and VI dimensions.

Out of the sixteen scenarios, in eleven situations the respondents clearly preferred to endorse collectivist items over the individualist ones. It appeared that the students preferred to *describe* them selves as co-operative and dutiful, were happy making lots of friends and by getting status and respect in the society, were interested in a book which guided them regarding how to make friends and how to fulfill one's duties, believed in strengthening family ties and respecting one's parents, showed preference for the value of equality on the one hand, and handing over decision power to the group leader on the other.

Furthermore, the students took care that the entertainment band they arranged for an official function, pleased their friends and seniors, and preferred to choose the Student Council's leader who was influential and was the choice of their friends. It was only in three situations that they preferred to endorse individualist choices. For example, if they had to buy a set of expensive furniture for personal use, introduce them selves with the help of an attribute, and choose a vocational paper. It appeared that the students decided to take individualistic position in situations that had direct reference to their very personal and individual matters. In such situations they preferred to be guided by personal liking, scope for being benefited and excelling others in competition.

Since no significant difference in was found between the percentage of respondents who chose different types of the cultural dimensions, in the present study and the one by Verma and Triandis (1999), it may be said that the scenarios may be seen as a reliable measure for measuring the cultural orientation of a particular cultural group. Minor changes in the content of the situations, did not bring about any significant difference in the observations of the two studies.

APPENDIX 1

Verma and Triandis (1999) used the following 16 scenarios in their cross-cultural study. These were used again in the present study but with minor changes here and there for making the described situations and the description of the different cultural dimensions, more familiar for the Indian respondents. Note that changes either in the content of the scenarios or in the description of the alternative cultural dimensions (*i.e.*, HI, HC, VI, VC) are reported in *italics*.

Scenario 1. You and your friend decided spontaneously to go out to dinner at a restaurant. What do you think is the best way to handle the bill?

HC Split it equally, without regards to who ordered what.
VI Spilt it according to how much each person makes. ***The richest among the friends should pay the bill and get appreciation of his/her friends.***
VC The group leader pays the bill or decides how to split it.
HI Compute each person's charge according to what that person orderd.

Scenario 2. You are buying a piece of art for your office. Which one factor is most important in deciding whether to by it? Buying a "piece of art for your office" was replaced by:

Buying an expensive reading table and some furniture.

VI It is a good investment.
HC Your coworkers will like ti.
Instead of ***coworkers*** it was ***your sisters, brothers, friends and others will like the furniture***
HI You just like it.
VC Your supervisor will approve of it. Instead of ***supervisor*** it was ***your parents or guardians will approve of it.***

Scenario 3. Suppose you had to use on word to describe your self. Which one would you use?

HI Unique.
VI Competitive.
HC Cooperative.
VC Dutiful.

Scenario 4. Happiness is attained by

VC Gaining a lot of status in the community.
HC Linking with a lot of friendly people.
HI Keeping one's privacy.
VI Winning in competitions.

Scenario 5. You are planning to take a major trip which is likely to inconvenience a lot of people at your work place during your absence. With whom will you discuss it, before deciding whether or not to take it? Instead of this it was said:

You have got a job in another city far away from your home. Tell us whom would you consult before taking the job?

HI No one
VC My parents.
HC My spouse or close friend.
VI Experts about the place I plan to travel so that I can decide if I want to go there.

Scenario 6. Which one of these four books appears to you to be the most interesting?

HC How to make friends.
VI How to suceed in business.
HI How to enjoy yourself inexpensively.
VC How to make sure you are meeting your obligations.

Scenario 7. Which is the most important factor in an employee's promotion, assuming that all other factors such as tenure and performance are equal? Employ is or has:

HC Loyal to the corporation.
VC Obedient to the instructions from the manager.
HI Able to think for him/herself.
VI Contributed to the corporation much in the past.

Scenario 8. When you buy clothing for a mojor social event you would be most satisfied, if. In this case, "major social event" was replaced by "***marriage ceremony***"

HI You like it.
VC Your parents like it.
HC Your friends like it.
VI It is so elegant that it will dazzle everyone.

Scenario 9. In your opinion an ideal society's national budget will be determined so that:

HC All people have equal income to meet basic needs.
VI Some people will be rewarded for making brilliant contributions.
VC There will be maximal stability, law and order. Inwtead of this it was said: ***Where the poor and the rich both are benefited.***
HI People can feel unique and dself actualized.

Scenario 10. When people ask me about myself, I

VC Talk about my ancestors and their traditions.
HC Talk about my friends and what we like to do.
VI Talk about my accomplishments.
HI Talk about what makes me unique.

Scenario 11. Suppose your wife and your parents do not get along very well. What would you do? Since the studnets were unmarried the scenario was presented as follows:

Suppose your younger brother or sister behaves according to his/her own whims, tell us what would you do in a situation like this.

HI Nothing.
VI ***I will tell my younger sibling that I do not like his/her whims."***
HC ***I shall tell him/her that he/she should make efforts to be one with the family (meaning must behave in a manner which is in harmony with the family expectations).***
VC ***I shall remind him/her that one's parents and family is very important and he/she must hehave according to the desires of the family members.***

Scenario 12. Teams of five people entered a science project contest. Your team won first place and a prize of $ 100. You and another person did 95% of the work on this project. How should the money be distributed? ***Dollars replaced by 1000 Ruppes.***

HC Split it eqully, without regards to who dis what.
VI The other person and I get 95% of the money and the rest goes to the group.
VC The group leader decides how to split the money.
HI Divide the money the way that gives me the most satisfaction.

Scenario 13. Imagine you are selecting a band for a fund raising event given by your organization. Which are the most important factors in making your decision?"Fund raising event given by your organization" was replaced by, *responsibility to select a band for the college sports day.*

HI really like the band.
HC My friends approve of this band.
VC The administration of my organization approves of the band. ***My college authorities approve of the band.***
VI The bandd will draw a large crowd. ***People will be impressed by my selection.***

Scenario 14. You need to choose one more class for next semester. Which one will you select?

Instead of saying, "one more calss for next semester" it was said, ***you have to select a vocations/professional paper for further studies."***

VI The one that will help me get ahead of everyone else.
VC The one my parents said to take.
HC The one my friends plan to take.
HI The one that seems most interesting to me.

Scenario 15. You are at a pizza restaurant with a group of friends. How should you decide what kind of pizza to order?"***Pizza***" ***was replaced by "dosa."***

VC The leadder of the group orders for everyone.
HI I order what I like.
HC We sedlect the Pizza that most people prefer We select the ***dosa*** that most people prefer.
VI We order the most extravagant pizza.

Scenario 16. Which candidate will you vote for the President of the Students' Union?

HC The one that your friends are voting for.
HI The one I like best.
VI The one who rewards me personally.
VC The one who is member of an organization important to me. The status of the organization will improve if that candidate is selected.

REFERENCES

Bontempo, R., & Rivero, J. C. (1992). *Cultural variation in cognition: The role of self-concept in the attitude behavior link.* Paper presented at the meeting of the American Academy of Management, Las Vegas, Nevada, August.

Davidson, A. R. Jaccard, J. J., Triandis, H. C., Morales, M. L., & Diaz, W. B., Matsumoto, Y., Ting-Toomey, S., Nishida, T., & Karmi, H. (1994). *Measuring self construal across cultures: A derived etic analysis.* Paper presented at the International Communication Association Convention. Sydney, Australia, July.

Kim, U., Triandis, H. C., Kagitcibasi, C., Choi, S. C., & Yoon, G. (Eds.), (1994). *Individualism and collectivism: Theory, method, and application.* Newbury Park, CA: Sage.

Mills, J. & Clark, M. S. (1982). Exchange and communal relationships. In L. Wheeler (Ed.), *Review of personality and social psychology.* Volume 3. Beverly Hills, CA: Sage.

Markus, H. & Kitayama, S. (1991). Culture and self: Implications for cognition, emotion, and motivation. *Psychological Review, 98*, 224-253.

Rokeach, M. (1973). *The nature of human values.* New York: Free Press.

Scheffe, H. (1957). *The analysis of variance.* New York: J. Wiley.

Singelis, T. M., Triandis, H. C., Bhawuk, D. & Gelfand, M. (1995). Horizontal and vertical dimensions of individualism and collectivism: A theoretical and measurement refinement, *Cross-Cultural Research, 29,* 240-275.

Sinha, D., & Tripathi, R. C. (1994). Individualism in a collectivist culture: A case of coexistence of opposites. In U. Kim, H. C. Triandis, C. Kagitsibasi, S. C. Choi, G. Yoon (Eds.), *Individualism and collectivism: Theory, method and Application,* (Pp. 123-136). Newbury Park: Sage.

Triandis, H. C. (1989). The self and social behavior in differing cultural context. *Psychological Review, 96,* 506-520.

Triandis, H. C. (1990). Cross-cultural studies of individualism and collectivism. In J. Berman Ed.), *Nebraska Symposium on Motivation,* 1989 (pp. 41-133). Lincoln, Nebraska: University of Nebraska Press.

Triandis, H. C. (1995). *Individualism and collectivism.* Boulder, Co: Westview Press.

Verma, J. & Triandis, H. C. (1999). The measurement of collectivism in India. In W. J.Lonner, D.L. Dinnel, D. K., Forgays, & S. A. Hayes (Eds.), *Merging past, present, and future.* Selected Proceedings Of The 14th IACCP (Pp. 256-265). The Netherlands: Swets & Zeitlinger.

Yamaguchi, S. (1994). Empirical evidence on collectivism among the Japanese. In U. Kim, H.C. Triandis, C. Kagitcibasi, S. C. Choi, & G. Yoon (Eds.), *Individualism and collectivism: Theory, method, and application* (pp.175-188). Newbury Park, CA: Sage.

5

Similarities and Variations in Facial Expressions of Emotion Across Cultures

MANAS K. MANDAL and MITHILESH SINGH

Introduction

Darwin (1872) emphasized that emotions are crucial to human existence and expressions of emotion serve important adaptational functions. The theory was little debated for nearly a hundred years and evidence in support of the theory was put forward using facial expressions of different emotions across cultures. Of late, the claim of the universalists that facial expressions of emotions are expressed or understood panculturally has been challenged by the cultural psychologists or social constructivists. The cultural school of thought grew up as a challenge to 'universal' (*i.e.*, emotion is the basic function of human beings that is relatively invariant across cultures) or 'differential' (*i.e.*, emotions are differentiated on the basis of accompanying physiological response patterning) theories in the experience of emotion (Scherer & Wallbott, 1994). Averill (1992), for example, argued that emotions are expressed or experienced within a social network and individuals understand emotional behaviour on the basis of their knowledge of the social norms or rules.

The view of cultural psychologists on the subject reflected in a recent meta-analytical study on facial expressions of emotion by Russell (1994) who commented that "facial expressions and emotion labels are probably associated but the association may vary with culture". Universalists like Izard (1994) argued that facial expressions of emotion are "innate (but not displayed in adults of all cultures) or universal (because of culture - constant learning) but show individual and cultural variability in the semantic meaning attributed to it". The argument in favour of universality was originally put forward by Ekman (1972, 1992) who viewed that facial expressions of emotion are panculturally understood and expressed. Ekman's proposition however accommodated the fact that facial expressions of emotion are moderated to some extent by culture-specific display norms, such as, intensification, deintensification, masking, neutralization, etc. Available studies have shown that the cultural background of the encoder as well as the decoder influence judgment of facial emotions (Matsumoto, 1990). Matsumoto *et al.* (1998) maintained that display rules are learned within socio-cultural contexts that 'dictate the management of emotional expressions'. They observed cross-national differences in the management of display rules (see also Matsumoto & Hearn, 1989) that covary with the construct of individualism - collectivism. Research in this direction has revealed that people belonging to individualistic culture display facial emotion more intensely and for longer duration. In collective societies, especially in Asia, negative emotions are expressed less often (see also Mandal *et al.*, 1996) to avoid disruption in collective harmony (Matsumoto, 1992). In these cultures positive emotions, such as sympathy and happiness are more frequently expressed to promote communal harmony.

Although a sizeable number of studies have been conducted during the past two decades to resolve the controversy raised by universalists and social/cultural constructivists, little progress has been made in arriving at a consensus. One of the major reasons behind this state of controversy is probably the reliance on a single set of photographs depicting facial expressions of different emotions. Such a set of photographs is usually shown to observers of different cultures and the responses are examined to conclude in terms of culture-specificity or universality. Relatively few studies were conducted with sets of photographs displaying facial emotions within different cultures with the purpose of examining the universality hypothesis in a given culture. This approach is important because the recognition accuracy for 'in-group' (same ethnic group) and 'out-group' (different ethnic groups) may be compared to isolate the elements of universality and culture-specificity. The present study made an attempt in this direction with sets of photographs displaying facial emotions of Indian, Japanese and American subjects with two specific research aims. The first was to assess similarities and differences in the understanding of different cultural expressions by Indian observers. The second was to have an assessment of display rules (*e.g.*, intensification, deintensification, masking, neutralization) followed by different cultural groups during their facial expressions of facial emotions by asking the Indian observers to select the appropriate rule in their socio-cultural contexts. The existence and salience of display rules in social encounter were established long ago by Ekman (1972) and Friesen (1972). In their experiments, American and Japanese subjects produced similar facial expressions when alone. With an experimenter in front of them, the Japanese subjects masked their negative feelings. It is believed therefore that facial emotions "are a combination of biologically innate, universal expressions and culturally learned rules for expression management" (Matsumoto, Takeuchi, Andayani, Kouznetsova & Krupp, 1998). Some authors however assumed the salience of display rules nullifying the proposition of universality (for example, Fridlund, 1997).

Recent studies on facial expressions of emotion go beyond the debate of universality and culture-specificity. In their meta-analysis, Elfenbein and Ambady (2001) reported that emotions are universally recognised at better-than-chance accuracy; however, within cultures, there is an 'in-group advantage', that is, accuracy of recognition becomes higher when the perceiver and expressor have the same cultural background. With greater cross-cultural exposure, the in-group advantage becomes minimized. Support for these observations was obtained from a recent empirical study (Elfenbein, Mandal, Ambady, Harizuka & Kumar, 2001). In another study (Mandal, Harizuka, Bhusan & Mishra, 2001), it was found that cultural variability is reflected in the facial asymmetry (left, right) and valence (positive, negative) of emotion expressions. While the whole face depicts emotion that is universally recognized, the left face is more pronounced during emotion expression for Indians and Americans. For Japanese subjects, a right hemifacial bias for positive and a left hemifacial bias for negative emotions were observed. Based on these empirical observations and theoretical propositions, it was hypothesized that there would be an in-group advantage for recognition of facial emotions displayed by different cultural groups. It was also hypothesized that facial management techniques (display rules) during emotion expression would differ as a function of culture.

METHOD

Photographs

Three standardized sets of photographs depicting the facial expressions of six emotions (happy, sad, fearful, angry, surprised, disgusted) and a neutral state were selected for administration. These sets included photographs of facial emotions expressed by American (Ekman & Friesen, 1975), Indian (Mandal, 1986) and Japanese (Mandal, Harizuka, Bhushan & Mishra, 2001) subjects. The rationale behind using these three sets was to have facial emotions displayed by ethnically different groups. Pictures of facial affect (Ekman & Friesen, 1976) were developed by instructing subjects to make anatomically appropriate facial muscle movement. The Indian and Japanese sets of photographs were developed by asking subjects from the respective cultures to make socially appropriate expressions. During such expressions, subjects were encouraged to imagine appropriate affect-laden experience in their lives. The Indian and Japanese photographs were standardized following the method adopted by Ekman and Friesen (1976). Photographs that were recognized by 80% of the observers in the respective cultures were selected. Further the selected photographs were administered to a set observers (*N*=50) who were asked to rate every photograph on a 7-point scale, with neutral or no emotion at one end of the scale and the intended emotion at the other, for each of the given emotions. The photograph that yielded the highest rating for an emotion was retained. However, if the photograph was not discriminated by at least 2 points from the rest of the responses, the judgment was deleted. Photographs with at least 70% consensus were retained (Mandal, 1986). Finally, these three sets of photographs were administered to five experts for judgment in terms of intensity of expression. Only those photographs were selected that displayed a given emotion most intensely within the alternatives available for the set.

Two photographs (one male, one female) of seven expressions were selected from each set of photographs (3 sets × 2 sex of expressors × 7 expressions = 42 photographs). The age of the expressor and the intensity of expression were matched across sets of photographs as far as possible. All photographs were black and white and life-sized.

Observers

Fifty observers from rural educational institutions of India (male 28, female 22; Mean age 24.6 years; SD 4.36 years; Mean education 13.2 years) were asked to participate in the study. None of these subjects had the experience of face-to-face interaction with American or Japanese individuals. They however had exposure to films and televised clips containing facial expressions of American or Japanese persons. These subjects had 'Hindi' as their mother tongue. Because of their formal education (Mean education 13.2 years., SD 2.32 years), subjects were familiar with the Hindi equivalents of English language emotion words. Subjects did not differ in their ethnic origin or socio-economic status. Exposure to urban life however was quite variable amongst subjects.

Procedure

A two-stage study was undertaken. In stage-I observers were asked to recognize these photographs in terms of seven expression categories, happy, sad, fear, anger, surprise, disgust and neutral state. Photographs of a given culture were presented randomly to observers for judgment on a 7-category forced-choice response format. Each photograph was shown for a period of 10 second during which observers were encouraged to give judgment as early as possible. Photographs of Indian expressors were administered first, followed by Japanese and American expressors. Frequency of correct responses was the dependent measure. Emotion expressions with a given a set of photographs were presented randomly. Randomization between sets of photographs was not done because of the observation in a pilot study that observers' reorientation to physical characteristic to extra-ethnic faces distracts emotion judgment.

In stage-II, photographs were presented in an identical manner. Photographs within a given set were administered in an order different from stage-I. Observers' task was to indicate the type of display rule adopted by an expressor of a given culture for facial management. In giving such judgment, observers were asked to make an assessment in terms of self-reported behaviour (*i.e.*, what they themselves would actually express). Five response alternatives in terms of display management were given to observers: actual expression (expression of feeling as it is with no inhibition or intensification), deintensification (expression of feeling with less intensity than one's actual feeling), neutralization (expression of no feeling), and masking (expression of a different feeling in lieu of the actual one) [see Matsumoto *et al.* (1998)]. The frequency of observers accepting the response alternative (display rules) for each photograph was the dependent measure.

Results

Table 1 shows the frequency of correct recognition for seven facial expressions of three cultures (see also Fig.5.1 for overall recognition accuracy and Fig.5.2 for emotion-specific recognition accuracy). One-way ANOVA was done with the overall recognition score as the dependent measure. The difference was found significant, $F = 70.01$, $df = 2,149$, $p < .001$. Post-hoc analysis of data suggested that recognition accuracy for the Japanese expressors was the lowest

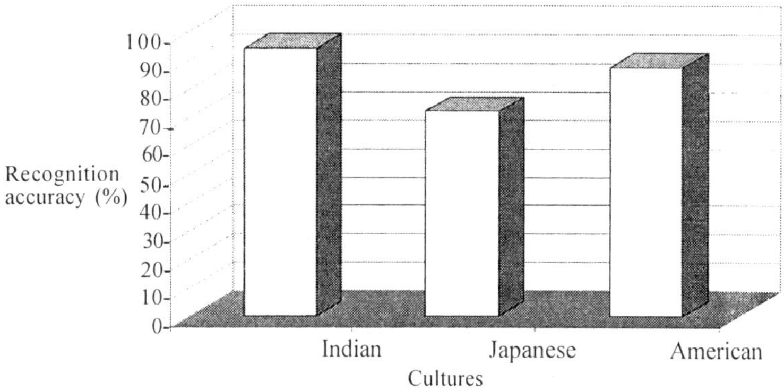

Fig. 5.1 Recognition accuracy (%) for facial expressions of three cultures

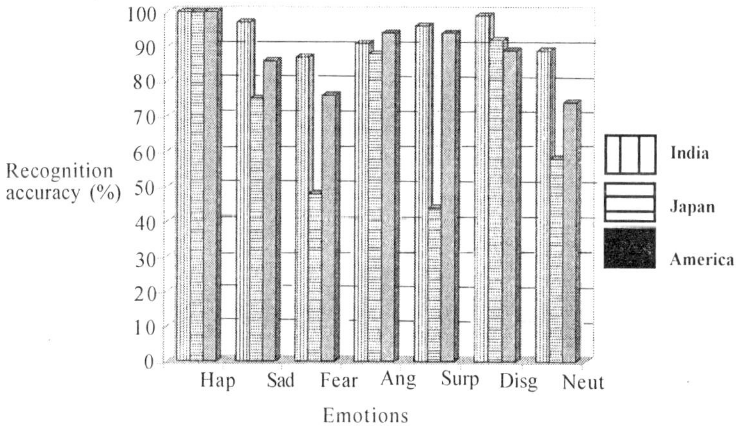

Fig. 5.2 Recognition accuracy (%) for facial expression of three cultures.

(*M* = 10.18, *SD* = 1.27; Tukey's *HSD* <.01) followed by the American expressors (*M* = 12.28, *SD* = 1.38; Tukey's *HSD* <.05) in comparison to Indian expressors (*M* = 13.18, *SD* = 1.24). The finding thus confirms the hypothesis that there would be an in-group advantage for recognition of facial expressions of emotion. The facial expressions of Indian subjects were best recognized by Indian observers. An emotion-wise analysis was done with the frequency of recognition for each culture as the dependent measure.

The difference in frequency of recognition was significant for fear ($\times^2 = 11.5, p<.01$), surprised ($\times^2 = 22.25, p<.001$) and neutral ($\times^2 = 6.52, p<.05$) expressions. Expressions of happiness, sadness, anger and disgust did not produce significant difference, the finding of which indicated the generality of these emotions across cultures.

Table 5.1 : Frequency of correct recognition (2 photos of each emotion × 50 observers) for seven expression categories

Emotions/ Groups	**Happy**	**Sad**	**Fear**	**Anger**	**Surprise**	**Disgust**	**Neutral**
India	100	97	87	91	96	99	89
Japan	100	75	48	88	44	92	58
N. America	100	86	76	94	94	89	74

Table 5.2 indicates the average frequency of times a display rule was chosen by observers across facial emotions (see also Fig.5.3).

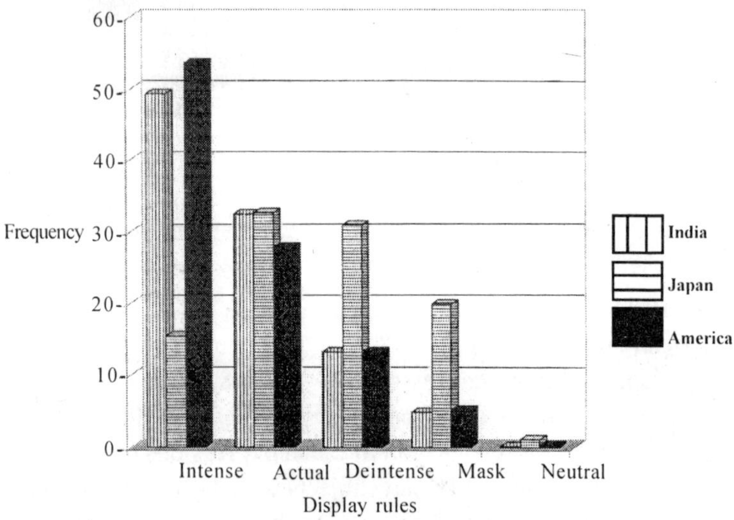

Fig. 5.3 Frequency of times display rules are chosen for cultures across emotions by observers

These data were treated with Friedman two-way ANOVA (F_r). It was assumed that if the cultural expressions (shown in rows, Table 5.2) were differentially related to display rules (shown in columns, Table 5.2), the set of ranks in each column would approximately be equal, yielding a non-significant index. Conversely, if the cultural expressions were not differentially related to display rules, a significant difference would emerge suggesting universality in facial display rules. To substantiate these findings, Kendall's coefficient of concordance (*W*) was also calculated to indicate the degree of association in judgment for three sets of cultural expressions. Findings yielded a non-significant index for judgments across emotions

Table 5.2 : Average frequency of times a display rule was chosen by observers (*N*=50) for facial emotions of different cultural origins

Display rules/ Groups	**Intensi-fication**	**Actual Expression**	**Disintensi-fication**	**Masking**	**Neutra-lization**
India	49.33	32.5	13.16	4.83	0.16
Japan	15.33	32.66	31.00	19.83	1.16
N. America	53.50	27.83	13.16	5.16	0.33

#maximum possible score for each cell = 100.

(F_r = 8.80, *df* = 4, *p* = .066; *W* = .733) indicating that cultural expressions were not differentially related to categories of display rules. Although the obtained level of significance did not reach the traditional level ($p<.05$), a close inspection of data indicated variations in the attribution of display rules by observers. Emotion-wise analysis was therefore done in an identical way. Emotions of happiness (F_r = 10.47, *df* = 4, *p* = .033; = .887), sadness (F_r = 10.06, *df* = 4, *p* = .039; *W* = .853), and disgust (F_r = 11.46, *df* = 4, *p* = .022; *W* = .955) yielded significant differences. These findings imply that observers uniformly treated these emotions across categories of display rules. However, the emotions of surprise

(F_r=7.40, *df*= 4, *p* = .116; *W* = .627), fear (F_r = 7.20, *df*= 4, *p*=.125; *W* = .60) and anger (F_r = 6.86, *df*= 4, *p* = .143; *W* = .581) did not yield significant difference for column totals (display categories), suggesting that cultural expressions were differentially judged across categories of display rules. Surprised expressions by the Japanese subjects were judged more often in the categories of 'deintensification' or 'masking' while such expressions by the Indian and American subjects were considered 'actual'. For negatively-aroused emotions (fear, anger), the Japanese expressions were adjudged identically as either deintensified or masked. The Indian and American expressions were judged more intense than actual display of emotions. Thus the hypothesis that facial display rules during emotion expressions would differ as a function of culture was partially supported. The hypothesis was confirmed for emotions like happiness, sadness and disgust and was rejected for emotions like surprise, fear and anger.

Discussion

The study had two general observations. First, facial emotions displayed by three cultures, Indian, Japanese and American, were not equally recognizable. Facial expressions of the Indians were best recognized followed by expressions of the North Americans and Japanese subjects. Second, facial emotions of happy, sad and disgust were judged to have displayed in a similar manner while emotions like fear, anger and surprise were judged to have displayed following culture-specific patterns.

The observation that recognition accuracy increases due to in-group advantage has been advocated recently by Elfenbein and Ambady (2001). The proposition is made following the observation that cross-cultural sample did not perform to the extent Americans performed for American facial stimuli. A number of factors were held responsible for this in-group advantage. One such factors was display rules or facial management technique (Ekman, 1992; Matsumoto, 1993) that modulate the emotion expressions to conform to the social construction embedded in a given culture.

As Buck (1984) has envisaged, the pancultural signals for decoding and encoding of facial emotions are discernable in non-social context-free conditions. Averill (1980, 1992), for example, argued that emotions are expressed or experienced within a social network and individuals understand emotional behaviour on the basis of their knowledge of the social rules or norms. He idealized 'emotion' as a form of social role that is enacted by an individual in the process of appraisal or reaction to a social situation. This behaviour is referred to as 'transitory social role' by Averill.

A second factor responsible for in-group advantage was language (Matsumoto & Assar, 1992), paralinguistic characteristics (Mesquita & Frijda, 1992) and semantic attributes (Russell, 1994). Russell (1994), for example, suggests that the association between emotional labels and expressions vary as a function of culture. Unlike the six basic emotions in Western literature (happy, sad, fear, anger, surprise, disgust; Ekman, 1972; Izard, 1971), the Natyasastra of Bharata in India (1st - 2nd century A.D.) mentions about 10 emotion words (anger, fear, disgust, heroism/valour, humour/amusement, love, peace, sadness, shame embarrassment shyness, wonder; see Hejmadi, Davidson & Rozin, 2000). These Hindu-Indian taxonomy of emotions do not correspond exactly to English - language emotion terms, especially the positive emotions. For example, happiness / pleasure has two connotations in Hindu Indian literature: worldly and heavenly pleasure. Worldly pleasure is derived from physical sources and is also attached to the feeling of pain. Heavenly pleasure is derived from desirelessness (absence of attachment) [Sinha, 1986]. A third factor responsible for in-group advantage may be motivation of the encoder to perform well for the 'out-group'. These factors were discussed in Elfenbein and Ambady (2001).

Although the present finding supports a cultural viewpoint, the universalists' notion cannot be ruled out. This is because the difference in recognizability was not absolute across emotions. It is quite possible that Indian facial emotions were better recognized by observers of the same culture due to culture-constant learning (Izard, 1994). Further, cultural acquaintance with the cranio-facial features of an ethnic group also facilitates recognition of an expressed emotion. In such case, the relatively poor recognition for the Japanese faces may be a function of the poor acquaintance with cultural norms or cranio-facial features of the target group. But paucity of such knowledge did not impair recognition beyond the level of chance accuracy. One may argue therefore that facial expressions of emotions are recognized universally although cultural acquaintance may facilitate recognition to a great extent. Ekman (1994) also pointed out that decoding accuracy is highly variable amongst cultures.

That certain emotions are expressed in a universal manner sparing others to follow culture-specific display rules is a finding juxtaposed between the notions of universalists and social/cultural constructivists. While universalists believe that facial emotions may be modulated depending upon culture-constant learning despite 'innate facial affect programme' (Ekman, 1992), social/cultural constructivists attribute such differences across culture on the process of socialization. Research has shown that knowledge of display rules is an important determinant for development (Malatesta & Haviland, 1982; Cole, 1985), socialization (Fridlund, 1997) and cultural elements like individualism - culturalism (Matsumoto *et al.,* 1998).

The present finding suggests that facial emotions of happiness, sadness and disgust were displayed in a similar manner across cultures. Happy and disgustful expressions were judged to have displayed more intensely (intensification) while sad expresions to have displayed in an inhibited manner (deintensification). Since observers' judgments were treated as the independent measure and facial management technique as the dependent one, the non-difference in cultural display rule was attributed to universality in the present study. Skeptics would however argue that the finding was a reflection of the cultural variation in perception rather than universality of expression in which the observers tended to perceive these expressions in a culturally approved manner.

Indian observers gave differential judgments about display norms for emotions like fear, anger and surprise, thus satisfying the convictions of cultural psychologists/social constructivists. Fear and angry expressions were judged to have displayed in an inhibited manner by the Japanese and in an intense manner by the North Americans and Indians. Earlier studies however suggested that the Japanese individuals, in comparison to the North Americans, favour restraint in their expressions, especially the negative ones (see Kitayama & Markus, 1994). Given such findings, universalists would argue that the difference in observation is a reflection of the perception of the social events rather than in expression management. Support for this assertion may be drawn from a study in which the Indian and North American observers rated fearful and angry expressions of the Indian and North Americans as significantly more distinctive (or intense) [Mandal, Bryden & Bulman-Fleming, 1996]. It is also argued that emotions that are more accurately recognized across cultures, are also displayed alike by individuals of different cultural origins. This presumption is partially justified by the present finding. The emotions of happiness, sadness and disgust were recognized and displayed without any cultural variation. The emotions of fear and surprise produced group difference either for recognition accuracy or display rules. These findings suggest therefore that the proposition of universality or culture-specificity depends largely on emotion categories.

The argument that 'basic' emotion categories should be universally recognized or displayed may not be true because cultural sanctions may inhibit an expression at the overt expressional level. The inner biological system may still respond to that emotion at a covert level (Izard, 1994). These observations lead us to believe that the debate on 'universality - culture specificity' is meaningless without taking into account the nature of emotion. In fact, the six basic emotions differ in terms of hedonic valence (positive-negative), arousal (arousal-non-arousal) and motoric direction (approach - avoidance) [Mandal, Borod, Asthana, Mohanty, Mohanty, & Koff, 1999]. Such variations in emotion expressions are taken into account in framing social rules and norms. Given such a background, it may be wise to ignore the universality—culture-specificity debate in favour of an integrated approach

(Matsumoto, 1998) wherein these two issues may be understood in a complementary rather than in a contrasting manner.

REFERENCES

Averill, J.R. (1992). The structural bases of emotional behaviour: A metatheoretical analysis: In M.S. Clark (Ed.), *Emotion.* Newbury Park, CA: Sage.

Boucher, J.D., & Carlson, G.E. (1980). Recognition of facial expression in three cultures. *Journal of Cross- cultural Psychology, 11,* 263-280.

Buck, R. (1984). *The communication of emotion.* New York : Guilford Press.

Burgoon, J.K. (1994). Nonverbal signals. In M.L. Knapp & G.R. Miller (Eds.), *Handbook of interpersonal communication.* London: Sage.

Cole, P.M. (1985). Display rules and the socialization of affective displays. In G. Zivin (Ed.), *The development of expressive behaviour: Biology-environment interactions.* San Diego, CA: Academic Press.

Darwin, C. (1872). *The expression of the emotion in man and animals.* London : Murray.

Ekman, P. (1972). Universals and cultural differences in facial expressions of emotions. In J.R. Cole (Ed.). *Nebraska Symposium on Motivation (1971),* Lincoln, Nebraska : University of Nebraska Press.

Ekman, P. (1992). Facial expression of emotion : An old controversy and new findings. *Philosophical Transaction of the Royal Society of London, B, 335,* 63-69.

Ekman, P. (1994). Strong evidence for universals in facial expressions: A reply to Russell's mistaken critique. *Psychological Bulletin, 115,* 268-287.

Ekman, P. & Friesen, W.V. (1975). *Unmasking the face.* New Jersy : Prentice-Hall.

Elfenbein, H.A. & Ambady, N. (2001). Of the universality and cultural specificity of emotion recognition: A meta-analysis. *Manuscript submitted for publication.*

Elfenbein, H.A. Mandal, M.K., Ambady, N., Harizuka, S. & Kumar, S. (2001). Cross-cultural patterns in emotion recognition: Accuracy and error beyond the "Diagonal". *Manuscript submitted for publication.*

Fridlund, A.J. (1997). The ethology of human facial expressions. In J.A. Russell & J. Fernandez-Dols (Eds.), *The psychology of facial expressions: Studies in emotion and social interaction.* Cambridge: Cambridge University Press.

Friesen, W.V. (1972). Cultural differences in facial expressions in a social situation : An experimental test of the concept of display rules. *Unpublished doctoral dissertation,* University of California, San Francisco.

Hejmadi, A., Davidson, R.J., & Rozin, P. (2000). Exploring Hindu Indian emotion expressions: Evidence for accurate recognition by Americans and Indians. *Psychological Science, 11,* 183-187.

Izard, C.E. (1971). *The face of emotion.* New York : Appleton-Century-Crofts.

Izard, C.E. (1994). Innate and universal facial expressions : Evidence from developmental and cross- cultural research. *Psychological Bulletin, 115,* 288-299.

Kitayama, S. & Markus, H.R. (Eds.) [1994]. *Emotion and culture: Empirical studies of mutual influence.* Washington, D.C.: American Psychological Association.

Malatesta, C. & Haviland, J. (1982). Learning display rules: The socialization of emotion expression in infancy. *Child Development, 53,* 991-1003.

Mandal, M.K. (1986). Judgment of facial affect among depressives and schizophrenics. *British Journal of Clinical Psychology, 25,* 87-92.

Mandal, M.K., Borod, J.C., Asthana, H.S., Mohanty, A., Mohanty, S. & Koff, E. (1999). Effects of lesion variables and emotion type on the perception of facial emotion. *The Journal of Nervous & Mental Disease, 187,* 603-609.

Mandal M.K., Bryden, M.P. & Bulman-Fleming, M.B. (1996). Similarities and variations in facial expression of emotions : Cross-cultural evidence. *International Journal of Psychology, 31,* 49-58.

Mandal, M.K., Harizuka, S., Bhusan, B. & Mishra, R.C. (2001). Cultural variation in hemifacial asymmetry of emotion expressions. *British Journal of Social Psychology,* In Press.

Matsumoto, D. (1990). Cultural similarities and differences in display rules. *Motivation and Emotion, 14,* 195-214.

Matsumoto, D. (1992). American-Japanese cultural differences in the recognition of universal facial expressions. *Journal of Cross-Cultural Psychology, 23,* 72-84.

Matsumoto, D. (1993). Ethnic differences in affect intensity emotion judgements, display rule attitudes, and self reported emotional expression in an American sample. *Motivation and Emotion, 17,* 107-123.

Matsumoto, D. & Assar, M. (1992). The effects of language on judgments of universal facial expressions of emotion. *Journal of Non-verbal Behavior, 16,* 85-99.

Matsumoto, D. & Hearn, V. (1989). Display rules differences in the U.S., Poland and Hungary. Unpublished manuscript.

Matsumoto, D., Takeuchi, S., Andayani, S., Kouznetsova, N. & Krupp, D. (1998). The contribution of individualism vs. collectivism to cross-national differences in display rules. *Asian Journal of Social Psychology, 1,* 147-165.

Mesquita, B. & Frijda, N.H. (1992). Cultural variations in emotions: A review. *Psychological Bulletin, 112,* 197-204.

Russell, J.A. (1994). Is there universal recognition of emotion from facial expressons : A review of the cross-cultural studies. *Psychological Bulletin, 115,* 102-141.

Saarni, C. (1984). An observational study of children's attempts to monitor their expressive behaviour. *Child Development, 55,* 1504-1513.

Scherer, K.R. & Wallbott, H.G. (1994). Evidence for universality and cultural variation of differential emotional response patterning. *Journal of Personality and Social Psychology, 66,* 310-328.

Sinha, J. (1986). *Indian psychology : Emotion and will* (Vol.2). Varanasi : Motilal Banarasidass.

Sorenson, E.R. (1976). *The edge of the forest : Land, childhood, and change in a New Guinea protoagricultural society.* Washington, DC: Smithsonian Institution Press.

6

Culture and Counselling:

The Indian Paradox—Implications for Professional Psychology

SONALI BHATT MARWAHA

Introduction

In recent years, the inter-disciplinary field of "Cultural psychology" has emerged, on the interface of anthropology, psychology, linguistics, and philosophy. It promotes theory and research amongst different cultures in various domains of psychological functioning, including the cultural psychology of the self, cognition, emotions, and so forth. Cultural psychology is the study of how culture and psychology make up each other. The aim of cultural psychology is to document and explain divergences in the way in which the psyche functions across different ethnic and cultural groups (Menon & Shweder, 1994).

This paper proposes to highlight factors that prevent adequate application of psychological principles in the treatment and management of emotional and mental health issues with the Indian people. The factors contributing to the low turn out of individuals in seeking professional help can broadly be divided into professional, sociological and psychological factors.

We, as Indian professionals, arising from our idiosyncratic culture, trained in a largely western theoretical framework, practice within our diverse social milieu. Irrespective of our social and theoretical background, as professionals in the field of personal development, we hope to help individuals in their process of growth. More so, at times when they are at their wits' end in dealing with issues that life faces them with.

Astute professionals recognise the difference in the cultural ethos of their clientele and modify their methods and approaches in dealing with the local population. However, the primary difficulty Indian psychotherapists face irrespective of the approach they may choose to follow, whether it is a long-term process or a time limited approach, is in inviting potential clients for therapy or counselling.

Considering the population and the incidence of mental health problems, the number of people seeking professional help for personal problems is negligible. Help columns in newspapers and magazines receive tremendous response, due to the anonymity that it offers. The issues that help is sought for are varied. They range from academic / career problems, problems in relationships – with peers, family, significant others, serious marital problems, sexual problems, and psychiatric problems. In fact, the entire range of emotional issues, that we can possibly be faced with. When viewed in this light, the gap between professionals and potential clients is truly glaring.

Professional Factors

At the professional level, lack of adequately trained professionals is a felt need. In recent years, there has been a growing realisation that the discipline of psychology in India, as an academic venture and as a profession needs serious rethinking. It has been indicated that the teaching programmes in psychology do not adequately address the requirements of the discipline as a profession. Aside from the issue of following a western framework, most psychology departments concentrate on the academic aspect of the discipline, with scant attention to the applied aspects. Thus producing more academicians than practising psychologists. Those who opt to approach the applied field do so off their own interest, acquiring training on the field and from non-institutional avenues. This aspect of the status of psychology training in India has been well expressed by Mishra, Prakash & Verma (1999), Mishra & Verma (1995), Singh & Dalal (1988). In the absence of sufficient trained therapists and clinicians, the profession stands to lose in popularising its potentiality and role amongst the para-medical professionals. The public thus runs the risk of being exposed to untrained persons, posing as mental health professionals.

Aside from academic and institutional inertia, reasons for laxity of approach in training professionals may well lie in the sociological aspects of the issue. These factors make the practice of psychology economically unviable to attract sufficient motivation to enhance training facilities and for graduates to opt for it as a full time profession, thus feeding the vicious circle of lack of professionalism in the field.

Sociological and Psychological Factors

In dealing with any aspect of Indian life, one has to be aware that there is no pan Indian approach in its analysis. India lives in its developed cities, its developing towns, and its rural hinterland. Alongside is the life of the individuals in the upper, middle and lower economic groups. At the personal level, India also lives at different levels of awareness: of individuality and empowerment, of those aware of and hoping or trying to reach this level of individuality, and those mired in traditional mindsets having no awareness of or scope for options to choose from. Compounding all this are the varied cultures and sub-cultures that exist within the unitary framework of India. Considering this, the sociological and psychological factors that restrict the scope for psychotherapy and counselling are presented.

The diversity of backgrounds from which the people emerge makes it nearly impossible for a psychologist trained in urban centres to comprehend and empathise with the needs of the people. This is possible only if professionals from these diverse social milieus are trained. For instance, only a person from a rural or tribal background can effectively comprehend the socio-cultural and political dynamics of their people. Without sufficient knowledge of their beliefs and values, and the ground realities of life in these various settings, improvising methods based on western psychological principles would be inadequate to deal with their mental health issues. Awareness of this lacuna is a felt need.

Considering the diverse milieu, the relativity of what constitutes a mental health 'problem' also arises. For example, the religiously sanctioned concept of "Santhara", amongst the Jainas is a case in point. This ancient religious duty permits an individual to starve himself to death 'once he has fulfilled his worldly obligation'. The person opting for such a route is deified. From another perspective, this is viewed as suicide, which has socio-religious sanction. Recently there have been reports of an increasing number of persons, especially women, opting for this process. Although elderly persons (mainly widows) have been choosing this route, there have been instances of young girls choosing this method (Parihar, 2001). For the mental health professional in these regions, what criteria does he have to differentiate these from purely suicidal individuals? He runs the risk of inviting public wrath for assigning a 'merely human' motive for such a 'noble' act.

Another case in point is that of cleanliness and religious ritualism. Where do rituals end, and compulsive behaviours begin? Unless such behaviour interferes with the functioning or comforts or necessities of other family members, compulsive behaviours may be encouraged and lauded as religious behaviour. Thus, the family itself may not perceive it as a mental health issue, requiring professional help. The individual, so encultured, may perceive his personal distress as a moral transgression, for which the rituals offer a solution. The moot point is, which is the problem and which is the solution?

Issues dealing with sexuality and the myths and misinformation surrounding it, find their basis in our socio-religious texts. These are areas leading to anxiety, depression, paranoia, which are not dealt with professionally. Most commonly they are ignored or dealt anonymously through help columns in newspapers and magazines.

Why is this area, which causes us the greatest personal distress and pain treated in such an indifferent manner? Why are they not considered important, as they affect the health status of individuals and eventually society at large?

Within the urban and semi-urban population, ignorance of mental health issues and awareness of possible available help is an important factor contributing to the under-utilisation of psychological services. The concept of mental disorders being a result of some paranormal phenomena or a medical disorder prevails. Hence, the mode of treatment chosen is either visits to shamans, mystics, and religious groups or a medical mode of treatment, when the situation gets out of hand. Thus, prevention of problems by seeking timely help for personal problems is not a priority. In addition, with inadequate and expensive primary medical health care facilities, treatment for mental health issues is not in the reckoning.

The staunch belief in fate, karma, astrology, palmistry, and currently vasthu, governs the lives of Indian people. Therefore, all problems are attributed to these factors. Discord in personal lives, the emotional and health consequences of this discord are also attributed to these factors. Thus, personal and family dynamics as distress causing factors, and hence within one's grasp to handle, are not considered. Consequently, in the face of problems, choosing methods such as appeasing the troublesome planetary configurations or appropriate religious observations are opted for. The onus of a problem within lies in some external occurrence. This belief has its positive and negative consequences—providing rationalisation to cope or adapt with one's situation or surrendering to a situation over which one can have some control. Either way, this would imply the use of some defence mechanism to deal with emotional upheavals. The consequence of ignoring emotional issues may show up later.

Sinha (1990) has analysed the notion of psychological well being and observed that the "Indian view" emphasises a symbiotic relationship with the environment rather than dominating and controlling it. These analyses indicate a trend in favour of context sensitive strategies to conduct oneself rather than viewing the environment in conflict with oneself and confronting it as a threat and overcoming it." Mishra (1994), Mishra and Radheshyam (1995), in a study on self-construal in Indians, report an absence of a clear-cut polarisation in favour of either the independent or the interdependent mode of self-construal. They report that women were more interdependent and independent than men. Women considered themselves similar to others and perceived others to be similar to them. Conversely, they also differentiated themselves more from others than did men, as was their need to be different. There is thus a dichotomy in their perceived self-liking for group membership and their need to be different. This was found to be greater in women than in men. Thus, the women would experience a self – ideal disparity. The studies further indicate that those high on independence and low on interdependence had a more positive self-construal. The implications of this, is the experience of a negative self-construal that Indian women may perceive. An adequate understanding of Indian social psyche would indicate that the situation for Indian men might not be that different. Our social norms value external controls for its members. Individual differences point towards the need for greater independence or internal controls. Studies indicate a positive relation between an internal locus of control and stress (Shejwal & Palsane, 1988; Singh & Dalal,(1988). This stress, may be the result of a self-ideal disparity, and the difference between personal needs and social norms.

It is a truism to say that an Indian's personal identity is that of an individual enmeshed in the identity of his social group. The concept of individuality is against the cultural ethos. A person is first a member of his family, his social caste group, and if time permits, an individual. Hence, personalangst is not an issue of concern. This would seem to be one of the factors inhibiting a person from considering emotional distress on par with physical health problems requiring attention. However, this does not prevent an individual from experiencing stress in his environment.

It is stated that the Indian cultural ethos, with its importance on family values, extensive support of joint and extended family systems, reverence of adults within the family as mentors, and the availability of social networks, precludes the need for professional help. These networks exist. They may work for issues of minor concern. However, the effectiveness of these networks, in the event of psychological or personal problems, may be our socio-political myth. Enmeshed in this is our philosophical background, our socio-religious principles, and our gender issues. "Gender ideology is deeply embedded in the ideas of custom, tradition, and religion, which continue to be the guiding forces of normative behaviour" (Kapadia, 1999).

Internal family and social dynamics, of the individual under distress, is the soil in which the seeds of problems germinate. To seek effective help from this very source would be counterproductive to the needs of the individual. In addition, the ability of family members to provide relevant information and support is a question. Even in the presence of sound family dynamics, the tradition of communication patterns within the Indian family system prevents an openness that would permit a member to seek help for personal issues. Paintal & Pandey (1996), in a conflict based study of attitudes of adolescents towards their parents report a high intensity of conflict with fathers, who were perceived as unfriendly, uncaring, non-communicative and distant. Though one may argue that this is our traditional mode of behaviour in a patriarchal society, the conflict and its effects exist. Although this is changing, this state of flux creates its own discord that requires effective and timely help, both for the parent and child. The politics of perpetuating this myth of family support lies in our perception of seeking "the help of a shrink" as a western import and hence against the needs of the people. A deeper analysis of the issue, however, reveals factors that again arise from the Indian mindset.

The concept of shame is deeply embedded in the Indian psyche. Seeking outside help for personal, especially emotional issues is considered disrespectful to the reputation of the family hence shameful. Especially since these issues invariably reveal some family "secret". The family honour is of paramount concern. Hence, the ever-present fear of familial and societal disapproval and criticism proves to be a prime deterrent for acknowledging emotional issues. This is also a factor that prevents individuals and families to seek help from their social network. As in other societies, this is more so in issues related to sexual abuse. The individual, irrespective of gender, hides behind the iron curtain of guilt, rather than exposing misdeeds of close family members or acquaintances and the burden of this guilt, influences the future course of their personal well-being. However, there is a paradox here. The proverbial "grape vine" is ever present, and people are invariably aware of situations around them, but the factor of shame, transgressing social norms of conduct, fear of "interference" in others lives, prevent them from taking adequate steps to mitigate a situation. This is indeed a paradox in our interdependent culture. This is particularly seen in situations such as dowry harassment, family violence. On the one hand we pride ourselves on our group culture, on the other we pride ourselves on our family unit. The smaller units are confined within themselves, pride and honour being the guiding factors. Our group culture protects only to the extent of dealing with other groups. Although caste panchayats do exist, their application may be extended to socio-political issues rather than individual mental health issues.

Data has revealed that domestic violence is multi-determined, originating in the family, the individual, and the culture (Pageglow, 1984; Strauss *et al,* 1980). In a study on family conflict and violence patterns in India, Dhawan *et al.* (1999) concluded that women are victims of family conflict/abuse by their spouses and other family members and that gender role conditioning and cultural norms both contribute to this. The interplay of multiple social hierarchies, of gender and generation contribute to the perpetuation of domestic violence (Fernandez, 1997).

Thus, the social support system that purports to be the backbone of family life proves to be, from one side the perpetrator and from the other side, impotent. Issues that can be dealt effectively with professional help are left to fester. If the problem reaches to the point of becoming pathological, it would be considered all the more shameful, as it is equated with "madness", and hence something to be hidden. Medical help as a "curative" measure, is more readily availed of, rather than utilising the services of psychologists and social workers as preventive measures.

These factors interfere even in the course of responding to questionnaires that address intimate and personal issues. Evading, or even denying, such issues become the preferred mode. This would even interfere in our endeavour to collect systematic data on issues such as family discord and violence – both physical and psychological, and hence in obtaining adequate data on the presence and extent of personal distress.

In addition to these factors of shame and family honour, gender stereotypes prevent the recognition, acceptance, and hence need to address emotional problems. The man (with the culturally ingrained Rama Ideal), as strong, with his emotions well under control, with permission to express anger, at times even brutally, may not consider it needful to seek help for himself. The woman (with her culturally emphasised Sita Ideal), as mild mannered, meek, emotional, with an inherent ability to bear all pressures and burdens does not need help. Thus the need for help is not recognised, as anyone falling short of this stereotype would be considered as being inadequately endowed for womanhood. It would be shameful for not living up to expectations, and hence a fault with one's self therefore not requiring help.

Gender stereotypes also interfere in the therapists' perception of problems and their ability to assist the client through their problems. As the therapist also comes from the same social milieu, his perception of a woman's role, status, and problems may be biased and interferes with effective working through of a problem. What we must make note of, is that, the Indian man is as much a victim of stereotypes and social pressures to conform, as the Indian woman. At the individual level, he may also be suffering his personalangst in his efforts to achieve his personal freedom, from the fetters of social norms.

Enmeshed in this issue is that of individuality and change from traditional mindsets. Both the therapist and client, in the Indian set-up realise the difficulty in implementing self-assertive behaviour. Particularly for the woman, our social ethos does not permit assertiveness. Assertiveness is not synonymous with selfishness and aggression. One may argue that a western therapeutic goal of self-assertion and individualism is an antithesis to our interdependent cultural framework. From the individual's perspective herein lies the paradox of therapeutic work in the Indian set-up. For as she / he gets in touch with her / his private self, the realisation of our cultural binds also sets in. This dilemma of whether to move the client to a process of change or towards adjustment and adaptation to an unsatisfactory situation is a major obstacle. As therapists, we may all have faced situations where the most effective and necessary step from the clients' perspective, and welfare, would be the most radical one. Allan Watts (1961) expresses this most succinctly :

> "The task of the psychotherapist is to bring about a reconciliation between individual feeling and social norms without, however, sacrificing the integrity of the individual. He tries to help the individual to be himself and to go it alone without giving unnecessary offence to his community, to be in the world (of social convention) but not of the world."

He goes on to express that,

> "The therapist who is really interested in helping the individual is forced into social criticism. This does not mean that he has to engage directly in political revolution; it means that he has to help the individual in liberating himself from various forms of social conditioning, which includes liberation from hating this conditioning – hatred being another form of bondage to its object. But from this point of view the troubles and symptoms from which the patient seeks relief, and the unconscious factors behind them, cease to be merely psychological. They lie in the whole pattern of his relationships with other people and, more particularly, in the social institutions by which these relationships are governed: the rules of communication employed by the culture or group. These include the conventions of language and law, of ethics and aesthetics, of status, role, and identity, and of cosmology, philosophy, and religion."

Conclusion

With our understanding of human and gender rights, do we as mental health professionals assist the individual towards self-assertion or towards submission and compromise, in the larger interest of society and our cultural norms? In doing so, do we conform to cultural identity or do we encourage the individual to accept and move towards her intuitive needs? The answer to these questions may well lie within the strength of the individual client—to accept and move towards her intuitively identified needs, and the therapist—for recognising the inequalities of our cultural norms.

The aim of psychotherapy and counselling is personal growth. Within the Indian context, seeking help of a mental health professional for personal growth and development is a concept that is not recognised. There are two aspects to this issue. Firstly, it would be seen as self indulgence and imitating a western concept. Secondly, when the issue of personal growth is considered, recourse to our indigenous systems, with a primarily religious basis is the preferred mode. This stems from a basic difference in what is meant by 'personal growth', in the Western and Indian context. Awareness of the individual's personality, working through of personal problems, and achieving maturity and "person-hood", constitutes 'personal growth' in the Western context. In the Indian context, spiritual development, and working towards the final aim of life, moksha, constitutes 'personal growth'. Although all Indians reaching for 'spiritual development' may not be approaching it with this aim, the philosophy and methods used are aimed towards this goal.

Many questions are to be raised on the efficacy of these methods, of joining cults and ashrams as effective means of dealing with mental health issues. Are they effective for persons within the range of normality, *i.e.*, persons with 'normal' problems of life, or are they effective for persons with definitive problems of "real" life, and mental health problems as listed in the DSM or ICD categories? As these methods put forth the promise of 'bliss', are they an escapist measure of dealing with life's problems, rather than dealing with them in a practical manner? As many problems arise from the conflict between old and contemporary values, can these systems, effectively deal with contemporary issues? Or, do they entrap the individual in a conflict cycle of differing value systems? Or, do they provide a façade of effort? Despite the validity of these questions, these are not effectively addressed. Two factors contribute to this. Due to their strong link with religion and religious identity, an individual is given tacit social approval to choose these methods. Any attempt to question the validity of these methods would be perceived as an affront to our cultural ethos and religious sentiments. Secondly, the intensive dependency on external factors as causative agents for personal problems absolves the individual from taking any proactive measures in dealing with them. Especially since these factors are considered to be omnipotent in nature. However, the inherent dichotomy in this philosophy is not lost. As mentioned earlier, our belief system provides us adequate avenues to 'deal' with this omnipotence. These measures encourage the individual to ignore personal and emotional issues. As these are issues that he may not be really willing to address, any attempt to question the validity of indigenous methods would be faced with individual opposition.

To summarise, the orientation and nature of current training of psychologists, the economic viability of seeking help for personal problems, our belief systems of karma and fate, interdependent cultural ethos, our concepts of shame and family honour, gender stereotypes, and the dilemma of change, are some of the factors that hinder individuals from seeking professional help for personal problems.

In recent times, attempts are being made to raise the awareness of mental health issues and the concept of seeking help for emotional problems. However, these attempts are inadequate for the needs and scope of addressing these issues in the Indian context. Until these barriers exist, emotional distress will not be treated as a priority for requiring professional attention.

REFERENCES

Dhawan, N., Punetha, D., Sinha, Y. & Gaur, S.P. (1999). Family conflict / violence patterns in India. *Psychology and Developing Societies 11, 2,* 194-216.

Fernandez, M. (1997). Domestic violence by extended family members in India: Interplay of gender and generation. *Journal of Interpersonal Violence, 12(3),* 433-455.

Kapadia, S. (1999). Self, women and empowerment. In T. S. Saraswathi (Ed.), *Culture, Socialisation and Human Development: theory, research and applications in India.* New Delhi: Sage Publications.

Kitayama, S. & Markus, H. R. (1994). The cultural construction of self and emotion: Implications for social behaviour. In Kitayama, S. & Markus, H.R. (Eds.) *Emotion and Culture: Empirical studies of mutual influence.* American Psychological Association.

Menon, U. & Shweder, R. A. (1994). Kali's tongue: Cultural psychology and the power of shame in Orissa, India. In Kitayama, S. & Markus, H. R. (Eds.), *Emotion and Culture: Empirical studies of mutual influence.* American Psychological Association.

Mishra, G. & Radheshyam, G. (1995). Is Indian self predominantly independent? *Journal of Indian Psychology, 13 (1),* 16-29.

Mishra, G. & Verma, S. (1995). Social problem, psychology and social policy. *Journal of Indian Academy and Applied Psychology, 20,* 97-105.

Mishra, G. (1994). Psychology of control: Cross-cultural considerations. *Journal of Indian Psychology, 12 (1&2),* 8-48.

Mishra, G., Prakash, A. & Verma, S. (1999). Psychology in India: Perceptions and perspectives. *Psychology and Developing Societies, (Jan-Jun), 11 (1),* 25-53.

Pageglow, M. D. (1984). *Family violence.* New York: Praeger.

Paintal, H. K. & Pandey, N. (1996). A conflict based study of attitudes of adolescents towards their parents: Implications for parental counselling. *Indian Journal of Clinical Psychology, 23 (1),* 4-11.

Parihar, R. (2001). Death Defying. *India Today,* April 2, 2001.

Shejwell, B. R. & Palsane, M. N. (1988). Locus of control: A personality correlate in life events stress. *Psychological Studies, 31,* 177-182.

Singh, A. K. & Dalal, A. K. (1988). Psychology in India: A survey of doctoral students. *International Journal of Psychology, 23,* 525-533.

Sinha, D. (1990). The concept of psychosocial well-being: Western and Indian perspectives. *National Institute of Mental Health and Neurosciences Journal, 8,* 1-11.

Strauss, M., Gelles, R. J., & Steinmetz, S. K. (1980). *Behind closed doors: Violence in the American family.* New York: Anchor/Doubleday.

Watts, A. W. (1961). *Psychotherapy East and West.* Pantheon Books, Random House.

7

Role of Socio-Economic Background in the Development of Perceptual Exploration and Part-Whole Perception

MAMATA VERMA, S.K. UPADHYAY and R.C. MISHRA

Introduction

Perception is a process by which we gain knowledge about outrenvironment and about ourselves in relation to the environment. It involves the processes of exploration and differentiation of objects, places and events. According to Piaget (1947) the perception of young child is 'centered', in the sense that the child is not able to shift attention from one part of an object to the other. With increase in age new mental structures evolve, and the child's perception becomes increasingly more differentiated and logical. During early years of life perception is centered more either on parts or the whole of the object or picture. With increase in age, the child is capable of perceiving both parts and whole. It is clearly realised that both parts and whole have different as well as interrelated meaning in the picture.

Piaget's (1947) theory of cognitive developments is characterised by a series of hierarchical stages each of which has its own organizational properties and structures. The structures specific to one stage are incorporated into higher order structures, which appear later in the child's life.

One of these stages called pre-operational stage, occurs roughly between 2 to 7 years. The other stage, called concrete operational stage, occurs roughly between 7 to 11 years. The last developmental stage called formal operational stage, occurs after 11 years of age. In pre-operational stage the mechanism underlying responses of a child is 'centration'. While perceiving a figure, the child focuses only on parts and ignores the whole. This indicates that perceptual factors have a strong hold on the child at this stage. Children's cognition is less controlled by mental actions. However, as the age increases and the child enters into the concrete operational stage, 'decentering' in attention takes place. The child is capable not only of attending to both the parts and whole of a figure, but also using this information in several ways. The visual data available to the child can be manipulated mentally and thoughts get relieved from excessive pre-occupation with the part or the whole.

Piaget (1958) has acknowledged that perception is not an innately fixed mechanism for registering stimuli, but is a developing system, which becomes increasingly adaptive with age. In the young child, perception is passive and dominated by the "best" organization of the various field forces. With the development of perceptual operations (internalized actions), the child's perception becomes active so that it spontaneously restructures the field into many possible organizations. Within this framework, decentering (the ability to examine the perceptual field from several perspectives) and perceptual regulations are developmental achievements that allow older children to see both aspects — part and whole of the figures— and to perform the infralogical multiplication necessary to appreciate that an object can belong to two classes at the same time.

Several studies conducted in India (see Mishra, 1990; Sinha, 1982) show that socio-economic disadvantages suffered by children tend to have detrimental effect not only on their general development, but are also reflected in performance on various perceptual and cognitive tasks. Deficiencies in the environment, especially due to physical factors induced through socio-economic disadvantages, have their impact through failure in providing the necessary experiential base essential for the development of perceptual and cognitive skills. A facilitator influence of caste, social class, and schooling has been noted for those at the upper end of the continuum, whereas a negative influence of the same factors has been noted in the case of the disadvantaged (Misra & Shahi, 1977; Ghuman, 1978; Rath & Patnaik, 1979; Majeed & Ghosh 1981; Misra 1982, 1983, Murlidharan *et al,* 1984).

The adverse consequence of social disadvantage have been documented for children's verbal competence (Sahu, 1979, 1981), figurative perception (Usha Rani, 1985). Level II abilities that require elaboration and transformation of information input (Jachuck, 1982a, 1982b); category clustering in free recall (Agrawal & Mishra, 1983; Jachuck & Das, 1982). Raven's Progressive Matrices and short-term memory (Mohanty, 1980a, 1980b); and performance on perceptual tasks of varying level of complexity (Mishra, 1976; Shukla 1993; Sinha 1979).

Researchers have attempted to identify specific factors associated with socio-cultural disadvantages that may be responsible for a lower level of competence. The findings indicate that with intelligence partialled out, the advantaged children perform consistently better than those belonging to disadvantaged background. Among pre-school children, the quality and quantity of home stimulation has been found to affect the advantaged and disadvantaged groups in different ways (Sahu & Devi, 1982; Sahu & Sahu, 1982). For the advantaged children stimulation through toys, games and reading materials contributes maximally to the variance in scores whereas for the disadvantaged physical environment (as assessed through Caldwell's Home Inventory) contributes to the highest variance in their psycholinguistic abilities; both tribal unilingual and bilingual second graders perform as well as (in some cases even better than) non-tribal unilingual disadvantaged do on the tests of linguistic proficiency and psycholinguistic competence. The authors concluded that the superior performance of tribal children could have been due to the acculturation in the case of tribal unilingual group, or due to schooling facilities in the case of tribal bilingual group. Stimulation may take place due to a number of factors. Studies indicate that the urban residence enhances conservation and classificatory skills (Banerjee & Jain, 1982) due to greater sensory stimulation (Jain & Iyenger,

1976; Iyenger & Jain, 1979). Children exposed to comics and other pictorial materials perform more competently on tasks of pictorial interpretation and sequential perception (Mishra & Gupta, 1978, 1983; Singh, 1981). Training has a facilitating influence on the performance of both advantaged (Rao, 1976; Mohanty & Chowdhry, 1981), and disadvantaged populations (Rath & Patnaik, 1979), with the disadvantaged children benefiting more from the training than their advantaged counter parts (Mishra, 1990). Mishra and Vajpayee (2000) studied the relative effects of chronological age and experiential deprivation on pictorial recognition. The results indicate that experiential deprivation interferes with the growth of such as a basic skill as pictorial recognition.

Studies reveal that perceptual exploration and part whole perception requires the process of decentring which has been shown to develop with age, but has not been studied in the context of experiential impoverishment. The aim of the present study was to examine the development of perceptual exploration and part whole perception in relation to privileged and impoverished socio-cultural background of the child. It was hypothesized that children of impoverished socio-cultural background would present evidence of less decenting and less systematic exploration than those of the privileged socio-cultural background.

METHOD AND PROCEDURE

Sample

The study was carried out with 400 children aged 3–12 years drawn from four primary schools of Varanasi city. Each child's house was visited, and information was collected on parental literacy, occupational status, caste and per capita income. Families were rated on these dimensions. Socio-economic status was determined by adding up the scores on six variables, namely education of father, education of mother, occupation of father, occupation of mother, caste and per capita income per month (Chatterjee *et al.,* 1983). On the basis of these children rated as belonging to upper lower and lower class represented the "impoverished" group, those belonging to upper and upper-middle class represented the "privileged" group. In each age group 80 children were selected, 40 from the privileged and 40 from the impoverished background following a quasi randomization technique. The children belonged to five age groups, 3-4, 5-6, 7-8, 9-10, and 11-12 years.

Test Materials

Each child was tested with the help of the Picture Ambiguity Test (Elkind, 1964) and a self designed task of perceptual exploration.

Picture Ambiguity Test

Developed by Elkind (1964), this test consists of 9 ambiguous pictures. Each picture is drawn in black on a white card. The pictures can be perceived in two ways depending on whether all segments of the pictures are used in describing the object or only some parts of the pictures are used for object description. A third possibility is to perceive both and say, for example, a butterfly with a facial profile in each wing.

A pilot study with 50 children revealed some problems in recognition of objects on two pictures. Hence these two items were dropped in the final study. The remaining seven stimuli were used in the final study.

The pictures were shown to children. They were asked to name each picture. The responses and reaction time to each picture were recorded.

On the Picture Ambiguity Test the response to ambiguous pictures were scored with respect to the following measures :

1. *Reaction Time:* The time taken to react to each card.
2. *Centration:* The inability of the child to shift attention from figure to ground.
3. *Decentration:* The child's ability to perceive both the whole as well as parts in figures.

4. *Part, Whole and Part-whole Perception:* The responses which used either part or whole or both part and whole of stimuli to identify pictures.

Exploration Task

This task consisted of picture of 24 common objects *e.g.*, fruits, vegetables, animals and electrical appliances with which all children were familiar. The pictures were pasted on a 30 × 25 cm paper sheet in unstructured and structured manners. In the Unstructured Array (UA), the pictures were arranged randomly so that they did not suggest any particular form. The Structured Array (SA) consisted of two sets. In one the pictures were arranged so that they made a triangle (Δ). In another the pictures were so arranged that they represented cross (+) pattern.

The children were presented with these patterns in a random order. They were asked to name each picture on the sheet or point it out with a stylus. The responses were recorded on a sheet, depicting the placement of pictures on the card in the order in which the child pointed them out.

Responses on the Exploration Task cards were scored as follows.

(a) Errors

Each child's protocoı was examined for the errors of omission (failure to name a picture) and commission (name the same picture again). For each of these errors 'one' point was given.

(b) Patterns of Exploration

Each child's protocol was examined to discover the pattern of exploration employed in the naming of pictures. On the unstructured set the following patterns were identified.

1. Non-Systematic (NS): A child's exploration was called NS, if many (at least five) of the figures named were not spatially

adjacent, and if there was no pattern of directionality present in the over all exploration.

2. Left-Right (LR): It was evident if the exploration began from the left corner and proceeded to the right.
3. Right-Left (RL): It was evident if the exploration began from the right corner and proceeded to the left.
4. Top-Bottom (TB): When the exploration began from the figure at the top of the card and moved down to the figures at the bottom it was referred to as TB.
5. Complex Pattern (CP): It was revealed if the child used a combination of any of the above mentioned patterns.

On the structured set the following patterns were identified:

1. Triangular (Δ): It was evident when the child moved the triangle in naming figures.
2. Cross (+): It was evident when the child moved along the cross in naming the figures.
3. Left-Right (LR): This pattern was evident when the child's exploration moved from left to right.
4. Right-Left (RL): It was evident in exploration that moved from right to left.
5. Non-Systematic (NS): A child's exploration was called NS, if many of the figures named were not spatially adjacent and there was no pattern of directionality.
6. Complex Pattern (CP): It was revealed in exploration in which some combination of the patterns 3, 4 and 5 was used.

ANALYSIS OF RESULTS

Children were divided into privileged and impverished groups on the basis of their socio-economic status (SES) scores. Table 7.1 presents the percentage of privileged and impoverished children showing centration and decentration at different age levels. Though the percentage of impoverished children showing centration is higher and that of showing decentration is lower than that of privileged children at all age levels, the difference between privileged and impoverished children on these measures was significant only at the 11-12 years level.

Table 7.1 : Percentage of privileged and impoverished children showing centration and decentartion.

Groups	Centration	CR	Decentration	CR
Age 3–4				
Privileged	(40) 100.00	—	(—)	
Improverished	(40) 100.00		(—)	
Age 5–6				
Privileged	(33) 82.50	0.98	(7) 17.50	0.98
Impoverished	(36) 90.00		(4) 10.00	
Age 7–8				
Privileged	(21) 52.50	0.68	(19) 47.50	0.68
Impoverished	(24) 60.00		(16) 40.00	
Age 9–10				
Privileged	(11) 27.50	1.19	(29) 72.50	1.19
Impoverished	(16) 40.00		(24) 60.00	
Age 11–12				
Privileged	(1) 2.50	2.03*	(39) 97.50	2.03*
Impoverished	(6) 15.00		(34) 85.00	

* $p < 0.05$
Figures in parentheses indicate the number of children.

Responses of privileged and impoverished children were also analysed to examine if there was any difference between them in frequency with which both parts and wholes were perceived (Table7.2). A slightly higher percentage of privileged children giving part-whole response in various age groups as compared to impoverished children was in evidence but the difference between these percentages was significant only at the 11-12 years level.

Table 7.2 : Percentage of privileged and impoverished children making "Part", "Whole" and "Part-Whole" perception

Groups	Part	*CR*	Whole	*CR*	Part-Whole	*CR*
Age 3–4						
Privileged	(34) 85.00	0.68	(6) 15.00	0.68	(—)	(—)
Impoverished	(36) 90.00		(4) 10.00			
Age 5–6						
Privileged	(20) 50.00	0.90	(13) 32.50	0.24	(7) 17.50	0.98
Impoverished	(24) 60.00		(12) 30.00		(4) 10.00	
Age 7–8						
Privileged	(6) 15.00	0.59	(15) 37.50	0.23	(19) 47.50	0.68
Impoverished	(8) 20.00		(16) 40.00		(16) 40.00	
Age 9–10						
Privileged	(3) 7.50	1.07	(9) 22.50	—	(28) 70.00	0.71
Impoverished	(6) 15.00		(9) 22.50		(25) 62.50	
Age 11–12						
Privileged	(—)	(—)	(1) 2.50	0.23*	(39) 97.50	2.03*
Impoverished	(—)		(6) 15.00		(34) 85.00	

* $p < 0.05$
Figures in parenthesis indicate number of children.

The mean reaction time of privileged and impoverished children according to age levels were also compared (Table7.3). The privileged group had lesser reaction time as compared to the impoverished group at all age levels, however the difference between the means of the two groups was significant only at the 7-8 years level.

ANOVA revealed the main effects of socio-economic status and age to be significant ($F = 170.62$; $df = 1, 390$; $p < 0.001$; $F = 459.82$; $df = 4, 390$; $p<0.001$). The interaction effect of these variables was also significant ($F = 35.44$; $df = 4,390$; $p < 0.001$) indicating greater effect of impoverished background at the 3-4 years level than at other age levels.

Table 7.3 : Mean reaction time (in seconds) for privileged and impoverished groups

Age Groups	Privileged		Improverished		t–value
	Mean	S.D.	Mean	S.D.	
3-4 years	20.23	3.83	30.80	5.81	9.61**
5-6 years	20.40	4.39	25.70	3.60	5.90**
7-8 years	16.90	2.07	16.43	2.29	0.96
9-10 years	11.35	1.51	13.08	1.33	5.42**
11-12 years	5.50	0.91	8.93	1.25	14.02**

** $p < 0.001$.

The accuracy of responses of the privileged and impoverished groups was also analysed (Table7. 4). ANOVA revealed significant age effect on triangle (F = 185.28; df = 4,390; p < .001), for cross (F = 188.94; df = 4,390; p < .001) and unstructured patterns (F=348.70; df– 4,390; p <.001). It indicated that with increase in age the number of correct responses increased significantly with all patterns. The effect of socio-economic status variables was significant on triangle (F = 13.92; df = 1,390; p < .001) and the unstructured pattern (F=41.90; df= 1,390; p<.001) favouring the privileged group. The interaction effect was significant (F=5.96; df= 390; p < .001) only for the triangle pattern.

ANOVA was also carried out on the errors of omission and commission made on the structured and unstructured patterns (Table 7.5). On the structured patterns (triangle and cross) the main effect of age was found significant for the errors of omission triangle (F=45.50; df=3,151; p<.001), for cross (F=83.83; df=2,138; p<.001) for commission triangle (F=6.77; df=3,168; p<.001), and cross (F = 5.80; df = 3,160; p <.001). Age effect was also significant on the unstructured pattern omission (F=189.54; df=4,324; p <.001), commission (F = 12.14; df = 4,277; p < .001). These findings reveal that with increase in age children make less errors in perceiving and exploring visual field. The main effect of

Table 7. 4 : Mean and standard deviation of correct responses for privileged and impoverished children at different age groups

Pattern of stimuli	Age Groups									
	3-4 years		5-6 years		7-8 years		9-10 years		11-12 years	
	Mean	SD	Mean	SD	Mean	SD	Mean	SD	Mean	SD
TRIANGLE										
Privileged	15.10	4.70	20.68	2.90	22.70	1.30	23.95	0.20	24.00	—
Impoverished	13.60	4.50	17.38	3.60	23.93	1.40	23.33	1.70	23.95	0.20
PLUS										
Privileged	15.00	4.30	18.45	4.60	22.93	1.10	23.95	0.20	24.00	—
Impoverished	14.03	3.40	17.75	3.60	23.23	1.30	22.95	2.10	23.93	0.03
UNSTRUCTURED ARRAY CARD										
Privileged	10.93	3.10	12.53	3.60	16.65	3.10	21.73	2.10	23.85	0.30
Impoverished	7.95	2.90	11.65	2.80	15.03	3.20	19.40	3.10	22.75	1.40

Socio-economic status was significant only for the omission error on triangle and unstructured patterns (F = 24.80; df = 1,151; p <.001 and F = 27.28; df= 1,324; p < .001 respectively).

Interaction among the variables was not significant on any of these measures.

The frequency with which privileged and impoverished children employed different exploration strategies on structured (Triangle and Cross) and unstructured patterns was also analysed (Table7.6). In the 3-4 years age group a higher percentage of impoverished children employed non-systematic exploration strategies with a significant evidence for this on the unstructured picture (CR = 3.67 p < 0.001). It was also evident that while children of the privileged group showed greater systematization in exploration at 3-4, 5-6 and 7-8 years than those of the impoverished group the differences were not significant. No definite age trend was observed for *LR, RL* and complex patterns of explorations.

Discussion

The hypothesis that development of centering, decentring perceptual exploration and articulation processes are related to the socio-economic background of the child finds only a partial support. The results in general showed that socio-economic status was not a major factor in determining the development of perceptual differentiation measured in terms of centration, decentration and part-whole perception on ambiguous cards. The effect of this variable was evident only at the 11-12 years level. At other age levels the difference in the performance of privileged and impoverished children was minimal, though the impoverished group took significantly more time to respond to ambiguous pictures as compared to the privileged group. With respect to perceptual exploration the results demonstrated that children belonging to the privileged group showed systematization in perception at an earlier age than those of the impoverished group. The number of correct responses was significantly higher in the former than the latter group at all age levels. No difference was noted between these groups

Table7. 5 : Mean errors of omission and commission for privileged and impoverished children on three exploration cards

Pattern of ctimuli	Age Groups									
	3-4 years		5-6 years		7-8 years		9-10 years		11-12 years	
	Mean	SD	Mean	SD	Mean	SD	Mean	SD	Mean	SD
TRIANGLE										
OMISSION										
Privileged	7.05	2.32	2.48	2.16	1.64	1.04	1.00	0.00	—	—
Impoverished	8.53	3.03	5.55	2.88	1.90	0.57	1.50	0.58	1.00	0.00
COMMISSION										
Privileged	2.65	1.38	2.17	1.56	1.11	0.31	1.00	0.00	—	—
Impoverished	3.55	1.62	2.70	1.58	1.41	0.62	1.10	0.32	1.00	0.00
PLUS OMISSION										
Privileged	7.03	2.81	4.84	2.34	1.11	0.33	—	—	—	—
Impoverished	7.64	3.12	5.03	2.89	1.22	0.67	4.14	3.08	—	—
COMMISSION										
Privileged	3.03	1.78	2.64	2.22	1.45	1.06	1.00	0.00	—	—
Impoverished	3.16	1.73	3.94	2.26	1.50	1.40	1.63	1.77	1.00	0.00
UNSTRUCTURED ARRAY CARD										
OMISSION										
Privileged	9.03	2.98	7.40	2.62	4.28	1.95	2.42	1.20	1.00	0.00
Impoverished	11.05	2.82	9.35	2.08	5.13	1.71	3.26	2.23	1.70	1.17
COMMISSION										
Privileged	3.95	1.78	3.33	1.26	3.29	1.74	2.20	2.57	1.00	0.00
Impoverished	5.08	2.03	4.08	2.06	3.95	1.97	2.19	1.27	1.55	1.04

Table 7.6 : Percentage of privileged and impoverished children showing different patterns of organization on structured and unstructured array cards

Age	Triangle					Plus					Unstructured array card				
groups	NS	LR	RL	CP	<	NS	LR	RL	CP	+	NS	LR	RL	CP	TB
3–4 years															
Privileged	7.50	12.50	2.50	12.50	65.00	40.00	—	5.00	25.00	30.00	50.00	5.00	—	45.00	—
(40)	(3)	(5)	(1)	(5)	(26)	(16)	—	(2)	(10)	(12)	(20)	(2)	—	(18)	—
Impoverished	21.00	10.00	5.00	25.00	40.00	57.50	—	5.00	25.00	12.50	85.00	5.00	—	10.00	—
(40)	(8)	(4)	(2)	(10)	(16)	(23)	—	(2)	(10)	(5)	(34)	(2)	—	(4)	—
5–6 years															
Privileged	12.50	12.50	12.00	—	62.50	27.50	2.50	5.00	27.50	37.50	40.00	37.50	—	15.00	7.50
(40)	(5)	(5)	(5)	—	(25)	(11)	(1)	(2)	(11)	(15)	(16)	(15)	—	(6)	(3)
Impoverished	12.50	25.00	2.50	7.50	52.50	32.50	2.50	2.50	30.00	32.50	45.00	20.00	—	30.00	5.00
(40)	(5)	(10)	(1)	(3)	(21)	(13)	(1)	(1)	(12)	(13)	(18)	(8)	—	(12)	(2)
7–8 years															
Privileged	—	10.00	—	2.50	87.50	—	—	7.50	5.00	87.50	12.50	25.00	7.50	40.00	15.00
(40)		(4)		(1)	(35)			(3)	(2)	(35)	(5)	(10)	(3)	(16)	(6)
Impoverished	—	22.50	—	—	77.50	—	5.00	7.50	10.00	77.50	32.50	32.50	2.50	22.50	10.00
(40)		(9)			(31)		(2)	(3)	(4)	(31)	(13)	(13)	(1)	(9)	(4)

(Contd.)

Table7. 6 : *(Contd.)*

Age groups	Triangle NS	Triangle LR	Triangle RL	Triangle CP		Plus NS	Plus LR	Plus RL	Plus CP	+	Unstructured array card NS	Unstructured array card LR	Unstructured array card RL	Unstructured array card CP	Unstructured array card TB
9–10 years															
Privileged	—	—	—	—	100.00	—	12.50	2.50	2.50	82.50	2.50	52.50	7.50	15.00	22.50
(40)					(40)		(5)	(1)	(1)	(33)	(1)	(21)	(3)	(6)	(9)
Impoverished	—	5.00	—	—	95.00	—	12.50	—	7.50	80.00	7.50	25.00	7.50	42.50	12.50
(40)		(2)			(38)		(5)		(3)	(32)	(3)	(10)	(3)	(19)	(5)
11–12 years															
Privileged	—	—	—	—	100.00	—	12.50	—	—	87.50	—	60.00	7.50	15.00	17.50
(40)					(40)		(5)			(35)	—	(24)	(3)	(6)	(7)
Impoverished	—	—	—	—	100.00	—	17.50	—	2.50	80.00	2.50	32.50	12.50	35.00	17.50
(40)					(40)		(7)		(1)	(32)	(1)	(13)	(5)	(14)	(7)

Figures in parentheses indicate the number of children NS = Non-systematic, LR = Left to Right, RL = Right to Left
CP = Complex pattern, <= Triangle, + = Plus, TB = Top to Bottom

with respect to the directionality in exploration. These results suggest that socio-economic status alone is not responsible for the overall development of perceptual skills in children. Researchers (Mishra, 1976; Sinha, 1979; Mishra & Gupta, 1978,1983; Singh, 1981) have demonstrated the effect of socio-cultural disadvantages on the performance of perceptual tasks to be relative to the level of task complexity. It is indicated that differences are more evident on complex tasks than on the simpler. Studies also suggest that children who have exposure to pictorial materials at home perform better on tasks of pictorial interpretation and sequential perception than those who lack such exposure (Mishra & Gupta, 1978, 1983; Singh, 1981; Upadhyay & Agarwal, 1988). Agarwal *et al.,* (1992) have shown that home stimulation contributes maximally to cognitive development of children as compared to socio-economic status. This indicates that stimulation is more important in the development of perceptual and cognitive skills in children than socio-economic status.

Many researchers have documented the relationship between the levels of cognitive competence shown by young children and the children's home environment. There is a growing consensus among researchers that measures of specific environmental processes are more accurate indices of environmental quality and predictors of behaviour than either socio-economic status or family structure (Dave, 1963; Bloom, 1964, Caldwell, 1968; Backwith, 1971; Marjoribanks, 1972; White *et al,* 1973). This assertion is primarily based on data that indicate that families within each socio-economic status group differ widely in the kind and amount of stimulation they provide to children (Littman *et al,* 1957; Pavenstede, 1965; Malone, 1966).

The findings of the present study allow us to conclude that the development of basic perceptual processes like figure-ground perception is not greatly influenced by the socio-economic status of the child. These processes unfold more or less uniformly across all SES groups during the childhood years. The environmental conditions play a more important role in the development of other skills such as perceptual exploration. This indicates that while organism and environment are considered to be logically dependent on each other, the characteristics of psychological development of organisms do not always follow the rules of environment. As Piaget (1957) indicates, there may be adaptational variations simultaneously involving a structuring of the organism and an action of environment. Thus, some functions may show biological unfolding with minimal support from the environment, whereas the development of other functions may be largely contingent on the characteristic features of the children's physical and socio-cultural environment.

REFERENCES

Agarwal, D.K., Awasthy, A., Upadhyay, S.K., Singh, P., Kumar, J., Agarwal K.N. (1992). Growth, behaviour development and intelligence in rural children between 1-3 years of life. *Indian Pediatrics, 29* (4) : 467-480.

Agarwal, S. & Mishra, R.C. (1983). Some social disadvantages and development of category organization skill. *Psychologia, 26,* 54-61.

Banerjee, M. & Jain, R. (1982). Development of conservation of mass, number and volume in Indian rural and urban school children of ages 5-12 years. *Psychological Studies, 27,* 12-16.

Beckwith, L. (1971). Relationship between attributes of mothers and their infants IQ scores. *Child Development, 42,* 1083-1097.

Bloom, B.S. (1964). *Stability and change in human characteristics.* New York: Wiley & Sons.

Caldwell, B.M. (1968). On designing supplementary environment for early child development. *NAEYC Reports, 10,* 1-11.

Chatterjee, B.B., Singh, S.S. & Singh, R.P. (1983). *The effect of environmental process variables on school achievement (5½-11 years,.* New Delhi: Report of the Varanasi Centre, NCERT.

Dave, R.H. (1963). The identification and measurement of environmental process variables that are related to educational achievement. Unpublished doctoral dissertation, University of Chicago.

Elkind, D., Koegler, R.R. & Go, E. (1964). Studies in perceptual development : II part-whole perception, *Child Development, 35,* 81-90.

Ghuman, P.A.S. (1978). Nature of intellectual development of Punjabi children. *International Journal of Psychology, 13,* 281-294.

Iyenger, D., & Jain, U. (1979). Development of conservation in deaf and dumb children. *Journal of Psychological Researches, 23,* 135-170.

Jachuck, K. (1982a). Level I - level II abilities of socially disadvantaged children—

A test of cumulative deficit hypothesis. *Perspective in Psychological Researches, 5,* (2), 1-4.

Jachuck, K. (1982b). Pattern of cognitive abilities among boys of four sub-cultural groups. In R. Rath, H.S, Asthana, D. Sinha & J.B.P. Sinha (Eds.), *Diversity and unity in cross-cultural psychology.* Lisse: Swets & Zeitlinger.

Jachuck, K. & Das, J. (1982). Free recall of categorized materials : A cross-cultural examination of Jensen's two level theory. *Indian Psychologist, 1,* (2), 51-56.

Jain, U., & Iyenger, D. (1976). Conservation of liquid : A cross-cultural comparison. *Asian Journal of Psychology and Education, 1,* (1), 9-12.

Littman, R., Moore, R. Pierce-Jones, J. (1957). Social class differences in child rearing : A third community for comparison with Chicago and Newton. *American Sociological Review, 22,* 690-704.

Majeed, A. & Ghosh, E.S.K. (1981). Effect of ethnicity and social class on cognitive differentiation. *Journal of Psychological Researches, 25,* 84-88.

Malone, C. (1966). Safety first ! Comments on the influence of external danger in the lives of children of disorganized families. *American Journal of Orthopsychiatry, 36,* 1-12.

Marjoribanks, K. (1972). Environment, social class and mental abilities. *Journal of Educational Psychology, 63,* 103-109.

Mishra, R.C. (1976). Perception and comprehension of certain types of pictorial materials. D. Phil. Thesis. University of Allahabad, India.

Mishra, R.C. (1990). Cognitive stimulation training and perceptual—cognitive task performance by socially deprived children. *Indian Journal of Current Psychological Research, 5,* 1-9.

Mishra, R.C. & Gupta, V. (1978). Role of schooling and exposure in perceiving pictorial sequence. *Psychologia, 2,* 231-236.

Mishra, R.C. & Gupta, V. (1983). Schooling, exposure and the skill for pictorial comprehension. *Indian Psychological Review, 24,* 29-34.

Mishra, R.C. & Vajpayee, A. (2000). Intervention for cognitive development of disadvantaged children. In A.K. Mohanty & G. Misra (Eds.) *Psychology of poverty and disadvantage,* pp. 214-229, New Delhi : Concept.

Misra, G. (1982). Deprivation and cognitive competence. In D. Sinha, R.C. Tripathi & G. Misra (eds), *Deprivation : Its social roots and psychological consequences.* pp. 151-176, New Delhi.

Misra, G. (1983). Deprivation and development : A review of Indian studies. *Indian educational Review, 18,* 1-21.

Misra, G. & Shahi, B.P. (1977). Prolonged deprivation and development of form perception. *Journal of Psychological Researches, 21,* 185-191.

Misra, G. & Shukla, A. (1984). Recognition of pictorial material as a function of experiential deprivation and age. *International Journal of Behavioural Development, 7,* 95-103.

Mohanty, B. (1980a). Effects of socio-cultural deprivation on intelligence and short-term memory. *Indian Psychological Review, 19,* (4), 17-24).

Mohanty, B. (1980b). Effects of socio-cultural deprivation on some psychological characteristics. *Psychological Studies, 25,* 113-117.

Mohanty, A.K. & Chowdhry, M. (1981). Training for conservation by self-transformation and screening techniques. *Psychological Studies, 26,* 78-81.

Murlidharan, R., Malani, I. & Bevali, U. (1984). Effect on environmental process variables on the school achievement and cognitive development of Indian children of ages 5½ - 11 years. Unpublished manuscript. New Delhi: National Council of Eucational Research and Training.

Pavenstede, E. (1965). A comparison of the child varying environment of upper-lower and very low-lower class families. *American Journal of Orthopsychiatry, 35,* 89-98.

Piaget, J. (1947). *The psychology of intelligence.* London : Routledge & Kegan Paul, 1950 (First French edition).

Piaget, J. & Inhelder, B. (1956). *The child's conception of space.* London: Routledge & Kegan Paul.

Piaget, J. & Morf, A. (1958). Les isomorphismes partiels entre les structures logiques etles structures perceptives. In Piaget, J. (Ed.) *Etudes depistemologie genetique.* Vol. VI, Logique et perception, pp. 52-116. Paris : Presses Universitaires de France.

Rath, R., & Patnaik, N. (1979). Effect of training on some cognitive abilities. *Journal of Psychological Researches, 23,* 81-92.

Rao, S.N. (1976). An experimental investigation of children's concepts of mass, weight and volume. *Indian Journal of Psychology, 51,* 3, 212-220.

Sahu, S. (1979). Effect of social disadvantage on verbal competence and language achievement. *Psychological Studies, 24,* 66-72.

Sahu, S. (1981). Verbal competence of socially disadvantaged children. *Journal of Social and Economic Studies, 9* (1), 59-65.

Sahu, S. & Devi, B. (1982). Role of home environment in linguistic abilities and intelligence of advantaged and disadvantaged pre-school children. *Psycholingua, 3* (1), 25-30.

Sahu, S. & Sahu, S.K. (1982). Cultural influences on language achievement and Psycholinguistic competence. In R. Rath, H.S. Asthana, D. Sinha & J.B.P. Sinha (eds.), *Diversity and unity in cross-cultural psychology,* pp. 104-109, Lisse: Swets & Zeitlinger.

Shukla, A. (1993). A developmental study of pictorial perception in high and low facility schools. *Unpublished doctoral thesis, Banaras Hindu University.*

Singh, A.K. (1981). Impact of comics reading on perceptual skills. *Psychological Studies, 26*, 86-87.

Sinha, D. (1979). Cognitive and psychomotor skills in India. *Journal of Cross-cultural Psychology, 10*, 324-355.

Upadhyay, S.K. & Agarwal, D.K. (1988). Home environment, malnutrition and intellectual ability. *Proceedings of Nutrition Society of India, 34*, 93.

Usha Rani, N. (1985). Figurative perception in urban and rural school children. *Journal of Psychological Researches, 29*, 2, 64-68.

White, B., *et al.* (1973). *Experience and environment.* Englewood Cliffs, NJ: Prentice-Hall.

8

Effect of Training on Cognitive Performance of Socio-Culturally Deprived Children

APARNA VAJPAYEE and RAMESH CHANDRA MISHRA

Introduction

A historical inquiry into the origin of Hindu society would suggest that in ancient times, it was guided by the philosophy of coevolution *(saha marsnaih)* and coexistence (*Saha abhibhave*). This indicates a common sharing of life by all people in the society. The origin of the caste system, which was originally based on occupational specialization but got typified later on, failed to capture the spirit of our philosophy of life. Unaffected by this philosophy the society drew lines between the social groups that were identified on the basis of birth. Consequently, a stratified social system emerged. This tradition continued over the years, and people placed on the lower end of the stratification system, called low caste groups, were prohibited by people of the upper castes from sharing many of the experiences of life. They were forced to live a segregated life cut-off from the life of the high caste society. The term 'Internal Proletariat' has been used by Toynbee (1962), which means "people who are in the society, but not of the society."

This group of the society has been labelled as socially deprived or disadvantaged group that suffers from continuing inadequacy of physical, socio-cultural, psychological and educational experiences and opportunities. As a result of these limitations, they could not develop psychologically like other groups of the society. Their children were found to perform poorly on cognitive and linguistic tasks, show learning deficiencies as well as progressive achievement deficit. These were the children who showed stagnation in schools and turned out as drop-outs (Jachuck, 1979; Rath & Patnaik, 1979; Sahu, 1979).

In the course of history, some changes were introduced in the society through the effort of many social reformers. Attempts were made to abolish the various restrictions imposed on the low caste people. After independence discrimination on the ground of caste, sex, religion or place of birth was declared as illegal and punishable. However, the story of the last 53 years of independence, is a story of partial success. Psychologists and educationists have shown a major concern with the study of the problems faced by children of the scheduled castes and scheduled tribes. It is now widely believed that psychological deficiencies are not genetic in nature; instead they are associated with deficiencies of physical and socio-cultural environment that surrounds them.

Studies have tried to analyze the environment of children of different caste groups. Bronfenbrenner (1977) had proposed a model, called an ecological model, to delineate the effect of both proximal and distal influences of children's environment on their development. Based on Bronfenbrenner's model Sinha (1977, 1982) has developed an ecological model to comprehend the environment of the scheduled and non-scheduled caste children in Indian setting. A variety of relationships between environmental features of the groups and their perceptual and cognitive development has been pointed out in this model. Sinha's model conceptualizes the environment of children in terms of two concentric layers. The inner layer consists of child's home school and peer groups. Physical space available to children, their activities and role relationship with peer group members constitutes the major set of influences in the inner layer of ecology. The outer layer consists of geographical features of a child's environment.

Sinha (1982) has compared the scheduled and non-scheduled caste children in terms of both inner and outer ecological features, and has presented a contrast between the high and the low caste groups at both the layers of ecology. His studies on the development of perceptual skills among scheduled caste, scheduled tribe and non-scheduled caste children bring out favourable evidence for the prediction made in terms of the ecological model. Sinha (1982) has reviewed a wide variety of studies on pictorial perception, psychological differentiation and Piagetian conservation that clearly reveal the effect of the caste variable. The influences seem to be generally associated with experiential factors.

Intervention Programmes

The above mentioned findings have generated considerable hope among psychologists, particularly among those who do psychology with a sense of human welfare. Many of them have tried to look for their role by intervening into the process in such a manner that the difference in performance of scheduled and non-scheduled castes could be overcome. Two kinds of propositions regarding the change among scheduled caste children have been made in order to ensure life opportunities similar to those of other caste groups of the society. One advocates for structural changes that focus on changes in social, economic and occupational structures of the scheduled caste groups including changes in their educational structure (Singh, 1988). The government policy of reservation introduced for these groups reflects this change. Unfortunately the policy has delivered goods only to a limited number of people of these caste groups. The majority still lives on its traditional resources without much contact with people who have benefited from the policy.

Looking at the various difficulties involved in structural changes, some psychologists (*e.g.*, Dash & Rath, 1985; Mishra, 1990; Sinha, 1990) feel that the solution of the problems of scheduled caste children need to be searched out within their existing circumstances. They advocate the programmes of behavioural change, which are free from conflicts and the problems of disharmony among groups.

Effect of Intervention Programmes on Cognitive Development

It is believed that by intervening into the stream of ongoing behaviour, the predicted direction of development for these groups can be shifted from anticipated negative outcomes to positive outcomes. Sigal (1990), Evans, Stewart, and Bengs (1972), Flavell (1963), Hunt (1961), Seigal (1978), Silver and Lewine (1977), and White (1973) have given short-term intervention programmes to children and have found significant improvement in their cognitive skills.

Berry and Berry (1977) found significant gain in the development of cognitive ability by pre-school contributions. Almost in all the studies intervention related to developmental strategies showed a significant gain in I.Q. scores (Abelson, 1982; Lazer & Darlington, 1982). Similansky (1979) has noted that by creating such an environment, cognitive development can be made long lasting with the help of parents, otherwise the programme will dissipate over time. Nandurbarkar (1991) used a stimulation programme in which progress in motor as well as mental areas of infants was clearly noted. Padhy (1992) reported a stronger association between intervention and cognitive skills. The efficacy of training has also been revealed in other studies (Dash, 1993; Baksi, 1993).

The Problem and Hypotheses

A cognitive psychologist focuses on how individuals perceive certain events, and how providing different types of information to them can modify these perceptions. The preceding discussion has presented fairly clear evidence that there are certain conditions in which the cognitive abilities of children do not find opportunities for their full growth and development (Agrawal & Mishra, 1983; Rath, Dash & Dash 1979; Sinha, 1977, 1982). Children who are less capable of performing cognitive tasks are generally considered as having inadequate system of such cognitive abilities as perception, imagery, problem solving, remembering and thinking. The need for their overall psychological improvement is advocated by different organizations like UNICEF, UN Development Forum and UNESCO. Psychologists with an applied orientation also give emphasis on the development of cognitive abilities of these children (Mishra, 1976, 1990; Misra & Tripathi, 1980; Sinha, 1977, 1982). Relegated to lower socio-economic status these children are often rated as having a poor mental ability. They are perceived as backward and inferior to others, and are taken with a negative attitude. There is not only a need to develop positive attitude of the society toward them, but also a need to inculcate positive self-image to prevent them from the feelings of inferiority.

Several studies indicate a lower level of performance of low caste and deprived children on tests measuring competence in a number of cognitive domains. Low degree of frustration tolerance (Rai, Seth & Manjula, 1987), inferior scholastic achievements, and less use of reasoning and abstraction (Jensen, 1971) have also been found to characterize these children. There is also evidence for progressive and cumulative deficit among these children during their school years (Sinha, 1977, 1982).

Research with disadvantaged children suggests that in order to improve their performance on perceptual and cognitive tests/ tasks, the organization of intervention programmes and advent of increased opportunity of interaction with others are essential. Efforts made in this direction have generally found strong evidence for improvement in cognitive performance of these children contingent on intervention (Baksi, 1993; Das, 1993; Dash & Rath, 1986; Jachuck & Chatterjee, 1989; Padhy, 1992; Mishra, 1990). While all intervention programmes have anticipated positive outcomes, the evidence has been more in support of short-term effects.

The programmes have also suffered from a number of weaknesses. There has been no uniformity in the criteria adopted to assess deprivation. For example, Das and Rath (1986) studied the effect of cognitive stimulation, and found considerable improvement in test performance. The study did not indicate how the children were considered advantaged and disadvantaged, as neither high nor low caste groups are homogeneous. Flavell (1969), Hunt (1961), Rath and Patnaik (1979), Schaefer (1972), Seigal, McCabe, Brend and Mathews (1978), Silver and Lewine (1977), Evans, Stewart, and Bengs (1972) and White (1973) have given short-term intervention programmes and have found significant improvement in cognitive skills. These works do have theoretical import, but they do not reveal whether gain found in test scores of deprived children is of the same nature and magnitude as of the children of non-deprived groups. Some studies (*e.g.*, Jachuck & Chatterjee, 1989) have compared the children of rich, middle and poor SES families, and have reported economic status as a significant variable in test performance of children. Although they compared the deprived and non-deprived children, the children were not matched on any reliable measure of SES.

Studies reveal that the nature and amount of practice and training mediate the end-state of a child's performance (Baksi, 1993; Das, 1993; Dash & Rath, 1986; Jachuk & Chatterjee, 1989; Kaul, 1991; Nandurbarkar, 1991; Mishra, 1990; Padhy, 1992; Vashisth, 1990). Unfortunately in none of these studies has the effect of different levels and long-term cognitive gains of children been examined. For example, Similansky (1979) noted that improvement in cognitive performance by such programmes dissipates over time. Mishra (1990) found about 23 percent gain in performance of children, and the effects were found to persist with a loss of only 3 percent over a period of three months. The long-term effects of intervention on cognitive functions have not been assessed beyond a few months. The maintenance effect on perceptual and cognitive tasks has also not been assessed over different intervals of time. Intervention programmes often seem to have been designed and carried out at group level, largely with the help of school teachers or through *Anganwadi* workers. Individual-based intervention programmes have not been attempted in spite of the fact that psychology primarily focuses on the study of individuals.

The purpose of the present study was to explore the effect of three levels of training (of different duration) and evaluate both short-term and long-term effects on children's performance. In the light of the general findings and theoretical propositions in this area it was hypothesized that :

(1) Before training the performance of high caste children on perceptual-cognitive tasks would be better than those of the lower castes.
(2) Training with perceptual and cognitive tasks would level off the performance of high and low caste children.
(3) Children getting exposure to a longer duration of training would perform better on perceptual and cognitive tasks than those receiving exposure to a shorter duration of training.
(4) The positive effect of training would be maintained to the same extent by high as well as low caste children.

METHOD

Designing a training programme and evaluating its effects on perceptual-cognitive task performance of high and low caste children were the goals of the present study. Intervention through training was the independent variable and its impact on performance of high and low caste children was measured as a dependent variable. The comparison of performance of high and low caste children was made at four different points: (A) Before training (BT), (B) Soon after training (SAT), (C) One month after training (MAT_1), and (D) Six months after training (MAT_6). It was thought that the comparison at the point "A" would provide the baseline against which the effect of training could be evaluated (point "B"), and that comparisons of point "B" with points "C" and "D" would provide evidence for the "maintenance" of training effects. Thus, a "before-after" measurement was made at each of the three levels of training, *i.e.*, (A) Half an hour per week for two weeks; (B) Half an hour per week for four weeks, and (C) Half an hour per week for eight weeks.

Design

To assess the effect of different levels of training, three separate groups of children were used. They were matched on certain social and demographic variables, *e.g.*, age, education, family background and urban-contact. Each group consisted of 20 high caste and 20 low caste children. Each child was assessed for its level of "test sophistication". This reflected the degree to which the child felt comfortable in a test situation. Each group was exposed to the same type of training material. The two levels of caste were high caste (Brahmin, Kshatriya and Vaishya) and low caste (the scheduled castes). The combination of training and caste variables resulted in a 3 (training) × 2 (caste groups) distribution of the groups in a factorial design.

Sample

The study was conducted with 8-9 year age village children on the outskirts of Varanasi city. An equal number of high and low caste children were selected. The main occupation of the population, from which the children were selected, was agriculture. Children of 8-9 years were selected because it is around this age level that the maximum difference between the performance of high and low caste or deprived and non-deprived children has been reported (Shukla, 1991; Tripathi, 1991). The overall sample consisted of 120 children drawn through a quasi randomization procedure.

Initially some villages situated at the outskirts of Varanasi city were visited. In each village the Gram Pradhan (the head of the village) was contacted, and information about village population was obtained. The researcher was also introduced to the Head Masters/Mistresses of the primary schools in villages. The names of children, their date of birth and caste identities was obtained from the school register. A separate list of high and low caste children between 8-9 years of age was prepared. The high and low caste children were drawn from families characterized by a low level of income. About 20% of the children enrolled in each school were studied.

TEST MATERIALS

Two kinds of tests/tasks were used in the study.

Criterion Tests/Tasks

These were used to measure the child's ability to perform the test before and after training. Included in this category were the Pictorial Interpretation Test (Sinha, 1971) and Picture-Model Matching Task (Mishra & Sinha, 1991).

The Pictorial Interpretation Test (PIT) intends to study the skill for perception and interpretation of perspective in pictures. The task consists of three achromatic pictures of 13 × 9.5 cm size. These are (1) The cat and the rat, (2) Two warriors and lady, and (3) The man and the monkeys. Each picture is so drawn that certain objects depicted in it could not be visible to some of the characters in the pictures due to the interposition of other objects between them. However, all these objects are easily visible to the child. The child's task is to indicate whether an object which is "hidden" for a particular character in the picture, or is placed outside its field of vision, can be visible to that character or not. A correct answer is more likely if the child understands the relative positioning of objects in the picture.

Each correct response was scored "one" and each incorrect response was scored zero. Some questions in the test were asked to break the "response-set" of the child. Responses to these questions were not scored. A maximum score of twelve was possible on the entire test with a minimum score of "zero" for any child. The reasons advanced by children for the non-perceptibility of objects depicted in pictures were also scored qualitatively. When the response indicated the grasp of spatial cues in pictures (*i.e.,* one object is hiding another), the reason was categorized as "relevant". Reasons that did not involve the idea of interposition were categorized as "irrelevant". The number of such reasons was counted.

Pictur -Model Matching Task (PMMT) intends to study the skill for comparing pictures with models in the context of changing visual cues (nature as well as amount). The task consists of pictures of five objects quite familiar to children. These include Elephant, Duck, Cup, Cart and Happy Man. The pictures represent objects in three viewing positions: Frontal view, side view, and oblique view. The child is presented with various models in each of the positions, one at a time, and is asked to choose from a set of three pictures the one in which the concerned object is shown exactly like the model.

For each correct matching, "one" score was given to the child; the incorrect answers were scored "zero". Since the child had to make twelve judgements on the whole test, the score ranged from 0 to 12.

Training Tests and Tasks

These were used for inducting children into the process of testing, and making them learn the mechanisms or operations required on them. It was thought that an experiential enrichment would enhance the skills of children to perform better on the criterion tests and tasks.

These included: the Indo-African Embedded Figures Test (Sinha, 1984), Kohs' Block Design Test, Picture Comprehension Task (Mishra, 1976) and Object Perception and Classification Task (Vajpayee, 1995).

ANALYSIS OF RESULTS

Picture Interpretation Test

On this test, the performance was analyzed on the measures of interpretation, reasoning and relevance of reasoning.

Interpretation Measure

The mean scores of children of high caste (HC) and low caste (LC) groups at different intervals of time are given in Table 8.1. The performance of both caste groups shows an increase at all levels of training. As far as the maintenance of training effect is concerned, results indicate that its magnitude varies from two weeks through four weeks to eight weeks. Maintenance of training effect is highest for the eight week training groups. Some evidence of decline in training effect is noted for the two week training groups.

ANOVA revealed significant improvement in performance due to training ($F = 69.65$, $df = 1{,}236$, $p < .01$). The improvement was noted almost equally in both caste groups. The effect of duration of training was also significant ($F = 43.59$, $df = 2{,}114$, $p < .01$) suggesting a greater improvement in performance with eight than four or two week training for both the HC and LC groups. Further analysis of the effect of training duration revealed generally no evidence of significant difference among SAT, MAT_1 and MAT_6 conditions for any training duration. These indicated that the effects of all training duration on HC and LC children were stable over a period of six months.

Table 8.1 : Mean and SD of groups on PIT (Interpretation Measure)

			BT	SAT	MAT_1	MAT_6
Two Weeks	HC	Mean	1.35	3.95	3.70	2.95
		SD	1.49	1.46	1.52	1.40
	LC	Mean	2.45	4.95	5.75	5.00
		SD	2.17	2.20	1.67	1.75
Four Weeks	HC	Mean	2.95	5.65	7.40	7.10
		SD	1.07	1.96	1.24	1.51
	LC	Mean	3.10	4.50	6.80	7.30
		SD	2.18	1.40	1.57	1.55
Eight Weeks	HC	Mean	4.05	8.20	9.55	9.95
		SD	2.20	2.40	2.18	2.14
	LC	Mean	1.35	3.65	6.00	5.90
		SD	1.85	1.15	4.01	3.91

BT= Before Training; SAT= Soon After Training; MAT_1 = One Month After Training; MAT_6= Six Months After Training.

Reasoning Measure

The performance of children on the PIT was measured in terms of reasoning for the non-perceptibility of various objects. Table 8.2 presents the mean scores and SD of different groups. There is clear evidence for improvement in performance of each group due to exposure to training and maintenance of training effect over time. Successive improvement in scores up to six months is observable in the eight-week training group.

Table 8.2 : Mean and SD of groups on PIT (Reasoning Measure)

			BT	SAT	MAT_1	MAT_6
Two Weeks	HC	Mean	1.25	2.40	2.75	2.50
		SD	0.62	1.36	1.51	2.04
	LC	Mean	1.00	2.00	2.50	2.25
		SD	1.22	1.42	1.32	1.47
Four Weeks	HC	Mean	1.10	4.15	5.15	5.00
		SD	0.99	1.68	1.56	1.76
	LC	Mean	2.15	3.15	4.30	4.10
		SD	1.49	1.46	1.71	1.81
Eight Weeks	HC	Mean	3.55	7.90	8.75	9.65
		SD	2.25	2.90	2.36	1.80
	LC	Mean	4.95	9.10	9.95	9.94
		SD	2.35	1.84	1.83	1.56

BT= Before Training; SAT= Soon After Training; MAT_1= One Month After Training; MAT_6= Six Months After Training.

ANOVA revealed no significant evidence for the effect of caste. On the other hand, there was a significant effect of training ($F = 98.69$, $df = 1,236$, $p < .01$), almost of the same level, on both caste groups suggesting greater reasoning by children due to exposure to training. The effect of duration of training was also significant ($F = 109.12$, $df = 2,114$, $p < .01$) with evidence for greater reasoning with eight than four of two-week training. However, the effect of eight week training on reasoning scores was of greater magnitude for HC than LC children ($F = 3.47, df = 2,114, p < .01$). Further analysis revealed that generally the effect of two-week training was not long lasting. On the other hand, the effects of four and eight-week training were maintained fairly well up to six months in both caste groups.

Relevance Measure

Interpretations on the PIT were assessed in terms of the relevance of reasoning given to non-perceptibility of objects or characters. Table 8.3 presents the mean scores and SD of different groups.

Table 8.3 : Mean and SD of Groups on PIT (Relevance Measure)

			BT	SAT	MAT_1	MAT_6
Two Weeks	HC	Mean	0.20	1.70	2.25	2.20
		SD	0.60	1.35	1.48	1.44
	LC	Mean	0.55	1.20	1.80	1.70
		SD	0.92	1.20	1.29	1.20
Four Weeks	HC	Mean	0.70	3.15	3.85	3.90
		SD	0.78	1.71	1.98	2.02
	LC	Mean	0.90	2.05	3.30	2.95
		SD	1.41	1.65	1.68	1.77
Eight Weeks	HC	Mean	2.90	7.20	8.10	8.15
		SD	2.10	2.93	2.38	2.55
	LC	Mean	2.65	6.05	7.20	7.02
		SD	1.74	2.04	1.78	1.95

BT= Before Training; SAT= Soon After Training; MAT_1= One Month After Training; MAT_6= Six Months After Training.

In general training appears to have brought about an improvement in the relevance of children's reasoning. So far as the maintenance of training effect over time is concerned, there is clear evidence for it at all levels of training for the HC group. In the LC group, on the other hand, the effect of two week training tends to get dissipated, whereas the effects of four and eight week training are maintained up to six months after training.

ANOVA revealed the effect of training to be significant (F = 62.14, df = 1,236, p<. 01) with evidence for greater improvement in the performance of HC than LC children (F=4.88, df= 1,236, p<. 05). On the other hand, the effect of duration of training (F=48.85, df=2.114, p<. 01) was found to be of the same order for HC and LC children. Further analysis revealed significant differences between BT and SAT scores. The differences among SAT, MAT_1 and MAT_6 conditions were not significant either for HC or LC children. This suggested that the effects of all training duration were maintained up to six months.

Picture-Model Matching Task

On this task, the performance was measured in terms of the accuracy of matching of models with pictures. The mean scores of HC and LC children are presented in Table 8.4. There is clear evidence for the effect of four and eight week training on performance. On the other hand, two-week training did not influence the performance of children.

Table 8.4 : Mean and SD of groups on PMMT

			BT	SAT	MAT_1	MAT_6
Two Weeks	HC	Mean	3.05	6.20	4.60	4.00
		SD	1.96	2.73	2.13	2.00
	LC	Mean	3.85	4.35	4.00	3.80
		SD	1.82	2.71	2.30	2.27
Four Weeks	HC	Mean	4.60	9.60	10.50	10.00
		SD	2.42	1.80	1.75	2.12
	LC	Mean	4.50	8.00	9.15	9.15
		SD	2.36	3.37	3.10	3.37
Eight Weeks	HC	Mean	4.55	10.89	11.50	11.80
		SD	2.67	1.44	1.02	00.51
	LC	Mean	5.60	9.65	11.20	11.12
		SD	2.44	1.80	1.12	1.28

BT= Before Training; SAT= Soon After Training; MAT_1= One Month After Training; MAT_6= Six Months After Training.

The findings also revealed that a longer duration of training had more beneficial effect on performance than a shorter duration of training. The improvement of performance of groups due to training was generally maintained over time.

ANOVA revealed a significantly better performance by HC than LC children ($F = 4.40$, $df = 1{,}236$, $p < .05$) and improvement in children's performance due to exposure to training ($F = 81.78$, $df = 1{,}236$, $p < .01$). Both the HC and LC children benefited from training almost equally. The effect of duration of training was also significant. ($F = 6.73$, $df = 2{,}114$, $p < .01$). Longer the duration of training, better was the performance of HC as well as LC children. The findings also revealed that two-week training was not at all effective for LC children. Four and eight-week training led to significant improvement in performance of both caste groups, and the effect was maintained up to a period of six months.

Discussion

Intervention programmes have shown their worldwide importance. In the present study the findings revealed that prior to training, the performance of high caste children on various tasks was better than that of the low caste. The difference in performance of the two groups was largely levelled off after training. Children having exposure to longer duration of training performed better than those having exposure to shorter duration of training did. A positive effect of training was evident not only soon after training, but also up to a period of six months, showing a kind of "maintenance effect" of training. Such an effect was observed almost with all levels of training and for both the caste groups.

There are number of issues that require discussion. We will like to address these issues in the context of the problems that are often raised with intervention studies.

The Effect of Training

A significant improvement in the performance of children due to their exposure to training programme brings out the importance of practice or training in psychological test performance. Various studies of transfer basically deal with these effects. Experience and learning opportunities have been considered as important factors in the performance of cognitive tasks from early days to more recent years (*e.g.*, Rogoff, 1981, 1990). Change in individual's performance due to training can be explained in terms of familiarity with content and operations, which often increase with training. These are called "non-test factors in test performance". Irvine (1983) has noted that the effects of these factors are more pervasive on the performance of people of the Third World countries than those in the Western hemisphere. Our findings give us a similar indication. What is interesting to note is that the effect of training has been more pronounced on the performance of low than high caste children. The differences initially noted between the performance of the two caste groups were levelled off after training, and this effect was evident till the last measurement of their performance (*i.e.*, up to six months).

The Effect of Duration of Training

Numerous studies indicate that the degree of learning influences significantly the retention of the learnt materials. While an under learnt material is more susceptible to forgetting over time, the interference that occurs due to number of intervening activities between learning and the retention test does not influence much the retention of materials that are overlearnt.

We had hypothesized that duration of training would significantly influence the performance of subjects not only soon after training but also over a longer period of time. A synoptic analysis of the effect of duration of training showed considerable improvement in children's performance with four and eight weeks of training, whereas the effects produced by two weeks of training were generally not significant for either caste group. The positive effect of practice has also been noted in several other studies (*e.g.*, Mishra, 1990).

The findings also reveal that the effect of training was not only evident immediately after training, but it was also found to be maintained over a longer period of time. Maintenance of training effect was evident in all groups up to a period of six months. However, with eight-week training, there was a successive improvement from immediate test performance to six months showing that a longer duration of training not only helps the maintenance of its effect, but also leads to progressive improvement in performance. The phenomenon of improvement appears to be similar to 'reminiscence' reported in studies of Ballard (1913). It appears that tasks that arouse interest are rehearsed automatically. This latent rehearsal may be held responsible for improvement in children's performance on various tasks over the period of six months.

Issues Related to Intervention

During the last two decades psychologists all over the world have shown concern with the development of Third World nations (Jahoda, 1975; Kagitcibasi, 1990; Wagner, 1986). The development of human resources through some kind of intervention has been considered important for achieving the goal of national development.

An analysis of intervention programmes would suggest that they have been largely designed for weaker sections of the society. A tacit assumption is that through intervention programmes, the weaker sections can be brought to the level of functioning of other sections of the society. There have been numerous criticisms of the "policy of reservation" by those engaged in intervention research. It has been argued that a reservation policy devoid of time frame generates at the individual level a tendency to "look to other", a feeling of dependency, and reduced vigor to compete with others. At the societal and national levels, it generates a variety of conflicts under the slogan of "distributive justice" (Eldering & Vedder, 1993).

Many other programmes have been developed in other parts of the world. These include programmes like Success for All (SFA) (Slavin & Madden, 1993), Turkish Early Enhancement Programme (TEEP), (Kagitcibasi, 1993) and Home Intervention for Pre-Primary

Youngsters (HIPPY), (Eldering & Vedder, 1993). These programmes have brought out a number of psychological dimensions, which may influence cognitive development of children. In all these programmes the basic assumption is that it is the functional isolation of children from others in the community that affects their cognitive development (Levitsky & Strupp, 1984). Thus as long as a programme can encourage participation of a child into the larger activities of a community by some psychological support extended over a definite period of time, it can ensure an optimum development of children of the deprived communities. Poortinga (1993) has argued that the intervention programmes have provided us with certain universal principles. What we need to do is to have a "cultural tailoring" of these programmes according to the local needs of individuals or groups. The finding of our study allow us to conclude that a training programmes with long-term goals in mind and carried out with a precise set of tasks (Poortinga, 1993) can bring about fruitful outcomes.

A number of critical issues have been raised with regard to the evaluation of the impact of intervention programmes. There has been some evidence to suggest that even programmes that have not been well implemented (Slavenburg, 1993), and programmes in which people have not directly participated (Dubey, Mishra, & Pandey, 1987) have also resulted in positive effects. Despite showing failure at the short-term level, many of the intervention programmes have shown positive effects in the long-term. One way to reconcile with this contrary evidence is to state these effects in personal terms (*i.e.*, test scores, school success, etc.), or in social terms (*i.e.*, reduced inequality in test performance or competence of two different groups). There is also evidence to suggest that short-term effects are generally evident at the individual level, whereas long-term effects are largely evident at the societal level.

Policy Implications

The findings of the study have some clear policy implications. There is a philosophical issue that needs to be addressed before designing any intervention programme for the development of deprived sections of the population. In the Western model of development the best way to bring about desired changes is to facilitate disadvantaged groups, which tends to help the people catch up with economic growth. Individual development in the Indian perspective is different from the norm of Western countries. Development related to modern technology can facilitate us for a comfortable style of life. It is not sufficient for the development of a human being, whose social development is seen as a consequence of actions of individuals who have attained self-realization and are acting in the interest of society (Tripathi, 1996). In Indian philosophy the stage of development was perceived with the stage of self-extension. It is also argued that social development based on value system may enable the society to move faster.

Even if we decide to ignore this philosophical debate on development, we can find other issues to derive policy implication of intervention studies. It may be noted that the government policy has delivered blind support to people on the basis of caste for the last five decades. The profit has gone mostly to those who are the least in need of any special assistance. There has been inadequate representation of people of the deprived sections of the population. Thus, degeneration from *varn vyavastaha* to caste system still continues in the society, resulting in negative consequences of caste consciousness, caste glorification and caste conflicts in place of a harmonious relationship of groups in our society.

There is another dimension of intervention effects. If we provide a readymade cake to eat, one can eat it once and enjoy it, but if we introduce the process of making cake, people can eat and enjoy forever. Thus, a struggler group can be made in place of a handicapped group. That is what Baba Amte, and other social reformers have done for the disabled people of the society. Through intervention we should generate the capability and awareness in the society so that people can multiply their innate resources for development.

The present policy is based on an 'organized-set' of action plans, which provide all people of the low caste groups with a common path of development without knowing the particular needs of the groups. There is need for an extensive survey of the circumstances of life of these groups to ensure the adoption of proper strategies for successful implementation of development programmes (Sinha, 1988).

REFERENCES

Abelson, W.D. (1982). Is an intervention programme necessary in order to improve economically disadvantaged children's IQ. scores? *Child Development, 53,* 304- 318.

Agrawal, S. & Mishra, R.C. (1983). Disadvantages of caste and schooling and development of category organization skill. *Psychologia, 26,* 54-61.

Baksi, A. (1993). *Developing and implementing an infant stimulation programme to mothers through Anganwadis workers.* Ph.D. Synopsis, University of Baroda.

Ballard, P.B. (1913). Oblivesence and reminiscense. *British Journal of Psychology Monographs* (794).

Berry, R.J. & Berry, A.V. (1977). Evaluation in the pre-school kindergarten. *Journal of Genetic Psychology, 440* , 91-107.

Bronfenbrenner, U. (1977). Towards an ecology of human development. *American Psychologist, 32,* 513-531.

Dash, A.S. & Rath, S. (1985). Effect of cognitive stimulation on disadvantaged and non-disadvantaged pre-school children: An experimental study. *Journal of Psychological Researches, 29,* 121-129.

Dash A.S. & Rath, S. (1986). Testing the limits of Reven's Progressive Matrices: An experiment. *Psychological Studies,* 32.

Das, R. (1993). *Testing for the effect of practice on attention and planning performance of high and low achievers.* Master's Thesis, Utkal University.

Dubey, V.K., Mishra, R.C. & Pandey, K.N. (1987). Radio in support of women's empowerment for child survival, protection and development in India. *Interaction, 5,* 1-14.

Eldering, L. & Vedder, P. (1993). Culture sensitive home intervention. The Dutch HIPPY experiment. In L. Eldering & P. Lisemen (Eds.), *Early intervention and culture.* The Netherland: UNESCO.

Evans, J., Stewart, P. & Bengs, T. (1972). Effects of pre-school language training on later academic achievements of children with language and learning disabilities. A descriptive analysis. *Journal of Learning Disabilities, 5,* 5-12.

Flavell, J.H. (1963). *The developmental psychology of Jean Piaget.* Princeton N.J.: Reinhold.

Hunt, J.M. Jr. (1961). *Intelligence and experience.* New York: Ronald Press.

Irvine, S.H. (1963). Testing in Africa and America: A search for routes. In S.H. Irvine & J.W. Berry (Eds.), *Human assessment and cultural factors.* New York: Plenum.

Jachuck, K. (1979). *Level I and Level II abilities of socially disadvantaged children in primary school.* Unpublished Ph.D. Thesis, Utkal University.

Jachuck, K. & Chattergee. R. (1989). Effect of pre-school education on cognitive abilities of high and low caste children. *Indian Psychologist, 6,* 79-84.

Jahoda, G. (1975). Cross-cultural psychology applied to the Third World. In J.W. Berry & W.J. Lonner (Eds.), *Applied cross-cultural psychology.* Amsterdam: Swets & Zeitlinger.

Jensen, A.R. (1971). Two level theory of mental abilities. In A.R. Jensen & W.D. Rohrer, Jr. (Eds.), *An experimental analysis of learning abilities in culturally disadvantaged children.* Washington, D.C.

Kagitcibasi, C. (1990). Home-based intervention. In R. Brislin (Ed.), *Applied cross- cultural psychology.* Sage: Newbury Park.

Kagitcibasi, C. (1993). A model of multipurpose non-formal education : The case of the Turkish early enrichment project. In L.Eldering & P. Liseman (Eds.), *Early intervention and culture.* The Netherlands: UNESCO.

Kaul, S. (1991). *Assessment of impact of non-formal pre-school education of integrated child development services on children's specific abilities.* Ph.D Thesis, M.S. University of Baroda.

Lazer, I. & Darlington, R. (1982). Lasting effects of early education: A report from the consortium for longitudinal studies. *Monograph of the Society for Research in Child Development, 47, (195).*

Levitsky, R.A. & Strupp, K. (1984). Functional isolation in rats. In J. Brozek & B. Schurch (Eds.), *Malnutrition and behaviour: Critical assessment of key issues* (pp. 411-420). Lausanne: Nestle Foundation.

Mishra, R.C. (1976). *Perception and comprehension of certain types of pictorial materials.* Doctoral Thesis, Allahabad University. Allahabad.

Mishra, R.C. (1990). Cognitive stimulation, training, and perceptual-cognitive task, performance by socially deprived children. *Indian Journal of Current Psychological Research, 5,* 1-11.

Mishra, R.C., & Sinha, D. (1991). *Acculturation, cognitive changes and interpersonal adjustment: A study of some changing tribes in Bihar.* New Delhi: ICSSR Project Report.

Misra, G. & Tripathi, L.B. (1980). *Psychological consequences of prolonged deprivation.* Agra: National Psychological Corporation.

Nandurbarker, A. (1991). *Enabling mothers of mild and moderate mentally retarded infants for fostering their infant development by planning and empowerment: A stimulation program.* Master's Thesis, M.S. University of Baroda.

Padhy, M. (1992). *Assessment and training of cognitive skills of Nolia children through play methods.* Ph.D. Thesis, Utkal University.

Poortinga, Y. (1993). Orientation on culture: Some comments on intervention programs. In L. Eldering & P. Liseman (Eds.), *Early intervention and culture.* The Netherlandss: UNESCO.

Rai, S.N., Seth, U. & Maujula, D. (1987). *Social deprivation and frustration tolerance: A study of the effect of caste and locale.* Presented in UGC seminar on strategies for the development of deprived section of Indian society, Department of Psychology, N.K.P. College, Dehradun, December 25-27.

Rath, R., Dash, A.S. & Dash, U.N. (1979). Cognitive abilities and school achievements of the socially disadvantaged children in primary schools. New Delhi: Allied Publishers.

Rath, S. & Dash, A.S. (1986). An experimental study of effects of cognitive stimulation on disadvantaged and non-disadvantaged pre-school children. *Psycho-Lingua, 16,* 17-26.

Rath, R. & Patnaik, N. (1979). *Cognitive abilities and school achievements of the socially disadvantaged children in primary school.* Bombay: Allied Publishers.

Rogoff, B. (1981). Schooling and the development of cognitive skills. In H.C. Triandis & A. Heron (Eds.), *Handbook of cross-cultural psychology, Vol. 4,* Boston: Allyn & Bacon.

Rogoff, B. (1990). *Apprenticeship in thinking.* New York: Oxford University Press.

Sahu, S. (1979). *Psycholinguistic competence and language achievement of socially disadvantaged children at primary school level.* Unpublished Ph.D. Thesis, Utkal University.

Schafer, E.S. & Aronson, M. (1972). Infant education research project: Implementation and implication of the home tutoring program. In R. Parker (Ed.), *The pre-school in action.* Boston: Allyn & Bacon.

Shukla, S.N. (1991). *Learning and memory among socially deprived groups: A developmental study.* Doctoral Thesis, Avadh University.

Seigal, L.S., McCabe, A.E., Brand, J. & Mathews, J. (1978). Evidence for the understanding of class inclusion in pre-school children: Linguistic factors and training effects. *Child Development, 49,* 688-93.

Sigal, J.E. (1990). Psycho educational intervention: Future directions. *Merrill-*

Palmer Quarterly, 26, 159-172.

Silver, R.A. & Levine, C. (1977). The role of art in developing and evaluating cognitive skills. *Journal of Learning Disabilities, 19,* 27-35.

Similansky, M. (1979). Priorities in education: Pre-school, evidence and conclusions. Working Paper No. 323. *Washington DC : World Bank.*

Sinha, D. (1977). Some social disadvantages and development of perceptual skills *Indian Journal of Psychology, 52,* 111-132.

Sinha, D. (1982). Socio-cultural factors and the development of perceptual and cognitive skills, In W.W. Hartup (Eds.), *Review of child development research, Vol.* 6. Chicago: Chicago University Press.

Sinha, D. (1984). Basic Indian values and behaviour dispositions in the context of national development: An appraisal. In D. Sinha & H.S.R. Kao (Eds.), *Social values and development: Asian perspectives.* New Delhi: Sage.

Slavenburg, J. (1993). Critical issues in the evaluation of pre-school intervention programs. In L. Eldering & P. Liseman (Eds.), *Early intervention and culture.* The Netherlands: UNESCO.

Slavin, R, & Madden, N. (1993). Success-for-All: Prevention and early intervention in elementary schools (working paper). The Hague: Netherlands Commission for UNESCO.

Toynbee, A. (1962). *The study of history.* New York: Oxford University Press.

Tripathi, N.M. (1991). *Family experiences and cultural background as factors in the development of pattern reproduction skill.* Doctoral thesis, Banaras Hindu University.

Tripathi, R.C. (1996). *Culture as a factor in community interventions.* Paper presented the symposium on "Applications of Psychology in Social Change and Development, XXVI International Congress of Psychology, Montreal, Canada, August 16-21.

Vajpayee, A. (1995). *Training and cognitive task performance: A comparative study of high and low caste children.* Ph.D. Thesis, Chaudhary Charan Singh University, Meerut.

Vashisht, S. (1990). *Enabling mothers of infants (0-3) months affected by cerebral palsymental retardation to foster infant development by planning a stimulation program.* Master's Thesis, M.S. University of Baroda.

Wagner, D.A. (1986). Child development research and the Third World: A future of mutual interest. *American Psychologist, 41,* 298-308.

White, B.J. (1973). *Experience and environment: Major influence on the development of the young child.* Englewood Cliffs, N.J. : Prentice Hall.

9

Variation in Sexuality and Cognition :
A Review of Research and Synthesis

GEORGE KURIAN

Introduction

According to psychoanalytic literature, higher forms of cognition result when libidinal strivings undergo sublimation. A perusal of the race differences research in the domains of cognition and sexuality will inform any discerning student the fact that in the past, it were those racial and ethnic groups capable of greater degree of sexual restraint, and developed manifold forms of sexuality, which generated great cultural products such as the arts, literature, science, technology etc. It can also be noted that those cultures and races which had elegant cultural products in abundance and were pioneers in mastering the nature were also the ones which not only developed elegant treatises on sexuality, but also practiced imaginative and diverse sexual modes and created exquisite art forms.

Two related aspects need emphasis here: firstly, restraints in the form of delay of immediate gratification of libidinal strivings can enhance the ratiocinative capabilities, which also gives rise to rich representational forms, paving way for the creation of culture and civilization. Secondly, sexual restraint may enhance the possibility of not only the development of forms that approximate the desired goal in manifold ways, but may also find further expression in the objectification of the goal through diverse means.

Most convincing arguments for a possible link between

sexuality and cognition can be extended from the data available on race differences in sexuality and cognition. Recent times have witnessed an enhanced interest in the study of race differences in the varied aspects of mental functioning, and their possible implications for theory building in the general psychological domain (see Rushton, 1989a; 1989b; Rushton & Bogaert, 1987; 1988; 1989). Most of the research reported in these works bring to the surface the psychobiological implications of these observed race differences, more than merely listing the differences. There is sufficient ground to believe that race differences have their roots in the biological substratum that constitute the races themselves, and the different behaviour patterns exhibited by different races of the mankind have a predictable nature. This leads to the assertion that inquiries such as exploring implications of race differences in sexuality and cognition may legitimately fall within the framework of modern psychobiological approach.

The Scope of Psychobiological Enquiry

The basic tenet of modern psychobiology is that mental events – whether they are internal events like dreams or fantasies or externally expressed ones like stated preferences or attitudes – can be studied and explained in terms of their psychobiological origins, although behaviour in any condition can be explained and understood at the functional level itself. Thus, while acknowledging that there are levels of explanation possible, the sanction to fall back upon proximate causes such as neuro-hormonal factors gives rise to greater explanatory power. While analyzing the psychogenesis of mental events or behavioural processes, we acknowledge the phylogenetic and ontogenetic history of the organism and its interaction with the milieu within which behaviour is expressed. Psychologists now generally agree that all behaviours are the proximal effects of neuro-hormonal factors and also the distal consequences of evolutionary pressures (Nyborg & Boeggild, 1989). Thus, the psychobiological approach to behaviour makes the central assumption that behaviour can be understood like any other biophysical structure. These structures - behaviours - are a product of hundreds of thousands of years of evolution and are assumed to be conserved, unchanged, across generations (Crawford & Anderson, 1989). Hence, there is a strong case for the study of behaviour in their natural setting, and the study of race differences in psychological parameters may yield rich insights into such proximate and distal causes of behaviour.

According to Dobzhansky (1965), scientifically it is far more viable to approach the issue of races from a population perspective than in terms of specific types. The current conception of races is in terms of populations with similar distributions on certain hereditary traits, but which differ from other similar populations within the species (Karen & Thompson, 1967).

In the following an attempt is made to review some of the pertinent literature on race differences in sexuality and cognition, and then analyze these within the Freudian framework to explore their implications for culture building and creativity.

Race and Civilization

Oriental and Mongoloid culture and civilization are acclaimed to be the oldest. Literature shows that science, technology, arts and scholarship flourished in these lands much earlier than the Greek and Roman civilizations. Artifacts unearthed from MohanJoDaro, and Harappa sites, and other archaeological evidence attest to this. Scholarship was exceptionally well developed which is evident from the several thousands of years old orally transmitted wisdom in fields as diverse as drama, music, religion, grammar, sexology, governance, etc.

If development of cultural products is any indication of the complexity of cognition the different populations were capable of, then it can be seen that the Bronze Age — an important milestone in the transition from the use of stone to the use of meta — originated in the Asia Minor, and regions surrounding it about 4000 BC. On the other hand, "The Bronze Age of Europe did not begin until 2000 BC, or later, and it was more retarded or entirely absent in parts of

Asia, most of Africa and all of Oceania" (Langer, 1952, p. 11). The same picture emerges with regards to the Iron Age also. Earliest use of iron began around 1400 BC, in the Asia Minor, in Europe around 11th or 10th century BC. However, use of iron was not prevalent in certain parts of Africa till many centuries later.

The particular population that could be credited with these early innovations can also be identified with certain amount of certainty. The Indian subcontinent was originally inhabited by a group of Mongoloid and/or of the Caucasoid races – the Veddoid and the Dravidian. According to Langer (1952), "... the invasion from the Iranian plateau by *Aryans* of uncertain antecedents, who gradually conquered or pushed back from the rich plains of northern India the earlier black Dravidian and Austro – Asiatic Munda population. The conquest is variously placed at 2000 -1200 BC" (p. 41).

It has also been pointed out that early developments in agriculture, and domestication of animals spread in India and in the Far East. The Dravidians and the Chinese renovated the idea of agriculture in their own terms and derived their own culture independently. According to Birdsell (1975), "... in the old world, early civilizations must be credited to three major racial groups — Caucasoids, Veddoids (aboriginal Indians), and the Mongoloids" (p. 546).

A comparable profile emerges when one examines the domain of sexuality too. Here erotic art forms provide some clue to the various culture's, conception of sexuality and the range of erotic sensibilities.

Going by the available literature on erotic art in ancient times, it can be seen that the ancient Greek and Roman erotic art belongs to 1st to 3rd century AD, whereas the oriental erotic art as found in India especially can be traced back to a much earlier period, probably 300 to 200 BC. It has been found that the Greek and Roman erotic art depicts conventional heterosexual postures with few variants on anal intercourse. On the other hand, erotic art forms found in India, show erotic themes of the most varied and sensuous kind. Here it is important to reflect upon two aspects of erotic art in India, which is of considerable importance to the discussion on sexuality - cognition linkage. Firstly, the proximity of erotic art to religious places like temples : There is considerable evidence in the form of temple carvings, sculptures and drawings scattered all over India, which show the intimate linkage between sexual strivings and a spiritual- philosophic view of life. According to some scholars, the association between eroticism and spirituality implies an absence of antagonism between the two. Both *Yoga* and *Bhoga* were considered as equally desirable and essential aspects of human existence. In the first case, the teacher inculcates in the learner the masculine discipline of *Yoga*, while in the second case, the sensual female help-mate takes on the role of *Sakthi*. The male initiate assumes the role of *Shiva*, and "both attain together a realization of the immense within themselves of the cosubstantiality of the Goddess and the God" (Zimmer, 1964, p. 130). Secondly, the variety of sexual activities depicted in the art forms provide an approximate measure of the contemplation on the theme of sex by the people of that time. The oldest depictions of intercourse can be dated back to about 300 to 200 BC. There are numerous other portrayals of precoital activities such as kissing, etc. (Bhattacharya, 1987). The following are some of major depictions found in various temples in the Southern, Western, Central and Eastern parts of India : Orgies involving two or more partners, two women with one man, two men with one woman, attendants helping the partners in coitus, partner(s) caressing attendant's genitals while in coitus and other forms of group sex. In addition to this, there are depictions of varied coital positions and other stimulation techniques such as manual and oral stimulation of sex organs etc. (Bhattacharya, 1987).

These two facts, the intimacy between sexuality and spiritual—philosophic strivings like *Tantra* and *Yoga* and the abundance of sexual themes in art, are glaring instances of the unique approach to life in these lands.

The former–sexuality–spirituality linkage–signifies the essential unity of them. The ratiocination that leads to higher forms of cognition as manifested in religious philosophy is also the one that adds a sensual touch to the human spirit. Both coexist not only as dynamic transformations of each other, but also in the intrinsic integrality of both, as conceived in *Shiva* or *Maheswara* (the Great Hindu God), who is also *Ardhanareeswara*—the symbol of androgyny.

It can be argued that the whole essence of the linkage between higher forms of thought and sexuality is personified in *Shiva* as *Purusha* and *Prakriti* – one exemplifying the masculine spirit and the other, the feminine sensuality. Creation and sexuality is thus captured in this singular unity.

The latter aspect—variations in sexuality—as depicted in the art forms, shows the pre-occupations of the great minds of those times on matters of eroticism. This is possible only when the mind is capable of delayed overt — response, or reflective action, as opposed to impulsive act, or immediate gratification of an instinctual impulse. The former allows for the development of ratiocinative capabilities resulting in the genesis of representation.

Apart from such graphic portrayals of sex, ancient India can be also credited with the first ever elegant treatise on the art of love and sex – *Vatsyayana's Kamasutra*. This 'aphorisms on love and sex' which has been found to belong to the 5th century AD, probably may be a codified form of the oral tradition on sexuality dating back to several centuries earlier.

In addition to the great legacy of representational forms such as graphics and treatises, the ancient Oriental civilization can also claim possession of great variety in their sexual modes. Homosexuality—one such non-procreative sexual variant-although prevalent in almost all cultures (Ford & Beach, 1951), appears to have originated in the Orient according to some scholars. According to Von Schrenck–Notzing (1895), homosexuality started spreading from the Orient to other countries. He notes that "From Asia, uranism (earlier label for homosexuality) was spread by the Phoenicians or Lydians first to Crete, and from there all over Greece" (p. 130). There is evidence to the effect that in *Kautilya's* time – about 4th century BC – homosexuality, whether among men or women was not considered a serious offense, in contrast to the heavy punishment meted out to heterosexual offenders. In the *Arthasastra*, there is mention of lesbianism and women's masturbatory practices (Chunder, 1970). In ancient China, homosexuality was tolerated, if practiced between consenting adults. There was no moral or religious sanction against it. *Taoism*, in fact favoured love between men because it brought two *Yang* elements together. Female homosexuality was also prevalent in ancient China. The dukes and emperors were entitled to 9 and 12 concubines respectively. This provided avenue for the close proximity of women and the long idle hours nourished the development of love among women. Also, lesbianism was encouraged by the husband, since it helped conserve his sexual energy (Lieh - mak, O'hoy & Luk, 1983).

This trend in homosexual practices appears to be prevalent in the present times too, as is evident from a recent report (Diamond, 1993). According to this author bisexuality is as high as 7.1 % to 15% for males and females respectively, in Japan. In China, it is approximately 7.6% for both male and female homosexuals combined. This is higher than the overall world estimate of 5 - 6% for males, and 2 - 3% for females.

Further support for the possible association between a culturally refined life-style and heightened eroticism comes from the close relationship found between homosexual practices and learning in ancient Greece. In Athens and Sparta, homosexuality was at its peak during the "golden age of Greece, with the greatest works of art and science, and that without endangering in any way masculine strength and activity" (Von Schrenck–Notzing, 1895, p.130). Greek boy–love had its intimate links with education and physical activity. The Gymnesia provided ample opportunities for the display of naked human body, which appealed to the aesthetic and erotic sensibilities of the Greeks. In the field of education, the tutor and the student formed a love-pair, with the lover becomes the guide to the beloved in all walks of life.

Presently we will briefly survey some recent research on race differences which has shown significant differences between the races in matters of sexuality and cognition. It can be seen that the behavioural studies comparing individuals belonging to different racial groups present a pattern similar to the one noted above with regard to cultural products.

Patterns of Race Differences

The following brief review of race differences research makes a strong case for the ordering of the races in the following form : On some psychobiological parameters the Mongoloids are higher than the Caucasoids who in turn are higher than Negroids (M > C > N) and on certain other parameters the Mongoloids are lower than the Caucasoids, who in turn are lower than the Negroids (M < C < N). It is important to note that whether in the ascending order or in the descending order, the sequence remains invariant, with the Mongoloid and the Negroid at the two ends and the Caucasoid placed in between. It is worth noting in this context that the computation of genetic distances places the Caucasoid in between the Mongoloid and the Negroid with regard to the separation of the races from their ancestral populations (Loehlin, Lindzey & Spuhler, 1975; Noble, 1978).

Race Differences in Cognition

Available literature points to the superior performance of the Mongoloid and the Orientals on various measures of cognitive functioning. Although Rushton (1985b) can be given the credit for recasting the whole spectrum of race differences within a firm theoretical mould, there are a number of findings in the earlier literature on this, except that most of the research involved only a few cognitive parameters.

Musical Ability

There is good amount of evidence to show the heritability of musical talent. Majority of the muscially talented had one or both the parents (64% to 68%) or their siblings (52%) or other relatives (54%) also to be muscially talented (Noble, 1978). It has been observed that qualitatively different musical forms have been produced by different racial groups. For example, note the Africans popularity for their Jazz. A survey conducted in the 1930's showed that the Caucasoid and the Jewish sub-population to be over represented in the professional musicians group. No comparative studies with the Mongoloids and Orientals have been reported.

Perceptual Speed

Noble (1978) reports that on discriminative reaction time (DRT), Asiatic Mongoloids and Indo-Dravidian Caucasoids perform at about the same level as American Caucasoids, while Negroids perform at a very low level.

Todas of Southern India have been found to be superior to Caucasoids on visual and cutaneous discrimination (Rivers, 1985/1986). Mongoloids have been found to be superior to average Caucasoids on spatial visualization. On Porteus Maze tests, Caucasoids performed better than Mongoloids, who in turn performed better than the Negroids.

Physical Development

On body size and physical development, Noble (1978) found Negroids to be superior to the Caucasoid, who in turn were found to be superior to the Mongoloid. Negroid children are invariably more precocious on various milestones of physical development than Caucasoids, who in turn were found to be more advanced than the Mongoloids. Codwell's (1949) study on male high school students of Negroid, Caucasoid and mixed races showed that the Negroid students performed far above others on five out of six standardized tests of physical fitness. According to Miller (1994), both Negroid men and women have a more mesomorphic body build than whites and Mongoloids. Mesomorphy is an index of muscularity and Negroids of both sexes are more muscular than other races.

These kind of findings have led Jensen (1973) to argue that these racial groups can be ordered on their evolutionary ages with respect to features such as developmental period, frequency of multiple births, and intelligence. According to Jensen (1973), these race differences might have occurred partly due to the sub-species differences in the evolutionary periods in their transition from

Homoerectus to Homosapiens. Even if Jensen's (1973) hypothesis regarding the differential timing of phylogenetic separation is discarded the role of evolutionary pressures in the selection of certain behavioural traits cannot be disputed. Ruston (1994) suggests that the migrating homosapiens from the African continent to Eurasia met with extreme cold conditions. Survival in these harsh environments prompted hunting, clothing, lighting of fires, protection of young ones etc., thus leading to a more cohesive social organization than a mere hunting – gathering system would demand for. This gains further significance in the light of the observation that infant motor development is inversely related to intelligence quotient (IQ).

Information Processing

In more recent times, Jensen (1980) has reported race differences in elementary and complex information processing. Black-White differences have been found to be more pronounced on complex reaction time tasks than on simple reaction time tasks. This kind of chronometric analysis of mental processes are very good approximators of real time information processing capabilities of the nervous system. A linear relationship has been reported between reaction time and the number of choices to be made. If processing latency can be taken as a measure of the complexity of the task, then it can be seen that the mean Black-White differences on reaction time tasks increase linearly as a function of the mean latency of processing (Jensen, 1985).

It has become possible now to say that reaction time tasks, unlike other paper and pencil measures are not very much affected by motivational, attitudinal or other extraneous influences. This is important because the task requirements and the format of the task in the chronometric paradigm are such that most of the processing involved take place much faster than the time required for the conscious registration of the stimulation. Libet (1965) has shown that it takes about 500 milli seconds for a peripheral stimulation to reach the conscious awareness of the subject. Usually, reaction times are far below the 500 milli seconds barrier (Jensen, 1982). This has other implications. Recent research has also shown that the variance in intelligence as shown by reaction time and similar other information processing tasks may be resulting "primarily from simple differences in fundamental properties of central brain processes" (Haier, Robinson, Braden & Williams, 1983, p. 598). Cortical evoked potentials show a significant positive relationship (r =.80) with full Wechsler Adult Intelligence Scale (WAIS) IQ. Measured intelligence correlates not only with electrophysiological parameters but also with such gross anatomical variables as brain weight and head circumference (Rushton, 1989b; 1990). Although Negroids are superior to Caucasoids, who in turn are superior to Mongoloids and Orientals in body size (Miller, 1994) when brain weight to body weight ratio is taken into account, the ordering of the races get reversed into M > C > N (Rushton, 1990). Beals, Smith and Dodd (1984) from a worldwide survey on cranial capacity obtained the following findings. Asiatics have a mean cranial capacity of 1380 c.c., Europeans, 1362, and Africans, 1276 c.c. A similar profile was presented by Rushton (1994). When crude measures of brain size such as head circumference is used, the correlation between IQ and brain size is between .18 to .20. However, the correlation increases significantly (r =.35), when IQ is correlated with brain size, the latter being measured using magnetic resonance techniques (Rushton, 1990). Similarly, Erhart, Marler, and Morrow-Tlucak (1987) found a correlation of .14 between Stanford-Binet IQ at age 3 and head circumference at birth (p<.05). The correlation between head circumference at the age of 3 years and Stanford - Binet IQ at 3 years has been found to be .22 (p<.001). Similar relationships between intelligence and brain weight, cranial capacity, number of extra neurons etc., has been noted.

Intelligence and Scholastic Ability

Rushton (1994) observed that the ordering of the races with respect to their relative cranial capacity is similar to the one obtained for measured intelligence. He reported that Asians in North America typically obtain mean IQs in the range of 101 to 106, Caucasoids, a mean around 100 and Africans between 70 to 90.

That brain size and information processing capacity are linked to intelligence and scholastic achievement can also find some support. Study of a variety of intellectual tasks performed by 1st grade and 5th grade boys was conducted by Uttal Lummis and Stevenson (1988). These investigators have found that both Japanese and Taiwanese children had higher achievement scores in both 1st and 5th grades compared to North American boys.

Thus the available evidence consistently show the higher performance of the Mongoloids and the Orientals on various measures of mental and behavioural processes.

Race Differences in Sexuality

Most of the research to be reported here has been taken from Rushton (1989a; 1989b) and Rushton and Bogaert (1987; 1988; 1989).

Sexual Precocity

It has been reported that Orientals have a very retarded development as far as sexual experience is concerned. The above cited research reports show that Africans have a very precocious sexual life compared to Europeans who in turn are far more sexually experienced than the Mongoloids and the Orientals. This trend is found for both the sexes. The extent of premarital sex is definitely a good indicator of sexual precocity. Christensen and Johnson (1987) compared the premarital sexual behaviour of blacks and whites in USA during 1968 and 1973. Black males and females were significantly more likely to engage in premarital sex compared to whites. Blacks of both sexes had more number of premarital sex partners too.

More recently Weinberg and Williams (1988) reported findings which support the above mentioned data. Both black males and females engage in premarital coitus much earlier in their life and much more frequently than white males and females. Black men and women also tend to have more number of sexual partners. Similar profile appears in the case of extramarital sex too.

This reduced restraint on sexual behaviour may have implications for other domains such as reproductive knowledge and other aspects of personality. Although the research to be noted here do not address the question of race differences, it can be seen that lack of sexual restraint is associated with various personality traits which makes possible more frequent conception and consequently more number of children as found in the case of Africans. Werner (1988) studied 200 men and women on their level of reproductive knowledge and personality. It was noticed that high and low reproductive knowledge in this group were associated with distinct personality characteristics. High reproductive knowledge was associated with high level of impulse control and women with high reproductive knowledge were found to be high on ascendancy, independence and unconventionality, compared to women with low reproductive knowledge. Predictably, low reproductive knowledge was associated with high valuation for stimulation – seeking and impulse expression.

Frequency of Intercourse in Marriage

Rushton and Bogaert (1987) report a higher rate of marital coital frequency among Africans (range : 3-10 per week; mean 3.8/ week) compared to Europeans (range : 1- 4 per week), and Japanese Mean=2 per week). The frequency found among Japanese is still less than the mean frequency of 2.5 per week found by Kinsey and his colleagues (Kinsey, *et al.*, 1948; 1953). A more recent study in China found a still lesser rate of marital coital frequency (Mean=1.2 times per week). An earlier study in the Indian context showed a frequency (Mean = 2.8 times per week) which is comparable to that of the European data (Kapadia, 1966).

Kinds of Sexual Activity

From the data provided in Rushton and Bogaert (1987; 1988), it can be seen that compared to Whites, Blacks have very few variations in their sexual practices. In the prepubertal period, there is tendency among the Blacks to indulge in coitus more often (29%), while

Whites indulge in prepubertal coitus remarkably fewer number of times (.09%). This finding becomes more revealing when kinds of sexual behaviour indulged in marriage is studied.

Whereas about 54% of White men are reported to indulge the oral stimulation of their female partners, only 20% of Black men do so. In the case of Black women a majority (80%) have not orally stimulated their male partners; but only a half of White women (50%) have not done so (Rushton & Bogaert, 1987).

As far as coital positions are concerned, Whites are far more likely to adopt a female above position (16%) in comparison to Blacks 9%. The female above coital position provides far more manevourability to the woman and it is less strenuous for the woman compared to the conventional male above positions.

It is also possible that variations like homosexuality may also be rare among Africans. Although Ford and Beach (1951) report that homosexuality is prevalent in almost all cultures, it is doubtful whether homosexuality among Africans exist for the same reason as found among the Europeans and the Orientals. Homosexuality may be tolerated and maintained as a custom, and as a part of initiation into adulthood of individuals in certain parts of the world. Such ceremonial, customary homosexuality is a part of sequential bisexuality as found in Sumatra, Papua - New Guinea, Sambia etc. (Money, 1987). In Sambia, there is institutionalized homosexuality among prepubertal boys who have to go and live among mature, unmarried youths and participate in oral sex with them (Money, 1987). Once the prepubertal boy reaches marriageable age, he begins the heterosexual phase of his life. Money (1987) notes that "Full manhood necessitates a prior phase of exclusively homosexual experience. Thus homosexuality is universalized and is a defining characteristic of head-hunting macho manhood" (p. 385).

However, the question whether sequential bisexuality and prepubertal and pubertal homosexuality as found in these cultures is similar to the homosexual orientation and practice as found in Europe and in the Orient remains open. But, one important distinction is worth mentioning. Homosexuality in Europe and in the Orient, is a socially, legally, and morally forbidden form of sexuality. Therefore, the homosexual runs the risk of social ostracism and criminal prosecution, in addition to the individual's self - recognition of being at odds with the norm. The voluntary homosexual is therefore different from that homosexual whose act carries institutionalized sanction. This is of importance for our discussion on sexuality — cognition linkage. Given the fact that Africans are less likely to engage in oral sex and other sexual variants, which are mostly non—procreative, then self-acknowledged homosexuality can be a rarity among Africans. This is further supported by the finding that unlike in the West, where spread of AIDS is predominantly through homosexual contacts, AIDS transmission in Africa is predominantly via heterosexual contacts (Rushton & Bogaert, 1989). In Europe and North America, AIDS and other HIV related syndromes are prevalent among men, whereas in African and Caribbean countries, the infected male and female populations are approximately equal. As regarding the prevalence of AIDS in the Orient, in China and Japan the main channel is blood transfusion; however, information on homosexual practices in the Orient is not available (Rushton & Bogaert, 1989).

In addition to the above, there is another set of evidence which tends to show lack of variations in sexuality among the Africans. Weinrich's (reported by Rushton, 1987) study show that sexual activities can be scaled in terms of their likelihood of leading to conception. Sexual activities such as kissing, oral sex, petting and variations like homosexuality have the least probability of leading to conception, in contrast to heterosexual coitus, which is most likely to lead to conception. When races have been compared on their propensity to engage in these different activities, Weinrich observed that Africans typically engage in activities which are most likely to lead to conception like coitus and they have less variety in their sexual behaviours compared to other races. Lack of variability in sexual expression implies few other modes than coitus, which in turn means more conception. Available data endorse this pattern. Africans, compared to Europeans and Orientals engage in coitus more frequently and have a higher birth rate.

Cognition – Sexuality Linkage : The Freudian Perspective

The aforementioned research findings and other observations call forth a formulation that can capture the relationship implicit in them. Psychoanalytic literature offers a rich and viable framework within which the proposed cognition – sexuality linkages can be captured. This can be attempted at two levels : (i) the psychoanalytic formulation of sublimation of the libido, as the mechanism that leads to the creation of higher forms of cognition may help in explaining how sexual restraint is positively related to higher cultural accomplishments, and (ii) the linkage between sexual restraint and evolution of ever richer erotic forms and practices, and the latter's association with creativity may be attempted within the Freudian framework.

i) According to Freud (1938), sublimation is a process "through which *excessive* excitations from individual sexual sources are discharged and utilized in other spheres, so that no small enhancement of mental capacity results from a predisposition which is dangerous as such" (p. 625. Emphasis added). In 'Civilization and its Discontents', Freud (1952) offers great insights on the process of sublimation. Libidinal displacements without getting frustrated by the outer-world reality is the greatest accomplishment of the process of sublimation. It leads to greater intellectual achievements and man's pleasure in these achievements. "This kind of satisfaction", Freud writes, "such as the artist's joy in creation, in embodying his fantasies, or the scientist's in solving problems or discovering truth, has a special quality which we shall certainly one day be able to define metapsychologically" (Freud, 1952, p. 773).

In the early phases of civilization where the man had to gather resources for survival, his sexual life had to suffer a great deal. Freud says that, since men do not possess an unlimited quantity of libidinal energy, he can contribute to material enrichment only by distributing his libido judiciously. "What he employs for cultural purposes he withdraws to a great extent from women and his sexual life; his constant association with men and his dependence on his relations with them even estrange him from his duties as husband

and father" (Freud, 1952, p. 784). Probably here one can fix man's search for vicarious sexual satisfaction in imagery and fantasy and also in alternate sexual modes like homosexuality, when confronted with the task of culture building resulting in extended estrangement from heterosexual pleasures.

In addition to this initial sublimation of the sexual instinct, civilization itself once it evolves, imposes curtailments on sexuality and its expression. Development of monogamy and religion extracted more from man's libidinal strivings. In 'Moses and Monotheism', Freud (1974) outlines how religion succeeded in restraining man's sexuality. The transition from the paganish, polytheistic religion to a monotheistic religion itself was a great cultural advancement. This great abstraction – monotheism —demanded from man renunciation of his libidinal strivings. Without going into the details of the mechanism that resulted in sexual restraining with the advent of monotheistic religion, it can be shown that by strict abstinence and renunciation, the abstract God got delinked from sexuality, and was raised to the level of ethical perfection (Freud, 1974).

However, it should be noted that there are differences between cultures and races in their extent of delinking God from sexuality. The degree to which the cultures and the races effected this delinking has implications for the races or cultures approach toward sexuality and morality. A relative lack of restraint (as documented in the early part of this paper) among the Africans leads to very limited cultural advancement and lesser erotic imagery. On the other hand, a very severe injunction against libidinal strivings as found in the Judeo-Christian tradition, and which has become more strident in the so called 'Protestant Ethic', leads to a smothering of human spirit and freedom. The consequences are equally harmful, if not all the way as disastrous as in the case of lack of restraint. When the Oriental tradition, especially the very ancient Indian tradition is examined on this aspect, it can be seen that it imposed only a moderate or partial delinking of sexuality from God. *Shiva (Maheswara)* is both the creator—the God—as well as the symbol of eroticism. The ancient Hindu tradition picturizes *Shiva* as going through a cycle of asceticism and sexual intercourse each one lasting a thousand years (Bowes, 1978). This culture and civilization, which depicts its supreme God as both a *Yogi* and *Bhogi* thus, provide a more optimal psychic environment for human experience.

Mischell (1974) notes, in the context of cultural differences in delay of gratification that extreme delay in gratification as found in achievement oriented 'Protestant Ethic' culture gives rise to an emotionally crippled individual and society, whose strivings get postponed forever and ever. On the other extreme is that which strives impulsively toward the instant gratification of the impulses leading to a poorly developed 'self' and highly impoverished culture. According to Mischell (1974), both are maladaptive. It can be hypothesized that the aforementioned ordering of the races may have their source in these shades of libidinal deployments.

The suggestion being made is that, from the initial stages of the development of civilization, there has been a trend to impose restraints arising from inner psychic mechanisms or socio-religious sanctions on man's expression of his sexuality. Every instance of cultural advancement such as incest taboo, monogamy and monotheism was an attempt in this direction.

Adair and Shimkunas (1973), attempted a direct test of the Freudian hypothesis of sublimation and its implications for creativity. This study correlated the degree of suppression of sexual and aggressive impulses with intellectual and creative expressions. It was found that extent of sexual suppression (high sexual fantasy, low overt expression) was significantly correlated with creativity. Similarly, extent of suppression of aggression (high aggressive fantasy, low overt aggression) was also correlated significantly with verbal IQ, aesthetic and social interests.

When the race differences findings are viewed within the aforementioned theoretical perspective, it becomes apparent that the data support the Freudian thesis. The Oriental and the Mongoloid races, which are credited with the earliest civilizations, are also the ones which are high not only on sexual restraint, but also on variety in sexual modes and an ever vibrant eroticism, with an aesthetic quality.

ii) Restraining sexuality, especially when it is in excess and powerful, may lead to diversions which can approximate the original drive in diverse ways. Mischel (1961; 1974) has analyzed Freud's (1911) formulation of two principles of mental functioning in the context of delay of gratification. According to Freud (1911), the genesis of ideation lies in the delay of gratification of an instinctual drive. In ontogeny, initially, a wish fulfilling hallucinatory 'object' in the form of an image arises as a consequence of the delay, which at later developmental periods is replaced by thought forms. But the capacity for fantasy and imagination continue to persist all through life, in the primary process which aids in the generation of rich, unconscious and drive - related cognitive forms whenever delay occurs.

It can be argued that delay in gratification of an instinctual drive may lead to the process of 'regression in the service of the ego', which makes possible the reconstruction of the primeval cognitive forms, which are nothing but the original libidinal strivings. This may help explain the differences between the races in their erotic sensibilities. Races which are capable of extended delays in the gratification of their sexual drives stand the chance of unearthing the primeval forms and recasting them in more subtle ways which are socially acceptable such as erotic art, and literature. On the other hand, those races which are low on delay, may not get the chance for this kind of regression, and hence may not acquire the capacity for variant sexuality and their representational forms. There are some indications to the effect that Negroes have less tolerance for delay, are more impulsive, and have lesser behavioural restraint (Miller, 1994). Mischell (1961) suggest that Negroes are more tuned to immediate rewards than to delayed ones. Hilgard's (1962) reformulation of Freud's (1911) concepts of primary and secondary processes, fits well into this scheme. Primary process strives immediate, impulsive gratification of a drive that reaches a given threshold of intensity, whereas secondary process aims to break this direct linkage between the drive and its satisfaction by placing the intermediary of ordered thinking in between (Hilgard, 1962).

One historical example can be seen in the life and works of Marquise-de-Sade. Sade was imprisoned and kept in loneliness for long durations of time, but he had a rich and fertile, imaginative, sexual pre-occupation. Simon de Beauvoir (1953) captures this transformation thus : "For eleven years – first at Vincennes and then in the Bastille a man lay dying in captivity, but a writer was being born (…) He recovered possession of his intellectual powers fairly quickly (…) But his flesh surrendered and he sought compensation for his sexual starvation in the pleasures of the table (…). From 1782 on, he demanded of literature alone what life would no longer grant him : excitement, challenge, sincerity and all the delights of the imagination" (p.24). What Sade wrote was rich in sexual imagery and thus he transformed and unleashed his eroticism into a deeper meaning and expression of his whole existence (de Beauvoir, 1953).

This leads to the elaboration of more intriguing aspect of sexuality—cognition linkage—its implications for creativity. As already noted, Freud commented on the 'excess' aspect of libido which demands the sublimation process, indirectly leading to extended delays in the gratification of instinctual drives. Freud also hinted upon the unusualness of this process. He says : "It is only available in the few. It pre-supposes special gifts and dispositions which are not commonly found in a sufficient degree" (Freud, 1952.) It may found in those who are basically of the narcissistic type and this type is characterized by their special gifts and the degree of sublimation of which they are capable. These individuals, in contrast to the majority derive their satisfaction out of their inner psychic functioning. Freud (1938) also observed that in the gifted and the creative there may be a proportionate mixture of creative, productive ability, perversion and neurosis.

The consequences of sublimation for sexuality and creative production has been elaborated by Herebert Marcuse in his book 'Eros and Civilization' (1969). According to Marcuse (1969), "The regression involved in the spread of libido would manifest itself in the reactivation of all erotogenic zones, and consequently, in a resurgence of pregenital polymorphous sexuality and in a *decline of genital supremacy*" (p. 201 Emphasis added).

According to Havelock Ellis, "There cannot be the slightest

doubt that intellectual and artistic abilities of the highest order have frequently been associated with a congenitally inverted sexual temperament" (Ellis, 1942, p. 26). This is found in creative people of both the sexes. Witty and Lehman (1965) while analyzing the emotional life of creative people suggests that it is possible that sexual variations like homosexuality or bisexuality might have played a significant role in the creation of works by geniuses such as Sappho, Shakespeare, Walt Whitman, Oscar Wilde and many others. These authors suggest that in the case of Edgar Allen Poe, there is evidence emotional of maladjustment relating to psychic impotence, and Lord Byron was referred to as a narcissistic who took efforts to maintain his physical beauty. Freud (1947) was struck by Leanardo da Vinci's physical beauty and the historical account of his sexuality. While concluding his study on the psychosexual development of this great artistic genius, Freud observed that Leonardo da Vinci's artistic and intellectual accomplishments may have their roots in the biological substrates and that his physical beauty, his sexual interests along with his great powers of intellect provide evidence for this.

The present thesis is that variations in sexuality, like homosexuality or bisexuality and the propensity for higher intellectual pursuits, have their linkages in the biological substratum, which in the psychological sphere may manifest in the form of specific needs, preferences and achievements, and which may be at variance with that of the ordinary and the 'normal'. The psychological mechanisms that are at work in this have not yet been revealed to the investigators so far, but some linkages have been suggested. In the specific neuro–hormonal, and psychological constitution of the creative individual, sexuality gets integrated with higher order mental functions, including that of work and creative production.

Further, the independent and non-conforming character of the creative personality is also exemplified in his or her negation of the sharp separation of sexuality from other domains, by a mechanism which makes it possible to permeate the whole personality with a tone of sensuousness. This also shows the rebellious nature of the creative mind which militate against the subjugation of sexuality for procreation alone, and also against the social institutions which strive to safeguard the *status quo*. As Barron (1963) notes, in the creative individual there is a total rejection of externally imposed controls "with the tendency toward socially unlicensed phallic activity, or phallic exhibitionism in its more derivative forms, being simply another expression of the general rejection of regulation of impulses by others in favour of regulation of impulses by oneself" (p.2.2). According to Barron (1963), the creative personality is characterized by rebelliousness, disorderliness and phallic exhibitionism. Thus, while restructuring sexuality and integrating it with higher mental functions, the primacy of genital, procreative sex or to put it in Freud's (1948) own words : "to bring one's own genital into contact with someone of the opposite sex" (p. 25) is totally rejected (Marcuse, 1969). In the creative mind, the whole of psychic realm is raised to a higher level of functioning, the body and the mind more integrated than ever before and this process "by its inner logic, suggests and conceptual transformation of sexuality into Eros" (Marcuse, 1969, p. 20).

Conclusion

The race differences data give rise to some robust conclusions such as the Oriental and Mongoloid superiority on sexual restraint, and greater intellectual achievements compared to Caucasoids and Negroids. The former accomplishments are reflected in the great tradition of the Oriental erotic art and its intimate linkages with a spiritual–philosophic way of life, while the latter is manifested in the ancient, rich, culture and civilization found in these lands.

The relationships between sexual restraint and capacity for higher forms of cognition on one hand, and that between richness and variety in sexuality, and capacity for creation on the other hand have been discussed within the psychoanalytic framework. The conclusion that the mechanisms that yield great cultural innovations are also the ones that make possible a more rich and diversified sexuality is drawn on the basis of the discussion of research findings in this area.

REFERENCES

Adair, M.J. & Shimkunas, A.M. (1973). Sublimation of sexual and aggressive drives. *Proceedings of the 81st Annual Convention of the APA,* Montreal, Canada, Vol. 8, 169-170.

Barron, F. (1963). *Creativity and psychological health.* Princeton, New Jersey : Van Nostrand Co. Inc.

Beals, K.L., Smith, C.L. & Dodd, S.M. (1984). Brain size, cranial morphology, climate and time mechanisms. *Current Anthropology, 25,* 301-330.

Bhattacharya, N.N. (1987). *History of the tantric religion.* New Delhi : Manohar Publications.

Birdsell, J.B. (1975). *Human Evolution : An introduction to the new Physical Anthropology.* Chicago : Rand Mc Nally & Co.

Bowes, P. (1978). *Hindu intellectual tradition.* New Delhi : Allied Publishers Pvt. Ltd.

Christensen, H.T. & Johnson, L.B. (1978). Premarital coitus and southern black: A comparative view. *Journal of Marriage and Family. 40,* 721-732.

Codwell, J.E. (1949). Motor functions and the hybridity of the American Negros. *Journal of Negro Education. 18,* 452-464.

Crawford, C.B. & Anderson, J.L. (1989). Sociobiology: An environmentalist discipline ? *American Psychologist, 44,* 1449-1459.

De Beauvoir, S. (1953). *The Marquis de Sade.* New York : Grove Press Inc.

Diamond, M. (1993). Homosexuality and bisexuality in different populations. *Archives of Sexual Behaviour, 22,* 291-311.

Dobzhansky, T. (1965). *Heredity and the nature of man.* London : George Allen and Unwin Ltd.

Ellis, H. (1942). *Studies in the psychology of sex. Vols. I & II,* New York : Random House.

Ernhart, C.E., Marler, M.R. & Marrow-Tlucak, M. (1987). Brain size, and cognitive development in early pre-school years. *Psychological Reports, 61,* 103 -106.

Ford, C.S. & Beach, F.A. (1951). *Patterns of sexual behaviour.* New York : Harper & Brothers.

Freud, S. (1911). Formulations regarding the two principles in mental functioning. In *Collected Works,* Vol. 4, New York : Basic Books.

Freud, S. (1938). *The basic writings of Sigmund Freud.* A.A. Brill (Ed.). New York: The Modern Library.

Freud, S. (1947). *Leonardo da Vinci.* New York : Vintage Books.

Freud, S. (1949). *An outline of psychoanalysis.* New York : W.W. Norton.

Freud, S. (1952). Civilization and its discontents. In R.M. Hutchins (Ed.). *Great books of the Western World,* (pp. 767 - 802). Chicago : Encyclopedia Brittanica Inc.

Freud, S. (1974). *Moses and Monotheism.* J. Strachey (Ed.). London : The Hogarth Press.

Haier, R.J., Robinson, D.L., Braden, W., & Williams, D. (1983). Electrical potentials of the cerebral cortex and psychometric intelligence. *Personality and Individual Differences, 4,* 591-599.

Hilgard, E.R. (1962). Impulsive *vs* realistic thinking: An examination of the distinction between primary and secondary processes in thought. *Psychological Bulletin, 59,* 477-488.

Jensen, A.R. (1973). *Educability and group differences.* New York : Harper and Row.

Jensen, A.R. (1980). *Bias in mental testing.* New York : The Free Press.

Jensen, A.R. (1982). The chronometry of intelligence. In M.P. Friedman, J.P.Das & N.O'cornor (Eds.), *Intelligence and learning,* (pp. 255- 310). New Jersey: Erlbaum Associates.

Jensen, A.R. (1985). The nature of the black-white difference on various psychometric tests : Spearman's hypothesis. *The Behavioural and Brain Sciences, 8,* 193-263.

Kinsey, A.C., Pomeroy, W.B., & Martin, C.E. (1948). *Sexual behaviour in the human male.* Philadelphia : W.B. Saunders & Co.

Kinsey, A.C., Pomeroy, W.B. & Martin, C.E. (1953). *Sexual behaviour in the human female.* Philadelphia : W.B. Saunders & Co.

Karan, N. & Thompson, F.W. (1967). *Human evolution.* New York : Holt, Rinehart & Winston Inc.

Langer, W.L. (1952). *An encyclopedia of world history.* Boston : Houghton Mifflin Co.

Libet, B. (1965). Cortical activation in conscious and unconscious experience. *Perspectives in Biology and Medicine, 9,* 77- 86.

Lieh - Mak, F., O'Hoy, K.M. & Luk, S.L. (1983). Lesbianism in the Chinese Hong Kong. *Archives of Sexual Behaviour, 12,* 21-30.

Loehlin, J., Lindzey, G. & Spuhler, J. (1975). *Race differences in intelligence.* San Francisco : W.H. Freeman & Co.

Marcuse, H. (1969). *Eros and civilization.* London : Allen Lane, The Penguin Publication.

Miller, E.A. (1994). Paternal provisioning *vs* mate selection in human populations. *Personality and Individual Differences, 17,* 227-255.

Mischel, R.W. (1974). Processes in delay of gratification. In L. Berkowitz (Ed.), *Advances in Experimental social psychology,* Vol. 7, (pp. 249-292). New York : Academic Press.

Mischell, R.W. (1961). Father absence and delay of gratification : Cross cultural comprisons. *Journal of Abnormal and Social Psychology, 63,* 116-124.

Money J. (1987). Sin, sickness, or status ? *American Psychologist, 42,* 384 -399.

Noble, C.E. (1978). Age, race, and sex in the learning and performance of psychomotor skills. In R.T. Osborne, C.E. Noble & N. Weyl (Eds.) *Human Variation,* (pp. 287-378). New York : Academic Press.

Nyborg, H. & Boeggild, C. (1989). Mating behaviour : Moves of mind or molecules.

Behaviour and Brain Sciences, 12, 29-30.

Rivers, W.H.R. (1986). *The todas.* Jaipur : Rawat Publications.

Rushton, J.P. (1985a). Differential K. Theory and group differences in intelligence. *The Behavioural and Brain Sciences, 8,* 239-240.

Rushton, J.P. (1985b).Differential K. theory : The sociobiology of individual and group differences. *Personality and Individual Differences, 6,* 441-452.

Rushton, J.P. (1989a). Race Differences in sexuality and their correlates : Another look at physiological models. *Journal of Research in Personality, 23,* 35-54.

Rushton, J.P. (1989b). The evolution of racial differences : A response to M. Lynn. *Journal of Research in Personality, 23,* 7-20.

Rushton, J.P. (1990). Race, brain size, and intelligence : A reply to Cernovsky. *Psychological Reports,* 66, 659-666.

Rushton, J.P. & Bogaert, A.F. (1988). Race *vs* social class differences in sexual behaviour : A follow-up test of *r/K* dimension. *Journal of Research in Personality, 22,* 259-272.

Rushton, J.P. & Bogaert, A.F. (1989). Population differences in susceptibility to AIDS : An evolutionary analysis. *Social Science Medicine, 28,* 1211-1220.

Uttal, D.H., Lummis, M. & Stevenson, H.W. (1988). Low and High Mathematics Achievement in Japanese, Chinese and American Elementary-School Children. *Developmental Psychology, 24,* 335-342.

Von Schrenck – Notzing, A. (1895). *The use of hypnosis in psychopathia sexualis,* New York : The Julian Press.

Weinberg, M.S. & Williams, C.J. (1988). Black sexuality : A test of two theories. *Journal of Sex Research, 25,* 197-218.

Werner, P.D. (1988). Personality correlates of reproductive knowledge. *Journal of Sex Research, 25,* 219-234.

Witty, P.A. & Lehman, H.C. (1965). Nervous instability and genius : Poetry and fiction. In W.B. Barbe (Ed.), *Psychology and Education of the Gifted : Selected readings,* (pp. 258-270). New York : Appleton-Century-Crofts.

Zimmer, H. (1964). Art of Indian Asia. *Bollinger Series, XXXIX,* New York.

10

Adolescence, Sexuality and Health:
Awareness and Perceived Constraints among Out-of-School Slum Adolescents*

URMI N. BISWAS and C. N. DAFTUAR

Introduction

Field theory and its later supporters (Lewin, 1931, 1946) defined adolescence as a transition, which is characterized by deeper and far-reaching changes in life and differentiation in life space. In the stage of adolescence individual enters into a cognitively unstructured region that results in uncertainty of behaviour. Lewin, like Mead (1950) believed that the transition could come through either a sudden shift or gradually. If the transition period is prolonged and children as a group are clearly distinguished from adults, adolescents are left in the twilight zone of social situation in which their group belonging is not clearly defined. The adolescent in such an in-between period is known as (in Lewinian terminology) the 'marginal man', meaning that the adolescent may at times act more like a child, often when the adolescent wants to avoid adult responsibilities and at other times may act more like an adult and request adult

*The study is a part of the project 'A study of Sexuality and Health Seeking Behaviour among Out-of-School Adolescents in Anand', sponsored by Population Council, India (1999-2000).

privileges. The inconsistencies and the lack of commitment that is some times reflected in adolescent relationships can be understood in the psychological dichotomy of adolescents. The high degree of uniformity observed among adolescents can be explained as an attempt to structure the field, which is experienced as unstable by the individual. This leaves a very fertile area of enquiry *vis-à-vis* adolescents' sexual attitudes and behaviour with reference to groups s/he belongs to.

The theme of adolescence is 'search for self identity' and this crests in when the physical, cognitive social and emotional developments are at the peak. At the age of (say) 14, a boy has the body of man and a girl has the body of a woman, they are capable of adult sexual activity and advanced problem solving. They also know that soon they will be held responsible for their own lives. The decisions involving their choices, relationships and lives, beliefs and values are not easy to make. According to Papalia and Olds (1994) 'these choices are not easy and they are often accompanied by emotional turmoil. Understanding teenager's alternating high and low spirits are two major pre-occupations – 'identity and intimacy', the identity and intimacy in the adolescents' lives have components of sexuality also, which may have major implications for the adult life of the individual. Social development of the adolescents goes through dramatic changes by moving from the close friendships only with the people of the same sex to friendships and romantic attachments with members of the opposite sex. Perceiving oneself as a sexual being and coming to terms with the sexual stirrings and developing an intimate romantic relationship becomes a part of the adolescents social identity.

Adolescents' self images and relationships with peers and parents are bound up with sexuality. Adolescents become sexually active to enhance intimacy, want to seek new experiences, to prove their maturity, to keep up with their peers, to find relief from pressures and to investigate the mysteries and pleasure of love.

In the broad framework of individual's sexual and reproductive health behaviour, sexuality has been understood to mean the total sexual makeup of an individual. In addition to the physical aspects, sexuality also encompasses attitudes, values, experiences, and preferences of the individual regarding sexual behaviour (International Planned Parenthood Federation, 1989). In India, one-fifth of the population comprises of adolescents between the age group of 10-19 years. The period of adolescence is characterised by physical, cognitive, emotional and psychosocial changes (Hall, 1916).

The adolescents' effort to adjust to the changes, bring a period of 'storm and stress', which is also a period of intensely fluctuating emotions from which young people may emerge morally stronger. The physical, cognitive, emotional changes in the adolescent and the specific developmental goal of moral, sexual, and occupational identity that adolescents have to achieve results in their having distinct developmental needs which are very poorly addressed and studied. It is reported, in an epidemiological study, that 44% of the total AIDS cases occur in the age group of 15-29 years (NACO, 1996). The National Family Health Survey (1992-93) pointed out that limited knowledge regarding reproductive health results in increased risks of STD infection including HIV/AIDS, maternal morbidity, mortality, unwanted pregnancies, and unsafe abortions, thereby, endangering the physical and reproductive health and productivity of adolescents. It has also been reported that adolescent girls undergoing abortion constitute a disproportionate (25%) share of the 5 million abortions.

In the national convention of NIPCCD (1998), it was agreed that the challenges that confront adolescents in this country are manifold, one of which is to check early marriages, unwanted pregnancies, and unsafe sexual practices so that the adolescents would reach their full physical potential and maturity. To achieve the same, the following issues need urgent attention.

(a) The nation should address and study the issues related to the health damaging behaviour of adolescents;
(b) The need for information related to sexual and reproductive health by adolescents should be addressed;
(c) Effort should be made to generate critical thinking in adolescents to develop attitudes and values that aid

democratisation of family and egalitarian gender relations; and

(d) The adolescents should be equipped with confidence an skills to protect their reproductive health.

Although three major national programmes were designed and are now under full implementation to address sexual health issues [namely, National Family Planning Programme, National AIDS Control Programme and National Sexually Transmitted Diseases (STDs) control programmes], still the impact of these programmes is inconsequential for adolescent population. In a study of illiterate adolescents, it was reported that as many as 94 per cent of sexually active adolescents had engaged in unprotected sex (Bansal, 1992). In rural Gujarat where the majority of premarital sexual activity occurred with the commercial workers as many as 80 per cent of adolescent boys had never used condom. Though condoms were obtained freely from health care workers, a large (55%) percentage was ignorant of the effectiveness of condoms in preventing STDs and HIV (Sharma & Sharma, 1995). Moreover, qualitative data from medical practitioners serving in an urban slum community in Bombay suggest that sexually transmitted diseases (STDs) are not unknown among these groups, but treatment seeking tends to be delayed, presumably out of ignorance and embarrassment (Bhende, 1995). In spite of these and some other studies, we can say that not many studies have been reported in the Indian context. Since cultural domain is an important factor, we cannot rely only on Western data and draw conclusions about the Indian situation. For example, Mead (1950), a cultural anthropologist, who studied adolescence in the ethnic tribal cultures, emphasized the importance of cultural factors in the transition of adolescence. She observed that when the shift from childhood to adulthood is more sudden, where both the groups are well defined and with the puberty rites, the adolescent is pushed to the life of an adult, then the transition would be difficult. In societies, like that of Samoa, where the shift is more gradual, adolescence will be more stress free. There, the children see the adults', sexual activity, watch babies being born, engage in sex play, regard death as natural, do important work, show assertive and even dominant behaviour and know precisely what they will do as adults.

However, studies that explore the health seeking behaviour and sexual health among adolescents are scarce. Harvey (1984) asserts that a discussion of sexual health from the perspective of social work revolves around sexual attitudes. It is also asserted that sexual health involves understanding the place of sexual desire and behaviour in the repertoire of human behaviour overcoming outmoded biases that impede sexual fulfilment and assertive approach to meet sexual needs and sensitivity to the rights of others. It has been also emphasized that sexual health is more than a successful working of anatomy or complying with irrelevant reproductively based rules, it is the ability of individuals to express themselves as sexual beings (Harvey, 1984), as an object of love, spiritual relationship, and personal identity.

In this context, it will be useful to discuss certain ideas and points of views regarding the interplay of love, sex and sexual health. The three concepts are so inter-woven in reality that very often the three are confused for one another. Psychologists have not yet been successful in delineating the three explicitly from each other. For example, Spranger (1955) takes an interesting position concerning sexual and affective development during adolescence that makes an important distinction between the feelings of 'sexuality' and feelings of 'pure love' that adolescents separate in their affective domain distinctly. Sexuality refers to the conscious sexual body pleasures that result in sexual excitement and desire. 'Pure love' is a psychological function depending upon understanding sympathy and empathy. Sexuality and pure love originate in different layers of the psychological structure. Sullivan, (1953) similarly speaks of the collision between the 'intimacy need, and lust'. Bühler (1935) also differentiates between the sexual component and spiritual component of sexuality. Underlying all these assumptions is the belief that the development of each of the two components during adolescence takes place independently and separately.

Adolescents can be aware of both the forms, but the object of pure love may be different from that of sexuality. This division of the two aspects of sexual development frequently results in many adolescent behaviour implications, either having relationships only for sexual gratification and not as realization of pure love or, postponement of sexual gratification since the emotional aesthetic component acts as on inhibitor of sexuality. In certain ways, this distinction dealt by Spranger (1955), Sullivan (1953) and Bühler (1935) is related to Erikson's idea of searching for an ego-identity during adolescence.

In continuation with the earlier framework, Erikson (1968, 1970) maintained that falling in love in adolescence is not a sexual experience but an attempt to define one's ego-identity. By becoming intimate with another person and sharing thoughts and feelings, the adolescent offers up his or her tentative identity, sees it reflected in the loved one, and is latter able to clarify the self. Erikson believed that males cannot achieve intimacy until they have achieved a stable identity. Females, he thought, achieve intimacy before identity. An adolescent girl puts her identity aside as she prepares to define herself by the man she will marry. Definitely Erikson's standpoint suffers from gender bias. That may also add another dimension of belief and attitude towards sexuality. Positive beliefs and attitude can change physical proximity into psychological love and may extend to the whole gamut of sexual behaviour including sexual health and pregnancy.

Apart from Freud's and Erikson's early theories most of the other theories forwarded to explain the identity search in adolescents, treated them as one homogenous group. More recently Gilligan (1987) proposes that women define themselves less in terms of achieving a separate identity and more in terms of relationship with people. They judge themselves on their responsibilities and on their ability to care for others as well as for themselves. They achieve identity less through competition and more through cooperation. Marcia (1980) based on survey data on a large sample, concluded that, women do not wait to develop the capacity for intimacy after they have achieved identity as in Erikson's allegedly male-based pattern; for women intimacy and identity develop together. However, other research findings support that intimacy is more important for girls than for boys, even in grade school friendships.

On the whole, there appears to be little disagreement on the idea that adolescence is a transition period from childhood to adulthood, except that social learning theorists (Bandura, 1964) took a position that human development is a continuous process and not divided into stages. According to Bandura, adolescence has become a transition period for some individuals, where it seems social conditions are responsible, and not some intrinsic aspects of human development.

However, most of the theories discussed so far, explain stress and strain and emotional instability during adolescence and attribute it to several causes. Anthropological theories (Mead, 1950) advance the idea that continuity in cultural conditioning will decrease adolescent difficulties while discontinuities will increase them. For social learning theorists (Bandura, 1964) it is not the nature of the developmental processes that causes stress and strain during adolescence but the social pressures, social expectations, and other socio-environmental conditions that contribute to stress and strain and create a crisis in some individuals during this specific period in the human lifecycle.

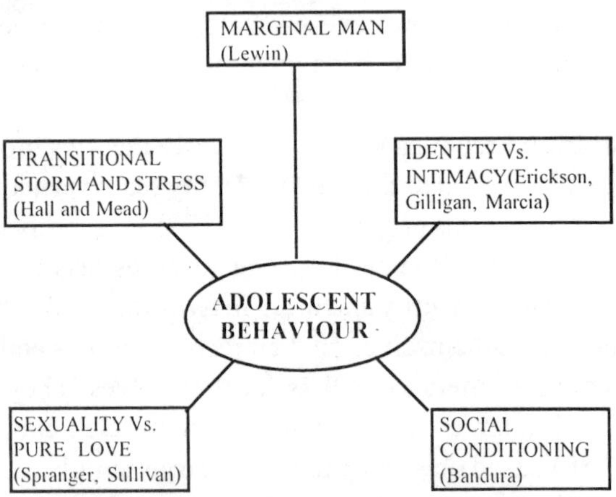

Fig.10.1: Different Viewpoints of Adolescent Behaviours.

Few studies have investigated the sources of knowledge and suggestions for information about sexual health in adolescents. Goraya and Prakash (1998) studied the knowledge level and practice of contraceptive use among pregnant teenagers. Findings suggest that school is the primary source of information about contraceptive methods. Considering school and education to be the major source, the out-of-school or never-been-to-school teenagers are supposed to be in a more disadvantageous position. Therefore, exploring their health care needs and perception of sexual risks seems important aspects to be studied. In the framework of these theoretical underpinnings of adolescent sexuality the present study focused on the adolescents of a slum community of Gujarat.

The present study attempted to discover adolescents' understanding and perception of their sexual needs, sexual health, and health seeking behaviour. Specifically, adolescents were assessed on their knowledge about pregnancy, childbirth, abortion, perceived sex related health problems and health seeking behaviour; suggestions for family health education and their beliefs and knowledge about family planning.

METHOD

Sample

The sample comprised 300 adolescents selected from a list of 'out-of-school' and 'never-went-to school' slum adolescent population of Anand town of Gujarat. The adolescents were categorised into two groups: Early adolescents in the age range of 12 to 15 years of age and late adolescents within 16 to 19 years of age range. A total of 162 male adolescents and 138 female adolescents were selected for the study.

Procedure of Data Collection

The study being exploratory in nature, it used both qualitative as well as quantitative approaches.

Phase I — Qualitative Approach

After identifying the slums, a door-to-door house listing was done in three major slums to identify the 12 to 19 years old school drop-outs or never-been-to-school adolescents. Rapport was established with the slum community as a whole and the key persons of the community were persuaded about the implications of the study for the health status and family welfare. The field investigators were well trained and well versed in the local language. After identifying the households the following qualitative techniques were used for data collection.

(a) *Social Mapping* : Initially to get acquainted with the slum society and its dynamics, two social mapping surveys (one for the boys and one for the girls) were conducted in each slum. Some key locations and key informants were identified during this exercise.

(b) *Focus-Group-Discussions (FGDs)* : Focused-Group-Discussions were held for groups of six to eight boys and girls, separately, in each slum. Through the FGDs, researchers could identify the code words, vocabulary used and shared by the slum adolescents relating to their sexual behaviour and practices. Moreover, the FGDs gave us a lot of insight into perceptions of accepted sex related beliefs and norms, different sexual practices, different sources of seeking sexual health care and services, etc.

Phase II — Quantitative Approach

Based on the information gathered through the qualitative phase described earlier, an extensive questionnaire was developed. The questionnaire was administered personally to the individual adolescents. The data were collected in only one session per person. Only those participants who willingly responded to the whole questionnaire were considered for the final analysis. On an average, collecting information from one individual took about two hours.

The Questionnaire : The questionnaire used for the quantitative survey consisted of nine sections. The questionnaire was developed and standardized for a large population, the sample of study of seven state level projects conducted in different parts of Gujarat and sponsored by Population Council, New Delhi. The first two sections covered background information of the respondents and their parents. The other sections dealt with exposure to mass media, knowledge regarding sexual behaviour, family planning, awareness and knowledge of sexually transmitted diseases, HIV, AIDS, actual sexual behaviour, substance abuse behaviour, sexual health seeking behaviour and respondents' suggestions for topics to be included in family health education.

Phase III — In-depth Interview

Depending on the openness, willingness to participate and availability, 15 boys and 15 girls were selected from the three slums for in-depth interviews about their sexual experiences, attitudes, health problems, awareness and knowledge about reproductive physiology, AIDS and HIV. Subsequently, the interviews were rewritten issue-wise, and processed for analysis.

Analysis

The study being exploratory in nature, only descriptive analysis (mostly in frequency count for respondents) was used. Frequency distributions for categories of responses were found for male and female groups of late-adolescents, and early-adolescents, separately. Moreover, the whole sample was divided into three groups depending on their exposure to the levels of education and compared across their responses to different knowledge and awareness questions.

RESULTS AND DISCUSSION

Pregnancy, Abortion and Family Planning

In the first section of the questionnaire adolescents were asked

Table 1 : Knowledge about pregnancy, abortion, and family planning (frequency distribution)

Variables	Male			Female		
	12 – 15	16 – 19	Total	12 – 15	16 – 19	Total
Problems in Early Pregnancy						
Prolonged labour pain	38	52	46	4	14	8
Risk to life of woman	37	58	49	34	59	46
Risk to life of child	35	58	48	23	53	37
Child may be very small	3	15	10	3	1	2
Risk of abortion	1	16	10	5	28	16
Other complications	5	7	7	2	6	4
Don't know	55	22	36	65	30	49
Abortion is acceptable	49	56	53	20	41	30
Reasons of not approving						
It is sin	45	40	42	46	30	38
Don't know	—	1	—	13	14	14
Is MTP legally approved						
Yes	1	1	1	11	20	15
No	4	2	3	13	23	18
Don't know	95	97	96	76	57	67
Pregnancy is preventable	45	85	67	29	70	49
How it can be prevented						
By using contraception	11	21	16	1	15	8
By abstinence	6	3	4	—	1	—
Washing vagina after sex	—	2	1	—	—	—
Doing physical exercises	—	3	2	1	1	1
Taking drugs (OCP)	31	56	45	12	44	27
Don't know	52	13	30	85	37	63
Sources of knowledge						
Parents	1	7	5	1	1	1
Brother/Sister	1	3	2	—	3	1
Other relatives	15	21	18	—	5	2
Teachers	1	6	4	—	—	—
School/book/course	1	10	6	—	—	—

(Contd.)

Table 1 : *(Contd.)*

Variables	Male			Female		
	12 – 15	16 – 19	Total	12 – 15	16 – 19	Total
Friends/Neighbours	41	78	61	9	21	15
Newspaper / Magazines	4	16	11	—	3	1
Audio Visual Media	42	55	49	11	58	33
Actually seen						
Condom	61	91	78	7	38	21
Pills	13	31	23	9	42	25
IUD	—	2	1	3	8	5
Using Condom	41	82	64	3	27	14
Using pills	1	13	8	5	38	20
Meaning of unprotected sex						
Sex using condom	3	4	4	1	1	1
Sex not using condom	18	14	16	1	11	6
Sex with other than the spouse	27	54	42	5	20	12
Sex using irregular contraceptive	3	2	2	1	17	9
Don't know	49	25	36	91	50	72
n =	71	91	162	74	64	138

about their knowledge and awareness about childbirth, abortion, pregnancy, and family planning. Responses of male and female young and late adolescents are presented in Table 10.1. Responding to the question 'what are the problems faced during pregnancy in an early age?' older adolescent boys reported risk to the life of the mother and the child is the most serious consequence. The next highest reported consequence was 'prolonged labour pain'. Younger adolescent boys also reported similar consequences to be the major ones due to pregnancy in an early age. Female adolescents, both old and young groups, also believed that risk to the life of the mother and child are major consequences followed by risk of abortion due to early (age) pregnancy. What seemed quite surprising was that both younger (86%) and older (30%) female adolescents showed ignorance about the consequences of early-age pregnancy.

Boys and girls indicated significantly different views on the approval of abortion issue. On the whole, 53 per cent of male adolescents approved abortion, whereas 70 per cent of female adolescents disapproved of abortion. When compared with the older group of adolescents, a large number of the younger group of both male and female adolescents disapproved abortion (51% and 80%, respectively). To understand why they disapproved of abortion, they were asked as to what were the reasons behind their disapproval. An almost uniform answer was that they considered abortion (male 42%, female 38%) as a sin.

Most male (96%) and female (82%) adolescents reported ignorance about the legal status of medical termination of pregnancy. However, 18 per cent of girls said that Medical Termination of Pregnancy (MTP) is legally disapproved whereas almost equal number of them (15%) said MTP is legally approved. In both the female adolescent groups, a higher percentage reported MTP as illegal.

Among the four groups of adolescents, the older group of female adolescents reported higher awareness about safe period for abortion. Yet, in all the four groups, specifically among the younger boys and girls, a serious lack of information (76% and 81%, respectively) was evident about the stage when abortion could be safe. Older adolescent boys reported that till 24 weeks of pregnancy, abortion could be safe which seems as bad as total ignorance. Looking at the ignorance level and myths about abortion and about the legal status of abortion and considering its salient health implications, there is an urgent need to educate adolescents about the reproductive physiology and health for a healthy society.

Among older age groups, a higher percentage of both males and females compared to the younger male and female adolescents believed that pregnancy is preventable (only 29% of the young female adolescents believed that). High percentage of older male adolescents perceived pregnancy as preventable. On being asked about the methods of preventing pregnancy, a very high percentage (85%) of younger groups of female and 52 per cent of male adolescents showed their ignorance. Both groups of older male and female adolescents reported taking oral contraceptive pills (OCP) considering as the most effective method. Using contraception was found to be the second most preferred method of preventing pregnancy. Looking at the percentage distribution, males appear to be more informed and more responsive than the female adolescents.

Identifying the methods of delaying or preventing pregnancy, 70 per cent of the male respondents as a whole, and 90 per cent of older male adolescents in particular identified use of condom. However, a high percentage of female respondents (31%) including older female adolescents (53%) suggested oral pills to be the most effective contraceptive method. The younger and older groups of adolescents again differed significantly in their awareness about the issue. Among young adolescents, 84 per cent of females and 51per cent of males displayed ignorance about other methods that can be used to delay or prevent pregnancy.

Male adolescents reported that friends and neighbours are their major source of information for knowledge related to family planning. Of course, audio-visual media was reported as the second major source followed by relatives as third important source. For female adolescents, audio-visual media seems to be the major source of information. Friends and relatives are only next to the media as the main sources of information. It appears that if we need to increase the level of awareness about family planning among our out-of school-adolescents, the girls' population can be targeted through advocacy programmes in audio-visual media, whereas for boys, groups training through peer education may be more effective.

Significantly, a higher percentage of late male adolescents (91%) than late female adolescents (38%) reported having actually seen condoms. 61 percent of young male adolescent reported that they had seen them actually, whereas, only 21 percent of all girls reported so. Regarding the oral contraceptive pills (OCP), 23 per cent of the adolescents reported that they had seen them. Between the two groups of female adolescents, there was a significant difference. 42 per cent of late adolescents reported that they had seen OCPs in contrast to only 9% from the young adolescents. Regarding Intra-Uterine Devices (IUD), less than 5 per cent of respondents from male (young and late) and young female adolescent groups reported that they had seen it. Only 8 per cent of the late female adolescent reported in the affirmative.

Knowledge about use of contraceptives was also investigated. 82 per cent of the older and 41 per cent of the younger male groups reported that they knew the use of condoms. Knowledge of using condom was reported by 27 per cent of late adolescents in female group compared to 3 per cent of the younger female adolescents. When asked about the knowledge of using condoms or OCPs, only 5 per cent of the young female adolescents showed awareness. Young male adolescents also reported complete ignorance about the use of the pills, but 41 per cent of them reported awareness about use of condom. Only 13 per cent of late male adolescents reported awareness about the use of the pills.

Knowledge and awareness of the young and older male and female adolescents regarding methods of family planning and their use showed interesting interactive trends. The variations in the responses among groups seem to be affected by the interactive effects of gender and age group. For confirmation, use of further inferential statistics is planned.

It was found that 36 per cent of male and 72 per cent of female adolescents did not know the meaning of unprotected sex, whereas a higher percentage of younger adolescent groups were unaware. However, a high percentage of male adolescents considered sex with other than the spouse as unprotected sex. They also believed that having sex without using condom was an act of unprotected sex. Female adolescents also reported sex with anybody other than spouse and irregular use of contraceptive as unprotected sex. They equated unprotected sex with promiscuity.

Knowledge of HIV/AIDS/STD

In the second section adolescents' perception about different sex related diseases and its consequences were explored. To understand the level of knowledge of adolescents about sexually transmitted diseases, they were asked whether they believed that diseases could

Table 10.2 : Knowledge about HIV/AIDS

	Male			Female		
Variables	12–15	16–19	Total	12–15	16–19	Total
Diseases by Unprotected Sexual Act	25	56	42	4	9	7
Types of diseases						
Chandi	12	42	29	3	3	3
Germi	11	23	18	4	6	5
Cancer	8	11	10	3	5	3
TB	10	10	10	1	1	1
Diarrhoea	—	3	1	—	3	1
Itching	3	2	2	—	—	—
Don't Know	—	1	—	—	—	—
Source of Information						
Parents	4	5	5	1	1	1
Other relatives	—	11	6	—	—	—
Teachers	1	1	1	—	—	—
School/book/course	3	4	4	—	—	—
Friend/Neighbour	22	47	36	1	6	4
Print Media	1	8	5	—	—	—
Audio-Visual Media	12	43	29	4	12	8
Don't know	—	1	—	—	—	—
Effect of Untreated STDs						
Infertility	10	23	17	—	1	—
Increasing risk of HIV/AIDs	31	29	30	3	5	4
Increasing risk of cervical cancer	7	8	8	1	—	—
Bad outcome of pregnancy	4	8	7	—	5	2
Affect the Newborn during birth	45	30	36	90	89	90
STD can be cured	53	70	63	5	12	9
Heard about HIV/AIDs	49	86	70	9	39	23
HIV/AIDs is a Fatal disease	43	69	58	7	25	15
Source of information						
Parents	1	9	6	1	6	4
Brother/Sister	1	5	3	4	5	4

(Contd.)

Table 10.2 : *(Contd.)*

Variables	Male 12–15	Male 16–19	Male Total	Female 12–15	Female 16–19	Female Total
Other relatives/friends	20	40	31	3	—	1
Teachers/Doctors	3	16	10	—	—	—
School/book/course	1	7	4	1	1	1
Friends/Neighbours	39	57	49	3	6	4
Slogan/Pamphlets/Posters	17	35	27	1	3	2
Print Media	7	6	7	—	3	1
Audio-Visual Media	39	46	43	8	44	25
HIV can occur to						
Male	6	8	7	—	1	—
Female	2	18	11	—	—	—
Both male & female	42	60	52	5	31	17
Don't know	49	13	29	95	67	82
Healthy looking person can have AIDS						
Yes	30	53	43	—	8	4
Don't know	56	17	35	96	80	88
Can AIDs be cured						
Yes	38	64	52	4	12	8
Don't know	56	21	37	96	79	88
n =	71	91	162	74	64	138

be transmitted through unprotected sexual acts. The distribution of patterns of responses is presented in Table 10.2. The results show that among the four groups of adolescents, highest percentage of older male adolescents (56%) agreed to the fact that unprotected sexual act can lead to diseases. Among young as well old female adolescents, very low percentage of respondents believed that unprotected sex could lead to diseases. When the two groups were compared, a higher percentage of younger male adolescents reported agreement to the statement (25%). On the whole, males reported significantly greater awareness about the probability of contacting a disease through unprotected sex than female adolescents.

When asked about the diseases that get transmitted through unprotected sexual acts, the adolescents reported a range of diseases from itching, diarrhoea, tuberculoses, cancer, gonorrhoea (*Germi*), syphilis (*Chandi*), etc. A very high number of them reported syphilis (*Chandi*) as a disease. Males' awareness about diseases seems to be significantly higher than females. Ninety-three percent of the female respondents reported that there could be no disease because of unprotected sex. The types of diseases reported by them are also less.

The major sources of information about the sexually transmitted diseases were friends, neighbours, and audio-visual media. Male adolescents reported friends and neighbours as their major source of information whereas, the female adolescents reported audio-visual media as their major source of information. For male respondents, the audio-visual media was reported to be the second major source and relatives as the third major sources of information.

The variations in findings reported by the male and female respondents related to the question 'how STD is transmitted' seem to be very interesting. Surprisingly enough, 84% of girls highlighted poor-hygiene as the cause of transmission. The high percentage of responses reported by the girls for this particular question shows their concern for STD transmission. The highest percentage was however from older adolescent males reporting unprotected sex with any partner as the major cause for STD transmission followed by poor hygiene as the second important cause. Younger groups of boys reported poor hygiene as a major cause followed by unprotected sex with any partner as the second prominent cause. Boys also perceived unprotected sex with spouse, as one of the causes of transmission of STDs. Younger female adolescents (89%) reported poor hygiene as the singularly responsible cause.

Consequences of unprotected sex were perceived in terms of infertility, increasing risk of HIV/AIDS, increasing risk of cervical cancer, bad outcome of pregnancy affecting newborn during birth, etc. Out of these consequences, highest percentage of young and old adolescents perceived the infant being affected at birth as the major one followed by increasing risk of HIV/AIDS. Infertility was reported as the third consequence. But 90% of females including a very high percentage in both young and old groups considered newborn baby being affected as the major consequence.

On the whole, the frequency distribution of response pattern to different questions pointed out that the female adolescents, in general, were non-responsive. This may be due to their ignorance. But they exhibited their concern about transmission of STD and believed that it is due to poor hygiene. They considered that untreated STD affects the health of the newborn baby. Older adolescent males were mostly aware of the causes and consequences of STDs. Younger adolescent boys also revealed a reasonable amount of awareness regarding these issues.

Adolescents were asked about their understanding and perception of HIV and AIDS. Out of the total sample, 70% of the male adolescents reported that they had heard about HIV/AIDS. On the contrary, 77% of the female adolescents reported that they had not heard about it. Comparing the age groups, a larger percentage from older adolescents from both sexes reported that they had heard about HIV/AIDS. A larger percentage of adolescent boys (58%) reported AIDS to be a dangerous disease compared to the girls (15%). Older adolescent boys seemed to be most aware of the fatal consequences of the disease followed up by the younger adolescent boys. Adolescent girls showed lack of awareness about the disease and its fatality.

Most male adolescents had heard about AIDS but very few girls had heard about it. Both groups believed that it was a contagious disease. Boys said that this is contacted from sex workers and, that is the reason why they did not visit sex workers. Few of them reported seeing AIDS advertisements on television. Even few of them believed that it could occur only if it was in one's fate. Raman, who described himself as a philander reports 'AIDS is a contagious disease, but you get the infection only if it is in your destiny - otherwise not. So I don't care'. Only 1 out of 14 males interviewed reported once having a venereal disease. However, condom use seemed to be very rare among boys. When OCP is largely used to prevent pregnancy, condom use is largely neglected and only one boy reported using it when he went to see a sex worker.

Sexual Health Problems and Health Seeking Behaviour

Adolescents' perception about the possibility of health problems related to sexual behaviour is also studied. High percentage of older male adolescents reported that they perceived chances of health related problems because of sexual intercourse. Compared to 79% of older male adolescents, only 20% of the older female adolescents perceived sex related health problems. In the younger group also, the disparity was high between male and female adolescents. Fifty-three per cent of younger male adolescents perccived sex related health problems compared to only 4% of younger females adolescents. On the whole, males seemed to be much more concerned about sex related health problems. Higher percentage of males reported AIDS as a possible health problem related to sexual intercourse. Only a few male adolescents believed pregnancy and STD as sex related health problems. On the contrary, older female adolescents reported pregnancy and weakness as possible sex related problems. Young adolescent girls seemed to be almost ignorant about this. Very few of them reported weakness as a sexual health problem.

When asked whether they had any health problems in the last three months, 22% of older male adolescents, 8% of the younger male adolescents, 9% of the older female adolescents and 4% of younger female adolescents reported having sex related health problems. Male adolescents reported different types of health problems varying from gonorrhoea to syphilis. The only health problem reported by female adolescents was itching in their private parts and similar other complaints. Among the 'range of sexual health problems' faced by the respondents, 6% of younger male adolescents reported gonorrhoea and 7% of older male adolescents reported having syphilis attacks.

Compared to the percentage of adolescents, who reported

having sexual problems in the last three months, very few adolescents sought any help or consulted anybody for treatment. Except for younger female adolescents, the percentage of male and female adolescents who consulted doctors for treatment was almost 50% of the number who reported having a problem. That means almost half of the suffering adolescents go untreated. This is a very serious issue and should be given a close consideration by all kinds of relevant professions.

Causes for not consulting a doctor were feeling shy and because of their expectations that the problem would vanish on its own after sometime. All female adolescents believed that the problem would vanish on its own. Very few adolescent boys (1%) and girls (2%) reported that there are provisions for government services for providing information and health services in the slum. The health departments and the social welfare departments need to look into it. In spite of the health department's claim, it seems that the services are not reaching to the intended target for various reasons.

Male adolescents showed a higher concern for health services in their slum than the female adolescents. Forty-four percent of younger male adolescents and 49% of older male adolescents expected the government to provide health services in their areas as compared to 17% of female adolescents. Moreover the demand for doctors far exceeded the demands for health workers, nurses, health centres, etc. In order to support the existing health services in these areas, the adolescents preferred health centres, government or private hospitals to be there in the slum itself. It is a good suggestion, which should be heeded to. The sex related problems are taboos in our society. Even educated, well to do people, are often reluctant to consult a doctor in such cases.

Expectations from Health Services

Male adolescents were more demanding in terms of their expectations from the public health service providers compared to the female adolescents. With respect to their expectations and suggestions about the types of health education they would need, both the female and male adolescents expressed their desire to know more about body hygiene, care during pregnancy and family planning. However, male adolescents showed more interest in reproductive physiology and care during pregnancy as possible topics for health education than the female adolescents did. Sex education and dissemination of knowledge about AIDS, STD and sexual education got a low priority from both female and male respondents.

On the whole, the major findings were :

(a) The girls seemed to have a very low level of awareness and knowledge about sexual and reproductive health. Within the group, the younger female adolescents seemed to be almost completely ignorant about these issues and concerns.

(b) Male adolescents, in contrast, seemed to be much better aware about the issues as well as about its consequences. Although younger male adolescents did report a lot of ignorance, older male adolescents seemed to be quite aware and concerned about sexual and reproductive health related issues.

(c) In response to almost all the questions about the sources of information, both younger and older male adolescents reported that friends and neighbours are the major source of information followed by relatives. Female adolescents, on the other hand, reported audio-visual media as the primary source followed by siblings. It suggests that males obtain knowledge and awareness about sexual and reproductive health related issues through their social network of friends, relatives, and neighbours. Girls, irrespective of reporting audio-visual media as the major source, remain quite secluded and are not conducive to the issues and concerns related to their sexual health. Female adolescents reported that their brothers and sisters are the major source of information. It implied that, for whatever reason, female adolescents have a very restricted social interaction and network. This may be the major cause of their lack of awareness.

Apart from these findings from the questionnaire, data collected through in-depth interviews revealed the ideas about love and sex among these urban slum adolescents that supplement the findings through quantitative data.

The pervasiveness of sexual behaviour was revealed with more clarity through in-depth interviews rather than through the survey (Daftuar & Biswas, 2000). Out of the 25 adolescents interviewed in-depth, almost 80 percent reported at least one sexual inflection. Most of the boys had their sexual initiation with older and married women. Only one out of the 14 boys seemed to have visited a sex worker for the initiation. Boys, who reported being initiated by elder married women, said they were seduced into the first intercourse. 'Sex per se' seems to be of much significance to the boys as compared to the girls. However, surprisingly, when sexual pleasure seems to be a very important ingredient of a successful marriage, premarital sexual relationships do not seem to have any implications for marriage. Most of the boys were very vocal about their sexual expeditions. For example, Kanubhai, a 17 year old sweeper with middle school education says, 'because of my salary, most of the girls in this slum know me more than any other boy. I spend a lot of money on girls; presently I have relation with three girls. I have loved only one girl, who is from a higher caste'. Similarly, Raman, a 19-year-old auto rickshaw driver, seems to have numerous sexual relationships. 'I have a habit of befriending girls. I hook girls by giving them a lift in my auto, offering them refreshments, taking them to movies, and gradually I get my way with them. After enjoying sex, I leave them. Even I got a girl impregnated twice and spent money to get it aborted. When she forced me for marriage, I left her.' Some boys even reported having sexual relationships with elder married women either out of sympathy or because 'she helps him in cash and kind'. On the whole, the in-depth interviews revealed that for male slum adolescents, sex is something exciting, desirable and they do not hesitate to give expression to their sexuality. But their sexuality does not lead to any commitment either to marriage or love.

The sexual relationships did not imply any serious emotional involvement. Mostly, for these male slum adolescents sexuality is a purely physical thing, but somehow, they also try to prove their identity, their efficiency through their sexuality. Female slum adolescents, on the contrary, revealed a different scenario. The female adolescents were committed to their partners of affairs. A broken affair meant a heartbreak, feelings of despondence and depression for them. For example, Gauni, a girl who is engaged but had an affair and physical relationship with another boy (her cousin) is adamant and is ready to break the engagement and face the wrath of her parents and the community for her love.

The findings of the study show that for male adolescents, identity and intimacy are separate domains. In the initial years of adolescence—sexuality is more or less channelised to form a part of their identity. But for girls, identity and intimacy seems to develop together. Identity is expressed through their intimate relationships. The gender dichotomy as proposed by Erikson (1968,1970) and Marcia (1980) is supported by these findings too.

The boys said that they help each other in understanding their sexuality and also in their sexual expeditions. They also support each other in carrying relationships and protect each other's interest. The girls seem to be socialized not to talk or share anything about their sexuality. They seem to have lot of inhibitions and constraints to open up about all this. What the researchers inferred to be the feigned ignorance of the girls from their non-responsiveness is basically because of the different social conditioning for boys and girls. In the in-depth interviews, girls even admitted about homosexual relationships as a very normal thing among the female slum adolescents, whereas in the survey, female adolescents emerged as a very non-responsive group and even reported ignorance about many pertinent issues like pregnancy and childbirth. The gender differences in expression of sexuality and the perspective of male and female adolescents confirms the stance of socio-cognitive theory. Socio-cognitive theorists like Bandura (1964,67) have suggested that adolescent problems are perceived differentially by different groups not because of transition that leads to storm and stress but because of the social conditioning and social environments of the community.

The major findings of the study focus on the large knowledge gap among female adolescents on sex, sexuality and health related issues, which in turn, implies that there is a strong need for community counselling to increase the awareness and acceptability of women's education and create a positive attitude towards gender equality and women's reproductive rights among slum adolescents.

REFERENCES

Bandura, A. (1963). *Social learning and personality development.* New York: Rinehart & Winston.

Bandura, A. (1964). The stormy decade: fact or fiction? *Psychology in the Schools, 1,* 224-231.

Bansal, R. K. (1992). Sexual behaviour and substance use patterns amongst adolescent truck cleaners and risk of HIV/AIDS. *Indian Journal of Maternal and Child Health, 3*(4), 108-110.

Bhende, A. (1995). Evolving a model of AIDS prevention education among underprivileged adolescent girls in the urban India. *Women and Aids Research Programme Report, Series No. 5.* Washington D. C.: International Centre for Women.

Bühler, C. (1935). *From birth to maturity.* London: Kegan, Paul, Trench, Trubner & Co.

Daftuar, C. N. & Biswas, U. N. (2000). *A study of sexuality and health seeking behaviour among out-of-school adolescents in Anand.* Small Research Grant Report Series No. 13, Population Council, New Delhi.

Erikson, E. H. (1968). *Identity: Youth and crisis.* New York: W. W. Norton.

Erikson, E. H. (1970). Autobiographic notes on the identity crisis. *Daedalus, 99,* 730-759.

Gilligan, C. (1987) Adolescent development reconsidered. In C. E. Irwin (Ed.) *Adolescent social behaviour and health.* San Franscisco: Jossey-Bass.

Goraya, A. & Prakash, M. (1998). Contraceptive knowledge and practice of pregnant teenagers requesting termination of pregnancy in inner city, London. *Family Practice, 15*(1), 914-515.

Hall, G. S. (1916). *Adolescence.* New York: Appleton.

Harvey, G. (1984). A social work perspective on sexual health. *Journal of Social Work and Human Sexuality, 2*(1), 11-20.

International Planned Parenthood Association (1989). *Preventing a crisis: AIDS and family planning work.* London: McMillan.

Lewin, K. (1931). Environmental forces in child behaviour and development. In C. Murchison (Ed.) *Handbook of child psychology.* Worcester, MA: Clark University Press.

Lewin, K. (1946). Behaviour and development as a function of the total situation. In L. Carmichael (Ed.) *Manual of child psychology.* New York: John Wiley and Sons.

Marcia, J. E. (1980). Identity in adolescence. In J. Adelsen (Ed.), *Handbook of adolescent psychology.* New York: Wiley.

Mead, M. (1950). *Coming of age in Samoa.* New York: New American Library.

Mead, M. (1952). Adolescence in primitive and modern society. In G. E. Swansen, T. M. Newcomb, E. L. Hartley, *et al.*, (Eds), *Readings in social psychology.* New York: Henry Holt.

NIPCCD (1998). *Report on National Convention on Family Life Education: Emerging Challenges,* held on 18-19 November, National Institute of Public Co-operation and Child Development, New Delhi.

Papalia, D.E. & Olds, S. W. (1994). *Human development.* Tata McGraw Hill, New Delhi.

Sharma, V. & Sharma, A. (1995). Condom promotion strategies: What we need to know? *AIDS, 9*(5), 537-538.

Spranger, E. (1955). *Psychologie des Jugendalters.* Heidelberg: Quelle & Meyer.

Sullivan, H. S. (1953). *The interpersonal theory of psychiatry.* New York: W. W. Norton.

11

Resilience of Low Income Working Couples

ABHILASHA SRIVASTAVA

Introduction

The Chinese character for crises represents a combination of the symbol for danger and the symbol for opportunity. Inherent in any profound challenge is the potential for one or the other of these outcomes. So far, psychologists have focused primarily on the 'dangerous' consequences of challenges. However, there has been a recent trend highlighting the opportunity for growth and change (O'Leary, 1998). Historically Freud and Maslow can be said to be the forerunners of the two approaches respectively.

Stress is ubiquitous. Suffering is a part of human experience and certain hardships, conflict make their way into everyone's life. Yet there are innumerable examples of individuals reflecting the power of human spirit to survive when the life seems hopeless. Some of the survivors of Nazi camp (*e.g.*, Anne Frank and Dr. Viktor Frankel) emerged as resilient individuals.

In psychology there has been a paradigm shift away from pathology toward a focus on the positive aspects of human strength. Moving away from the existing deficit/vulnerability model, which focuses on the stress-illness relation, the present study aims at understanding the positive aspect of human strength, which has long been ignored in psychology but is now receiving attention. Resilience is one such phenomenon reflecting human capacity to brave adversity.

Resilience may be considered as an encompassing phenomenon, a kind of psychological strength of individuals to overcome challenges, brave adversities, adapt effectively and grow within a context. The aim is to understand and conceptualize resilience as it exists in human beings at all levels, cutting across gender and nations. However for the present study, the focus is on a specific group and it has a specific context, that is, of poverty stricken masses. Among them, we find the example of both types of people—those who survive and grow and those who succumb and stagnate. In between these two extreme groups lies the majority. The study aims to tap this range of resilience, where there is manifestation of tremendous inner strength at one end and on the other extreme there is vulnerability.

Poverty by its very nature forces one to experience certain socio-economic stressors. People living in poverty experience dearth of financial resources and thereby deprivation of certain basic amenities. Not only this, socially also they are allotted a low status. They experience discrimination and ill treatment from their better off counterparts. It is presumed that resilience will influence the subjective perception or experience of these socio-economic stressors.

Poverty is a family characteristic rather than an individual characteristic *i.e.*, people are defined as poor or non-poor depending on the economic status of the family with which they live. In other words, poverty is not an individual level phenomenon, the whole family is affected by it. Therefore, another objective of the study is to investigate the quality of family life of these families. The aim here is to see the relationship between resilience of individual and his/her quality of family life.

Throughout the world, especially in the western countries the institution of marriage is breaking down. India has a relatively strong tradition of family. This study therefore, contextualized resilience in the family. In the West, resilience can be judged in terms of the individual's achievements and coping. But in India, it is more operative or manifested at the level of family.

Thus in brief, following are the objectives of the study :

- To conceptualize resilience and to develop a psychometrically sound measure of resilience in the context of poverty stricken sections of society.
- To see the relationship of resilience with certain concomitant variables *viz.* socio-economic stress and quality of family life (QOFL).
- To study gender differences regarding resilience, perception of socio-economic stress and QOFL.

The paper has been organised in the following sections. The first section describes the constructs related to resilience. In the second section the definition of resilience is given as evolved and used in the present study. The next section on Method deals with sample, variables and the measures used in the study, following which are the sections on Results and Discussion.

Resilience: Related Constructs

In the literature, constructs like hardiness, Sense of Coherence (SOC)), Dispositional Optimism (DO), Learned Resourcefulness (LR) and Competence come closer to the concept of resilience. A brief introduction of and discussion on these constructs may help to understand the concept of personal resilience. In all these constructs, there is a common thread running which helps in portraying a picture of a resilient person. However, there is a possibility of having some unique characteristics/qualities in a resilient person considering his/her socio-cultural and economic context. It is likely that the inherent quality of resilience is the same but its manifestation is different depending upon the socio-economic and cultural context.

The concept of *hardy personality* emerged from an existential theory of personality (Kobasa & Maddi, 1977). Hardy persons are considered to possess three general characteristics: 1. The belief that they can control or influence the events of their experience (Control), 2. An ability to feel deeply involved in or committed to the activities of their lives (Commitment), and 3. The anticipation of changes as an exciting challenge to further development (Challenge) (Kobasa, 1979). The highly stressed but healthy person is hypothesized to have, (a) Decisional control or the capability of autonomously choosing among various courses of action to handle stress, (b) Cognitive control, or the ability to interpret, appraise, and incorporate various sorts of stressful events into an ongoing life plan and, thereby, deactivate their jarring effects, (c) Coping skill or a greater repertory of suitable responses to stress developed through a characteristic motivation to achieve across all situations. In contrast, the highly stressed persons who become ill are powerless, nihilistic, and low in motivation for achievement.

Although commitment to all areas of life- work, social institutions, interpersonal relationships, family and self should be characteristic of highly stressed person who does not fall ill, commitment to self is considered to be the most important one.

According to Kobasa (1979), hardy individuals do not engage in irresponsible adventurousness. At the core of the search for novelty and challenge are fundamental life goals that have become, in adulthood, increasingly integrated in a widening diversity of situations.

Like Kobasa, Antonovsky (1988) tried to unravel the mystery of health. Unlike Kobasa he tried to do it by taking up a salutogenic orientation. A pathological orientation seeks to explain why people get sick. A salutogenic orientation (which focuses on the origins of health) poses a radically different question: why are people located or why do they move toward the positive end of the health ease/ disease continuum or why do they move towards this end, whatever their location at any given time? To answer the salutogenic question Antonovsky developed the concept of *Sense of Coherence*. SOC is a general global orientation towards life and it has three core components—comprehensibility, manageability and meaningfulness.

Comprehensibility refers to the extent to which one perceives the stimuli that confront one, as making cognitive sense, as information that is ordered, consistent, structured and clear, rather than as noise – chaotic, disordered, random, accidental, inexplicable.

The person high on comprehensibility expects that stimuli he or she will encounter in the future will be predictable or, at the very least, when they do come as surprises, they will be orderable and explicable. Nothing here is implied about the desirability of the stimuli. Death, war and failure can occur, but such a person can make sense of them.

Manageability is defined as the extent to which one perceives that resources are at one's disposal which are adequate to meet the demands posed by the stimuli that bombard one. The phrase "At one's disposal" may refer to resources under one's own control or to resources controlled by legitimate others – one's spouse, friends, colleagues, God, history, the party leader, a physician – whom one feels one can count on, whom one trusts.

The third component – meaningfulness – refers to the extent to which one feels that life makes sense emotionally, that at least some of the problems and demands posed by living are worth investing energy in, are worthy of commitment and engagement, are challenges that are "welcome" rather than burdens that one would much rather do without. Even when unhappy experiences occur like death of loved one, need to undergo serious operation, or being fired, he or she will willingly take up the challenge, will be determined to seek meaning in it, and will do his or her best to overcome it with dignity.

Antonovsky (1988) suggests that all the three components of the SOC are necessary but are of unequal centrality. The motivational component of meaningfulness seems most crucial. Without it, being high on comprehensibility or manageability is likely to be temporary. For the committed and caring person, the way is open to gaining understanding and resources. Comprehensibility seems to be next in importance, for high manageability is contingent on understanding. But if one does not believe that resources are at one's disposal, meaningfulness will be lessened and coping efforts weakened. Thus, successful coping depends on SOC as a whole.

Antonovsky has considered four spheres of life that should be of subjective importance to the person, in order to have a high SOC. These spheres or "boundaries" are – one's inner feelings, one's immediate inter-personal relations, one's major activity and existential issues (death, inevitable failures, shortcomings, conflict, and isolation). He has also distinguished between the calm confidence of a person with a very high SOC and the rigidity of inauthentic SOC.

Both Kobasa and Antonovsky have given theories of personal resiliency where at least few characteristic features should be there in a person, but Scheier and Carver (1985) have given a one-trait theory. According to them *dispositional optimism i.e.,* a consistent general positive outcome expectancy (or a generalized expectancy for positive outcomes) determines continued efforts in dealing with problems, hence, better coping. There is enough data linking optimism to physical well-being (Orr & Westman, 1990). Optimists are found to display coping patterns that involve continued positive striving and making the best of whatever situation they are confronting. Pessimists in contrast, try to deny stressors' reality, are pre-occupied with their emotional distress and tend to disengage from the goals with which the stress in interfering.

Another concept related to effective coping is *learned resourcefulness*. Rosenbaum (1988) conceives of learned resourcefulness (LR) as a personality repertoire which consists not just of a set of beliefs but also of skills and self-control behaviours which are thought in a typical stress inoculation-training programme. He has defined it as a set of behaviours and skills by which individuals self-regulate internal responses that interfere with the smooth execution of an ongoing behaviour (Rosenbaum, 1983).

Similar to LR, *competence* is another multi-dimensional concept related to personal growth, effectiveness and well-being. Competence has been defined either in terms of individual's intellectual, cognitive capability for learning and imagining, as motivational processes to maintain positive affective state or as behavioural effectiveness in the task of living, or as a social skill for maintaining proper interpersonal relationship. Jahoda (1958) described six criteria applicable to both competence and positive mental health, these were: 1. Attitudes towards the self, the self-concept, 2. Style and degree of growth, development of self-actualization, 3. Integration of personality, 4. Autonomy under social influence, 5. Perception of reality, and 6. Environmental mastery.

Tyler's model of psychosocial competence (1978) conceives of three simultaneously present characteristic attributes in a competent self. First it requires a perception of self as causally important in one's life. Secondly, it requires a moderate degree of optimism and interpersonal trust as a basis for constructive interactions with others. The non-competent person seems pessimistically distrusting and thereby builds a destructive pattern of interaction. Finally, it requires an active planful, invested coping style including high initiative, goal setting, forbearance and a capacity to build from both success and failure.

Definition of Resilience

In the present study, resilience is defined as individuals' perseverance and maximum or optimum utilization of resources (personal and of surrounding) to positively cope with socio-economic hardships.

Perseverance is continuation of efforts in a constructive, goal-directed manner. It operates at three levels: behavioural, emotional and cognitive.

Behavioural: Person continues his/her efforts till the task is completed/accomplished. The person has a fighting spirit and a tendency to finish a task by overcoming problems.

Emotional: The person regulates his/her emotions. He/she does not allow anxiety, fear and hopelessness to overpower him/her.

Cognitive: The person regulates his/her thoughts to remove the internal blocks and to become more active and task oriented. This helps in assessing the reality and also in keeping one's eyes open to change and possibilities to bring about changes. It is antithetical to constricted vision.

The underlying motive to persevere can be sense of responsibility, habit, optimism or commitment.

Utilization of resources has two components :

Internal resources refer to the beliefs, skills, self-confidence and correct utilization of one's time and energy. Here the person draws upon his/her previous experiences to solve present problems.

External resources refer to financial help, information, emotional support and opportunities to which one can get access.

Positive coping refers to the positive or optimistic approach towards oneself and life. The person accepts the present without a sense of resignation; is hopeful towards future. He/she is alert, active and involved in various spheres of life. The person enjoys life and shows an enthusiasm to learn and work.

METHOD

Sample

A sample of 100 low-income working couples (a total of 200 respondents) was drawn from fifteen slums of Allahabad, U.P. Both husband and wife were interviewed with the help of a questionnaire, simultaneously and separately by a male and a female interviewer respectively. This was done to gain their independent and unbiased responses. Since it was difficult to locate the working couples and to get consent from them, help of an NGO and/or Aanganwadi worker was taken to find a key-person in the locality who could facilitate the data-collection by identifying the working couples. However, it was made clear to all the respondents that the survey was done for academic purposes only and that the interviewers were students of psychology and were not from the NGO or any government agency. Approximately 45 minutes were spent on interviewing one individual.

Majority of the respondents were working in the unorganised sector *i.e.,* as household servants, unskilled/skilled labourers, vendors, engaged in petty business and so on. 88% of them were Hindu and 12% Muslims; regarding caste distribution 45% belonged to SC/ST, 40% to OBC and 15% to upper caste community. 80% of the respondents were from nuclear family, 19% from joint and 1% from extended joint family.

The mean age of the husband in the sample was 38.43 years and that of the wives was 31.80 years. The average monthly incomes of husband and wives were Rs. 1457.00 and Rs. 547.10 respectively. Regarding education 76 per cent of the women and 45 per cent of the men did not have any formal education.

Variables and Measures

The demographic variables of age, gender, religion, caste, education, type of family were elicited by single questions. They were also required to report their income, income of their spouse and that of other family members, number of family members (adult and children) and if the children go to school. The description of other variables is as follows.

Resilience

A four-point Likert type scale comprising of 32 items was constructed specifically to study the resilience of low income working women and their husbands.

Based on the literature and open-ended interviews with low income working women four dimensions of resilience *i.e.* Perseverance (PER), External Resourcefulness (ER), Internal Resourcefulness (IR), Positive Orientation (PO) were identified and items on each were constructed. A pool of about 100 items was the beginning point, from which 61 were selected for judges' rating and pilot testing, which further reduced the items to 32.

The alpha value for the overall scale is .86. The four dimensions and their corresponding alpha values (given in the bracket) are: Perseverance (.68), External Resourcefulness (.53), Internal Resourcefulness (.62), Positive Orientation (.69). (Please see Appendix for Item Total Correlation and Inter-dimensional Correlation.)

To counterbalance any possible response style bias twelve items were negatively worded and hence were reverse coded. A high score is indicative of high level of resilience.

Socio-economic Stress Scale

This scale consists of three sub-scales—Economic Stress (ES) Scale (4 items), Family Hassles (FH) Scale (3 items), and Relative Economic Deprivation (RED) Scale (3 items). The Economic Stress Scale comprised of four items adapted from the Perceived Poverty Scale (Pandey & Singh, 1985). The items assessed the lack of money (or economic difficulties) faced by the respondents regarding food, clothing and in the treatment of sick family members. The Family Hassles Scale is measuring the stress emanating from lack of time and work-load related to household chores and responsibilities. The RED Scale items focus on the social discrimination, ill-treatment and feeling of inferiority due to poverty. Reliability of the three sub-scales *i.e.,* ES, FH, RED as measured by Cronbach Alpha is .86, .69, .70 respectively and that of the total S-E stress scale is .83.

A four point rating scale is used in this scale also and a high score is indicative of high level of stress.

Quality of Family Life

This scale was developed for assessing the extent to which a healthy, harmonized interpersonal/psycho-social environment prevails in the respondent's family. The six items of this four point rating scale focus on the trust, mutual help, sharing, conflicts and conflict resolution and alcoholism in the family. A high score is indicative of a better quality of family life. To break the response set, three items were negatively worded and hence reverse coded. Cronbach Alpha for the scale is found to be .75.

Thus the questionnaire consisted of items on the above-mentioned variables on a four point Likert type rating scale. Apart from this each respondent was asked to narrate a stressful experience and the way he/she coped with it (This qualitative data is yet to be analyzed).

Results

The *t*-tests for paired samples were carried out to find out if husbands and wives differed significantly on resilience (and its dimensions), S-E stress (and its various facets) and QOFL. These results are given in Tables 11.1 and 11.2.

Inter-variable correlation matrix for husbands and wives are given in Tables 11.3 and 11.4.

Table 11.1 : *t*-Test between Husband and Wife on Resilience and its Dimensions

Dimensions of Resilience	Husband		Wife		*df*	*t*- Value
	Mean	SD	Mean	SD		
Perseverance	19.93	2.38	16	3.59	99	7.58**
External Resourcefulness	16.01	2.94	15.05	3.53	99	2.38**
Internal Resourcefulness	29.22	3.82	26.18	4.67	99	5.52**
Positive Orientation	33.07	4.91	30.70	5.72	99	3.36**
Overall Resilience	98.23	10.63	88.81	14.59	99	5.99**

** $p<.01$.

Table 11.1 shows that on all the dimensions of resilience and on overall resilience the mean scores of husbands are significantly higher that those of wives. The homogeneity on the scores is also more in case of husbands on resilience and its dimensions as reflected in the respective SD values of husband and wife on them.

Table 11.2 : *t*-Test between Husband and Wife on S-E Stress and QOFL

Variable	Husband		Wife		*df*	*t*-Value
	Mean	SD	Mean	SD		
Economic Stress	9.4	3.17	12.07	3.75	99	6.56**
Family Hassles	6.03	2.06	6.05	2.01	99	2.61**
Rel. Eco. Dep.	6.86	2.65	7.08	2.92	99	.56
Socio-economic Stress	22.29	6.25	26	7.24	99	4.45**
Quality of Family Life	19.4	2.395	17.53	4.13	99	4.33**

** $p<.01$.

Table 11.2 shows that wives have scored higher than their husbands on S-E stress and its various sub-scales. However the difference is significant in the case of Economic Stress, Family Hassles and S-E stress and not in the case of Relative Economic Deprivation. Husbands have scored higher on QOFL scale and their responses are more homogenous than their wives, as reflected in the respective mean and SD values. The SD values of women for ES, RED and S-E stress are higher than those of men indicating more heterogeneity in the case of women.

Table 11.3 : Inter-correlation among Resilience, Socio-economic Stress and QOFL for Husbands

	Resilience	Eco. Stress	Fam. Hassl	Rel. Eco. Dep.	S-E Stress	QOFL
Resilience	1					
Eco. Stress	–.55**	1				
Fam. Hassl.	–.499**	.53**	1			
Rel. Eco. Dep	–.46**	.33**	.47**	1		
S-E Stress	–.64**	.83**	.796**	.75**	1	
QOFL	.37**	–.15	–.19*	–.06	–.16	1

** $p<.01$ *$p<.05$

Table 11.4 : Inter-correlation among Resilience, Socio-economic Stress and QOFL for Wives

	Resilience	Eco. Stress	Fam. Hassl	Rel. Eco. Dep.	S-E Stress	QOFL
Resilience	1					
Eco. Stress	–.45**	1				
Fam. Hassl.	–.32**	.31**	1			
Rel. Eco. Dep.	–.42**	.42**	.25**	1		
S-E Stress	–.55**	.84**	.58**	.72	1	
QOFL	.36**	–.29**	–.18	–.30**	–.34**	1

** $p<.01$.

Tables 11.3 and 11.4 indicate that both in the case of husbands and wives resilience is significantly and negatively correlated to S-E stress and its various sub-scales. Resilience is found to be significantly and positively related to QOFL for both of them.

QOFL is found to be negatively related to S-E stress across gender. However, all the correlations are not significant. In case of husbands, FH and QOFL are significantly related, whereas for wives ES and RED are found to be significantly related, all in the negative direction.

Discussion

The aim of the present study was to investigate the relationship among three variables *i.e.,* resilience, S-E stress and QOFL and also to see the differences between husband and wife on these variables.

The results indicate that husbands are more resilient than their wives. This is true for all the dimensions *i.e.,* they are found to be more persevering, high on external and internal resourcefulness and have more positive orientation towards life. On the other hand, women are found to be experiencing more stress than their husbands do. This difference was significant for ES, FH and S-E stress. Although from the same family, husbands have rated QOFL in more favourable terms.

In India, about 72 million families live under absolute poverty situation. 39 per cent of the total population or 400 million people are living below poverty line. There are 300 million workers in unorganized sector and 40 per cent of them are women (Jhabwala, 1998). These 120 million women working in this sector are in a disadvantageous position on various accounts. They are low paid, have few options, come from the lowest strata of the society, are part of the workforce not by choice but by necessity, have to do a double duty, can not afford domestic help (unlike their better-off sisters), and are uneducated and mostly unskilled. Given these circumstances, it is not surprising that women are found to be more vulnerable than their husbands in the present study.

Women and their children constitute an increasingly large proportion of America's poor, this phenomenon has been called 'the feminization of poverty' (Pearce, 1979). In India also the women and children are the worst victims of poverty. Feminist critiques argue that women suffer poverty on a more widespread basis than men do and that their experience of poverty is quite different as a result of expectations about gender roles.

Traditionally women's place is confined to homes. Even though in the low-income group, they are forced to work, the broken dream to have a husband who could take care of the family was voiced by many women during the interview.

The depiction of women in Hindu scriptures, mythology and folklore has been uneven and ambivalent (Ramu, 1995). Although in Hindu mythology there are images of women who are strong— *Shaktiswaroopa— e.g., Durga* and *Kali*, yet when it is seen in everyday life the image of women as 'weaker sex' is reinforced (many a time to make a plea to rise above weakness). And the reasons for their weakness are elaborated upon. On the other hand, men in the patriarchal society have an edge over women. They are the protectors, the strong ones, and the head of the family. Thus, their 'resilient' image goes well with the traditionally ascribed role. In patriarchal society, women's dependence on men is unquestioned. Yet, when both are working, women's problems seem to increase, although they work to provide solutions (to the financial problems of the family). In the present study, their stress score is found to be consistently higher that that of men on all the dimensions and significantly so in case of ES, FH and S-E stress. Agonized by these stressors, women are further tormented by poor QOFL. Since, they are the ones who spend more time in the family, are traditionally (and therefore morally) responsible for household chores, are entrusted with the duties of taking care of sick and children, do not have palliative coping mechanisms like alcohol (and ironically have to put up with their husbands' drinking problems/habit), it is not surprising that they do not find their family life as happy and harmonized as their husbands do. During the interviews, frequent complaints of alcoholism, non-cooperation and careless attitude of husbands were made. Alcoholism amongst husbands, inflict severe problems on the poverty stricken families, the brunt of which generally women have to face.

Across gender, resilience and S-E stress are found to be significantly and negatively correlated. This indicates that higher level of resilience accompanies or is accompanied by lower level of stress. A resilient individual apparently experiences less stress. Resilience and QOFL are positively related. It is apparent that higher the level of resilience, better will be the QOFL and *vice-versa.*

Regarding the relationship between S-E stress and QOFL, an interesting pattern emerges when husband and wife are compared. For wives, FH is not significantly related to QOFL but ES, RED and S-E stress are found to have a negative and significant relation with QOFL (Table11.4). In the case of husbands the situation is just reversed. In their case, ES, RED and S-E stress are not significantly related to QOFL but FH has a significant and negative relation with QOFL (Table 11.3). It seems that women are more concerned with the economic hardships and with the conditions of poverty (poverty as compared to others) and this has a negative bearing on their rating/perception of QOFL. Even in the absence of a regression analysis this relationship seems to be logical. For men, day to day family hassles, workload etc., are deciding factors for QOFL or it can be interpreted that poor QOFL has bearing on the FH for men. To make any conclusive statement, regression analysis needs to be done. Since in the case of husbands QOFL does not relate to ES, RED and S-E stress, it may be indicative of certain amount of aloofness on the part of husbands towards these stresses or a genuinely positive orientation where QOFL remains high and independent of stress level. This finding, however, has to be interpreted with some caution. During interviews husbands also had expressed concerns and anxieties related to family matters, in particular, those related to children; some of the women as well as men cried during the interviews, their pain for some specific stressors especially for bereaved children was almost alike immediately after the incidence. However for women it remains a kind of an unhealed wound even after a long passage of time. Therefore, to corroborate the specific patterns of results for men and women, further analysis is needed and it also needs to be supplemented with the qualitative data and interviewers' observations to arrive at any conclusive picture.

To summarize, the picture that emerges from the present study reflects a scenario where men and women — both from the same family have different psychological realities (or perceptions). Both are husband and wife and hence they bring up the same family, yet the wife experiences the stresses more, although she is also earning to make both the ends meet. In their attempt to manage their two roles and double duty, their perception of the QOFL is less favourable than that of their husbands. Contrary to expectations, women's resilience is found to be lower than that of their husbands. This needs to be understood however, in the total context of a woman's psychosocial reality. The myriad demands on her expectations, responsibilities, duties, conditions and conditionings, biological and social roles, and inherent sensitivity, all combine together to give woman a ground which is a source of her strength as well as that of her vulnerability.

Appendix

Table 1 : Item Total Correlation for Resilience Scale ($N = 200$)

Item No.	Item Total Correlation	Alpha, if item deleted
1	.544**	.85
2	.386**	.85
3	.148*	.86
4	.549**	.85
5	.416**	.86
6	.226**	.86
7	.364**	.86
8	.257**	.86
9	.462**	.85
10	.475**	.85
11	.343**	.86
12	.394**	.85
13	.472**	.85
14	.404**	.85
15	.211**	.86
16	.511**	.85
17	.188**	.86
18	.448**	.85
19	.444**	.85
20	.306**	.86
21	.209**	.86
22	.448**	.85
23	.432**	.85
24	.260**	.86
25	.383**	.86
26	.197**	.86
27	.523**	.85
28	.579**	.85
29	.394**	.85
30	.405**	.85
31	.443**	.85
32	.379**	.86

** $p<.01$ * $p<.05$ Cronbach Alpha = .859 Standardized Item Alpha = .8653.

Table 2 : Correlation among Dimensions of Resilience

Dimension	Perseverance	Ext. Resource	Int. Resource	Positive Or.	Resilience
Perseverance	1				
Ext. Resource	.422**	1			
Int. Resource	.562**	.471**	1		
Positive Or.	.538**	.584**	.617**	1	
Resilience	.756**	.739**	.835**	.883**	1

** $p<.01$.

REFERENCES

Antonovsky, A. (1988). *Unravelling the mystery of health: How people manage stress and stay well.* San Francisco: Jossey Bass.

Jahoda, M. (1958). *Current concept of positive mental health.* (Joint Commission of Mental Illness and Health Monograph Series No. 1). New York: Basic Books.

Jhabwala, R. (1998). Minimum wages based on workers needs. *Economic and Political Weekly,* ***Vol. XXXIII***, No. 10.

Kobasa, S.C. (1979). Stressful life events, personality, and health: An inquiry into hardiness. *Journal of Personality and Social Psychology, 37,* 1-11.

Kobasa, S.C. & Maddi, S.R. (1977). Existential personality theory. In R. Corsini (Ed.), *Current personality theories* (pp. 243-276). Itasca, Il: T.F.Peacock.

O'Leary, V.E. (1998). Strength in the face of adversity: Individual and social thriving. *Journal of Social Issues, 54*, 2, 425-446.

Orr, W. & Westman, M. (1990). Does hardiness moderate stress, and how? A review. In M. Rosenbaum (Ed.) *Learned resourcefulness* (pp. 64-94). New York: Springer.

Pandey, J. & Singh, A.K. (1985). Social psychological responses to perceived and objective indicators of poverty in India. In R.I.Langunes & Y.H. Poortinga (Eds.) *From a different perspective:Studies of behaviour across cultures.* Lisse: Swets and Zeitlinger.

Pearce, D. (1979). Women, work and welfare : The feminization of poverty. In K.W. Feinstein (Ed.) *Working women and families.* Beverly Hills: Sage.

Ramu, G. N. (1995). Paid work, married women and family in India. In J. Frankle (Ed.), *Families of employed mothers.* Hamden, CT: Garland Publishing, Inc.

Rosenbaum, M. (1983). Learned resoucefulness as a behavioural repertoire for the self-regulation of internal events: Issues and speculations. In M. Rosenbaum, C. M. Franks & Y. Jaffe (Eds.). *Perspectives on behavior therapy in the eighties* (pp. 54-73). New York: Springer.

Rosenbaum, M. (1988) Learned resourcefulness, stress and self-regulation. In S. Fisher and J. Reason (Eds.), *Handbook of life stress, cognition, and health.* Chichester, UK: Wiley & Sons.

Scheier, M.F. & Carver, C. S. (1985). Optimism, coping and health: Assessment and implications of generalized outcome expectancies. *Health Psychology, 4,*219-247.

Tyler, F. B. (1978). Individual psychological competence: A personality configuration. *Education and Psychological Measurement, 38,* 309-323.

12

Exploring the "Culture of Silence" Through the Lens of Gender and Mental Health

SADHANA NATU*

Introduction

"Language is power and the silent majority if released into languages would not be content with a perpetuation of the conditions that have betrayed them. But this notion hangs on a special conception of what it means to be released into language not simply learning the jargon of an elite, fitting unexpectedly into the status quo, but learning that language can be used as a means of changing reality"(p.21, Rich, 1979).

Within language and linguistic discourse speech and its various patterns have been examined. But speech and silence are not merely linguistic tools. They also connote assertion, stifling of rights, freedom, oppression and so much more. The 'Culture of Silence' is all-pervasive in its poignancy among all the oppressed. There are various taboos associated with women, children, dalits, and tribals speaking up. It speaks of the caste, class and gender hierarchies that are inherent in our society and which control articulation. Hence it is also essential to look at silence and speech and make linkages

*I wish to thank my friends Sharmila Rege and Bhargavi Davar for our initial discussions on this paper and their valuable suggestions and comments.

with the psychosocial realm. Silence can be an indicator of oppression and negotiation with patriarchy when studied in its psychosocial contexts. The present paper makes a modest attempt to initiate such an inquiry.

The aim of this paper is to explore the realm of silence and its various shades and also the dichotomies of silence and speech in the context of gender, culture, and mental health. The paper is divided into four parts. Part I of the paper tries to illustrate how cultural practices and patterns of socialization engender both 'silence' and 'speech'. Part II tries to analyze how the 'culture of silence' is reinforced by pedagogical and classroom practices. The issue of sexuality is a definitive illustration of the culture of silence due to the taboos associated with it. The linkages between culture, sexuality and mental health are explored in Part III. This is done with the help of snippets from newspapers about the so-called 'sex scandals' that took place in Maharashtra in recent years. In Part IV the need for seeking alternatives within the paradigm of feminist therapies is underlined. The point that is emphasized here is that feminist therapies too give a lot of importance to articulation, whereas a lot of women need other forms of expression to be made available to them.

Cultural Patterns and Practices of Socialization

At the onset of puberty a clear-cut demarcation between the clothes, play, toys, mobility household tasks and modes of speech of boys and girls is seen. This is expressed, in the construction of 'legitimate' and 'proper' mode of speech, demeanour, behaviour for young girls. Girls are encouraged to speak, softly and to avoid abrasive – 'male' language. Boys learn to use all kinds of abuses; however, even if the milder abuses used by women are used by young girls, they are frowned upon. Girls are advised to exercise self-restraint, and talking and laughing loudly, or being argumentative is disapproved (Dube, 1988).

In one region of India, a 'loud-mouthed' girl is referred to as a malevolent goddess who brings pests and destruction. In another part of India being 'soft spoken and demure' qualifies a girl for being like Lakshmi (the goddess of wealth) while a loud and noisy girl is rebuked (Dube, 1988).

These taboos are not merely confined to speech but also extended to gestures and actions like whistling, clinking of bangles, and smiling which signify amorous inclinations. Shyness and modesty are considered natural and approved feminine qualities. Girls are often rebuked for jumping, running, rushing off to a place and hopping. These movements are considered a part of masculine behaviour, unbecoming to a female.

Cultural practices also reinforce gender stereotypes about men fitting the 'instrumental stereotype' (aggressive, independent) and women working along the 'expressive stereotype' (passive, subservient) (Bhogle, 1999).

A few Marathi phrases and proverbs are examined to illustrate how subtly silence and speech are engendered.

(1) *Lahan Tondee Motha Ghas Ghene* (which also has a synonymous Hindi phrase – *Chota Mooh Aur Badi Baat*). It means that those who are 'young' (in age, in the hierarchy of the household) should not speak (out of turn!). It is children and women who often fit this category, indicating a clear demarcation of boundaries for men and women *vis-a-vis* speech.

(2) *Uchalli Jeebh Lawlee Tallyala.* This suggests that when a person speaks bravely or assertively, it has been done unthinkingly, without logic and objectivity. If young girls or women 'dare' to participate in the public sphere they are often admonished with this phrase.

(3) *Tujhya Jeebhela Kahi Haad Ahe Ka ?* or Don't you know where to stop? Don't you know the limits of speech? This admonition is used with both men and women to make them cautious about what they are saying. This amounts to an admonition that one should use restraint while speaking.

(4) *Bolel To Kareel Kay, Garjel To Padel Kay.* This

proverb dissociates action from speech. It means that those who speak seldom act and a cloud that creates thunder does not burst, suggesting that if a person indulges in 'speaking' there is scarcely any time for 'doing' things.

(5) *Adhi Kele Mag Sangeetale* or You do things first then talk about them later. Here too, the stress is on 'doing' rather than expression.

A sample of two phrases which are indirectly about how speech/ assertion is scorned or looked at negatively is given below.

(1) *Kana Magoon Ali Ani Tikhat Jhali* or You are a new addition to the family [young daughter, daughter in-law, wife] and you have already started expressing or airing your opinions. There is a veiled threat here indicating that this kind of behaviour will not be tolerated, and that the person needs to be put firmly in her place.

(2) *Nakane Kande Solne.* This saying implies that somebody who sets high standards and expresses them is arrogant. What is left unsaid is that pride goes before a fall.

These stereotypes about 'who should speak' and 'how to speak' and 'whether to speak at all' are pan-cultural. This is indicated by the age-old English adage, 'Speech is silver but silence is golden'. It suggests that speech has some value attached to it but silence is greater in value!

Pedagogical and Classroom Practices

Classrooms in schools and colleges reinforce the stereotypical gender patterns of speech through student – teacher communication and through the syllabi and textbooks. Rich (1979) observes, "Language is a weapon – and what goes with language: reflection, criticism, renaming, and creation. The fact that our language itself is tainted by quality of our society, means that in teaching we need to be acutely conscious of the kind of tool we want our students to have available to understand how it has been used against them and to do all we can to ensure that language will not some day be used by them to keep the others silent and powerless" (pp. 24-25).

In schools and colleges, female passivity is rewarded and the female mind is not taken seriously. Girls and boys are indoctrinated in stereotypical gender roles. "In teaching women, we have two choices: to lend our weight to the forces that indoctrinate women to passivity, self-depreciation, and a sense of powerlessness. Or to consider what we have to work against as well as within ourselves, in our students, in the content of the curriculum, structure of the institution and in Society at large. This means believing that there is a unique quality of validation, affirmation, challenge, support that one woman can offer another, believing in the value and significance of women's experience, traditions, perceptions (p. 28, Rich, 1979).

Even in co-educational institutions young men and women do not receive an equal education. The content of the education itself validates men and invalidates women. The silences, unasked questions, blanks, women's facial expressions in the classrooms need to be studied. We have to "Listen to the small, soft voices often trying courageously to speak up, voices of women taught early that tones of confidence challenge, anger or assertiveness are strident and unfeminine" (p. 22, Rich, 1979).

In contrast, men allow themselves the physical and verbal space and assume that people will listen to them. Women are groping for language in which to express what is on their mind, sensing that terms of academic discourse are not their language, trying to cut down their thoughts to the dimensions of discourse not intended for them (for it is not fitting that women speak in public, deprecating their own work by a pre-judgment. We do not deserve to take up time and space) (Rich, 1979).

We have to consider the context within which women students think, write, read, study, project their own futures. We can refuse to accept passive, obedient learning and insist upon critical thinking. Young women need to have their intellectual lives, their work legitimized against the claims of family, relationships and service.

We have to listen in all disciplines: art, literature, social sciences to all the descriptions of silence: silence, absence, the nameless, the unspoken. The encoded – for there we will find the true knowledge of women. In breaking those silences, naming our selves, uncovering the hidden, making us present and taking charge of our lives.

Appropriate teaching styles have to be applied to recover the female experience and they can be applied to the education of all people. Although women have been particularly silent and silenced, official truths and traditional teaching methods have distorted the truths and experiences of minority and working class men and women (Maher, 1985).

Academic disciplines ignore and distort the experience of women as a group by structuring their subject matter and concepts around male – derived norms. The dominant pedagogical style of most classrooms discriminates against women's experiences and participation in a variety of ways, all of which reinforce female passivity. Teachers—male and sometimes female—tend to call on women students less in discussions to ask them less probing questions and to interrupt them more often. They make more frequent eye contact with men, are more attentive to male questions or comments (Thorne, 1975, cited in Hale & Sandler, 1982).

Classroom discussions and lectures reward "assertive speech", competitive interchanges, and impersonal and abstract styles. These modes of speech though not inherently masculine, seem more natural to men culturally. Women tend to be more polite, tentative, hesitant in their comments and thus are taken less seriously by teachers. Women who try to be more assertive face a double bind, they are perceived as 'hostile females' rather than as 'forceful men'. As a result of this treatment and the subject matter, women college students as a group are more silent than men. Like 'Freire's oppressed' they do not speak up, their experiences, interpretations, questions are not heard as often (Maher, 1985).

Teaching practices, which stress cooperative rather than competitive participation may encourage more women students (and more students) to question, examine and express. Interactive pedagogy, subject matter presentation, roles of teacher and student, structure of classes and courses also need to be analyzed.

Women often feel alienated in academic settings and experience 'formal' education as peripheral or irrelevant to their central interests and development. Girls and women have more difficulty than boys and men in asserting their authority, expressing themselves in public so that others will listen, in gaining respect of others for their minds and their ideas. Women grow up dealing with historically and culturally engrained definitions of femininity and womanhood with a common theme that like children, women should be seen not heard (Goldberger *et al,* 1986).

'Voice' and 'Silence' are metaphors for "Speaking up", "speaking out", "being silenced", "not being heard", "really listening", "really talking", "words as weapons", "feeling deaf and dumb", "having no words", "saying what you mean", "listening to be heard", having to do with sense of mind, self-worth, feelings of isolation from or connection to others. These findings are from interviews with women students (Goldberger *et al,* 1986).

Karlekar (1988) found in her study that at Class VI, VII girls were as assertive and definite in their points of view as their male peers were. At the higher levels they became quiet and reserved non-participants. Out side class, they wandered around in groups, while boys could be heard shouting lustily on the playing fields.

Sexuality and Culture of Silence

'In Kothewadi (Ahmadnagar district, Maharashtra) three rape victims came forward four days after the incident to register the complaint. ' In the Jalgaon sex scandal (where there were several incidents of molestation of young girls) a girl was threatened not to reveal anything. Her family also kept silent fearing that her marriage prospects would be hampered'.

'Delay in registering cases in the Jalgaon sex scandal. Only after repeated appeals from the police and women's groups cases were registered'. 'In the in- camera trial in the Jalgaon sex scandal, only two-three women came forward to present a strong testimony'.

'Jalgaon awaits a woman martyr (!) even as racketeers wriggle out of the case, due to political connections'.' Women's organizations urged the girls and women to shed their helplessness. They expressed that those who had given evidence in the sex scandal case had shown great courage and needed protection and government help'.

'In Malegaon one victim who had complained was ostracized by the parents for tarnishing the image of the community by reporting the matter to the police. A second victim had to run from pillar to post to three police stations. The police took two days to register her complaint.'

'In Malegaon one complainant and her supportive husband were persecuted. On one hand the victim earned respect for her courage and on the other—insults and abuses from prejudiced people'.

These snippets from newspapers underscore the fact that social stigma silences the victims of sexual atrocities. In the Indian culture sexuality is a taboo topic, rarely discussed in the public realm hence, the question of speaking about sexual atrocities is beset with problems. There is nothing that equips a girl or a woman to stand up and speak about such an atrocity.

Those who dare to speak up are socially ostracized and branded for life as "bad women/ sluts/ loose women" and driven to suicide. The issue does not remain an issue of violation of the body, mind and heart; instead it becomes an issue of 'morality'.

This creates an all-pervasive fear of disclosure and most women end up as victims 'suffering in silence'. These victims suffer doubly because of the pervasive victim blaming of women. Fearing exposure some women are also driven to suicide. This is really an indictment of society that fails to create an atmosphere of security for women in the first place. Then in extreme situations of sexual atrocities, women face the burden of confronting both sexuality (a taboo subject) and sexual atrocity (which destroys their self-esteem totally).

In such situations women are caught in a double bind. Conditioning forces the women to repress everything which is traumatic since speaking out would invite social wrath. How realistic is it then to expect such victims to speak up without creating enabling structures for them to do so in the first place?

Feminist Therapies and Articulation

Consciousness raising (CR) is a group process, in which people with some form of commonality share and explore their experiences to draw connections between the personal and the political. As practiced within the women's movement consciousness raising has helped women recognize that concerns about relationships, sexuality, feelings of inadequacy are not so much individual problems as they are manifestations of society's systemic oppression. CR has led to alternatives to mainstream psychotherapy like feminist therapy; self help groups and mutual support groups. These were identified as processes by which people promote their own healing (Kalinowski & Penney, cited in Levin, Blanch & Jennings, 1998).

Even though feminist therapies have tried to move away from the directive invasive mainstream therapies, speech is still given a lot of importance. Until now I have argued in this paper that cultural practices, patterns of socialization and classroom practices all engender silence. Issues like sexuality and sexual atrocities underscore the culture of silence. Against this backdrop, even in the therapeutic context 'speaking out' becomes very difficult.

In the Indian scenario, especially for rural women therapy remains an alien phenomenon. Hence, the entire exercise of seeking help and verbalizing in front of a therapist is something that they cannot relate to culturally. Very often other indigenous healing traditions hence become more viable choices for them.

Survivors of child sexual abuse, domestic violence and sexual harassment often find it difficult to verbalize about their experience in the therapeutic situation. In cases of women diagnosed with mental illness, who also have a history of physical or sexual abuse or both, the problem of articulation as a part of therapy becomes acute. Very often the survivors of trauma feel retraumatized due to lack of restraint. In their case often 'speaking out' is not a good choice (Carmen & Rieker, cited in Levin, Blanch & Jennings, 1998).

Survivors of trauma have very often been dominated in early life by the tyrannical demands and threats of the abuser. Their development of personal choice (which includes speech) is superseded by the need to placate the abuser, in the attempt to avoid violence, violation and sometimes death.

Even when there are women therapists and women clients in feminist therapy; there are barriers like caste, class, and race, disabilities and alternative sexuality that affect their therapeutic relationship.

To some extent alternative forms like dance, play, art, music therapy and indirect techniques like role-play and psychodrama are being tried out. However, they need to gain legitimacy and centrality and cannot be mere adjuncts to verbalization.

Conclusion

This paper is an exploratory attempt to highlight the nuances of silence and speech in the context of control and oppression of women. As Rich (1979) observed succinctly, "Where language and naming are power; silence is violence, is oppression (p. 27). Hence, the cultural suppression and suffocation of women needs to be addressed. On the other hand, in day-to-day life as well as in therapeutic situations, non-verbal patterns and practices also need to gain acceptance and popularity.

REFERENCES

Bhogle, S. (1999). Gender roles: The construct in the Indian context. In T.S. Saraswathi (Ed.), *Culture, socialization and human development: Theory, research and applications in India.* (pp. 278-300). New Delhi: Sage.

Dube, L. (1988). Socialisation of Hindu girls in patrilineal India. In K. Chanana (Ed.) *Socialisation, education and women: Explorations in gender identity.* New Delhi : Orient Longman.

Goldberger, N. R., (1986) (Ed.). *Women's ways of knowing: the development of self, voice and mind.* New York: Basic Books.

Hale, R. & Sandler, B. (1982). *The classroom climate: A chilly one for women?*

Project on the status and education of women. Washington D.C.: American Association of Colleges.

Karlekar, M. (1988). Women's nature and access to education. In K. Chanana (Ed.). *Socialisation, education and women: Explorations in gender identity.* New Delhi, Orient Longman.

Levin, B. L., Blanch, A. K., Jennings, A. (1998) (Eds.). *Women's mental health services: A public health perspective.* New Delhi: Sage.

Maher, F. (1985). Classroom pedagogy and the new scholarship on women. In M. Culley & C. Portuges (Eds.), *Gendered subjects: the dynamics of feminist teaching.* London: Routledge & Kegan Paul.

Rich, A. (1979). *On lies, secrets and silence: Selected prose 1966-1978.* New York: W. W. Norton.

13

Kerala Model of Development:

Some Socio-Psychological Fall-outs and Implications for Mental Health

NALINI BIKKINA

Introduction

The development experience of the southern Indian state of Kerala, widely referred to as the Kerala Model is the subject of this essay. In particular, the paper aims to explore the deep impact of the complex social, economic, cultural and political factors on the mental health of the people of this state.

The 29 million Keralites in this densely populated state (which has about 750 persons per square kilometer as per the 1991 census and a gross domestic product per capita lower than the Indian average), have won an international reputation for having accomplished comparatively high levels of health, education and social welfare, and for engendering a political culture where the people are conscious of their rights. The public distribution of food through fair price shops has been unusually extensive and efficient. The same goes for the public and private systems in health and education. By far the most consistent land reform in India was carried out here. Most workers are organized, and important labour laws including social security provisions have been implemented. Various social and religious reforms have broken up much of the rigid caste system, paved the way for coexistence between the many communities, and strengthened the position of women

(Tornquist & Tharakan, 1996). The cleanest and greenest state with the highest literacy rate in the country, Kerala can also boast of the most civic-minded population.

The United Nations and most of its affiliates—the UNESCO, UNICEF, UNDP as well as the World Bank and ILO—have acclaimed the achievements of Kerala and some even held it out as a model for the less developed world to emulate (Mathew, 1999). Kerala's development experience has been widely referred to as the 'Kerala Model', which is but a post-facto generalization of an experience historically evolved but promoted by public action, and sustained by social demands. The model is a specific set of social, political, cultural and economic experiences in a specific trajectory of historical development. Still dynamic and live, the model continues to be a paradigm meaningful for democracy and people's well being (Oommen, 1999). Kerala's emphasis on public services and egalitarian ideals is thus in contradiction with the models based on private accumulation and resultant inequalities. Out of the complex conjuncture of events and processes, Kerala's activists and intellectuals have fashioned the elements of a Kerala Model (Franke & Chasin, 1999).

Features of the Kerala Model

According to Franke & Chasin, the Kerala Model can be summed as having :

- A set of high material quality of life indicators coinciding with low per capita incomes, both distributed across nearly the entire population of Kerala.
- A set of wealth and resource redistribution programmes that have largely brought about the high material quality of life indicators.
- High levels of political participation and activism among ordinary people along with substantial numbers of dedicated leaders at all levels. Kerala's mass activism and committed cadre were able to function within a largely democratic

structure, which their activism has served to reinforce (Franke & Chasin, 1999).

The essence of the Kerala model is social justice. Kerala has brought most of its people up to the levels of the first world, in case of literacy (in terms of social awareness too rather than mere ability to read and write), life expectancy, and infant mortality. Kerala's achievements have largely transcended caste, class, rural/urban and gender limitations (Franke & Chasin, 1999). This achievement is all the more remarkable because it was made in the context of slow economic growth. Kerala model is influenced apart from the political economy, by its unique ecology, maritime culture, and role in Indian Ocean maritime history (Cassinder, 1995).

Kerala's development experience questions a widely held paradigm: first agriculture and industry have to develop and then, in due course, improvement in the standard of living of the masses would take place. Kerala is challenging this historical sequencing of economic growth and mass welfare endorsed by the experiences of the developed countries. One of the relatively backward states in India with per capita domestic production consistently below the national average, Kerala has been able to provide for the basic needs of most of its citizens. A composite index of quality of life taking into account various factors now places Kerala far above the general situation prevailing not only in India but also in most parts of the developing world.

With all this development to its credit, the Kerala Model however, holds out a peculiar paradox. While the state has recorded on the one hand, impressive levels of socio-economic development, as assessed by indicators such as literacy, including women's literacy, health care and so on, Kerala has also experienced several negative mental health and social fall-outs. For instance, the state has been reporting one of the highest suicide rates in the country, has registered an increase in crimes under the Narcotic Drugs and Psychotropic Substances Act and has reported one of the highest prevalence rates of schizophrenia among the Indian states.

Furthermore, in the latter half of the 1970s, as the achievements of Kerala in quality of life began to receive international recognition, the model itself was slipping into a major crisis. It was all-pervasive, but its important constituents were the severe stagnation in the spheres of material production, soaring unemployment, acute fiscal crisis and erosion of sustainability of the social welfare expenditure. Stagnation of the agricultural and industrial sectors has aggravated the unemployment situation in Kerala. Despite the high unemployment level, the state also experiences acute labour scarcity in many traditional occupations as job expectations tend to rise with education and the educated tend to withdraw from low status jobs (Isaac & Tharakan, 1995).

Social Fall-outs

The most important change that occurred in Kerala was the proliferation of nuclear families, of which the state today has the highest percentage in the country. The old are being increasingly neglected (Krishnakumar, 2000). For some years now, doubts have been expressed about the quality of education in the State's schools. (Krishnakumar, 1999). Recent reports (Isaac & Tharakan, 1995) suggest that there was a resurgence of casteism and communalism at least partly caused by the current developmental and social crisis (Tharamangalam, 1999). Despite the higher level of education and participation in grass roots level movements, women are conspicuously absent in the higher levels of decision-making (Isaac & Tharakan, 1995). The abuse of medical technology in perpetuating a social bias for sons over daughters is an emerging concern in the state (Verma, 2000). Thc actual state of women at home and in the workplace remains unchanged or has even become worse if one goes by the increasing number of gang-rapes and export of women for flesh trade (Satchidanandan, 1999).

Psychological Fall-outs

Krishna Prasad Sreedhar (cited in Krishnakumar, 2000) said that "Kerala is predominantly an 'intellectual state' and not an 'emotional state' as is evident in the sober response of the people to many events." But the flip side is that this society does not provide a release mechanism for the tensions that could build up within an individual as a result of the rapidly changing social climate around him or her. In the earlier days, Kerala society allowed certain popular release mechanisms, such as faith healing, hysterical dances in temples or exorcism, which however negative or undesirable they may have been, provided emotional outlets. With the rise in the level of education and the general advancement of society, such means naturally became the butt of social ridicule. But, a positive alternative did not evolve. A key question is whether the people of Kerala are worse off because they had better education and health (Krishnakumar, 2000).

From around mid-1970s, it was a period of rapid changes in Kerala society, probably the cumulative outcome of the revolutionary land reform measures initiated in the late 1950s, and later the boom in employment and remittances from the countries of the Gulf. Kerala has become materialistic. Increasingly, alien values replaced traditional ones and nuclear families took the place of a once predominant joint family system. It is today a very individualistic society, caught in a state of imperfect modernisation. Imperfect education and easy Gulf money have led to the creation of a society, which has great expectations but not enough resources and other means to bring them to reality. Rapid changes have taken place in the material culture, but there has been no change at all in the State's non-material culture. Kerala society is caught in a cultural lag (Krishnakumar, 2000).

The neo-rich culture of opulence without content, the spread of alcoholism that cuts across classes, the rapid increase in sexual, communal and political violence, the high rates of morbidity and suicide also seem to be symptoms and products of a larger social malaise generated by unemployment, loss of identity, economic uncertainty and social discontent prompted especially by the new disparities created by foreign remittances (Satchidanandan, 1999).

The expressions of worry are often countered by arguments that the seemingly higher figures are but a reflection of a high level of reporting, a better health care system and awareness among the people and that there is no objective evidence of morbidity rates being higher in Kerala than in other parts of the country. However, the constraints facing the health care system in the government segment and the increasing commercialization in the health sectors are worrisome. It is in this context that the state now faces the phenomenon of rising suicide rates and trends that point towards problems in the state of the mental health of the population (Krishnakumar, 2000).

High Suicide Rate

For some time now, Kerala has been reporting one of the highest suicide rates in the country – and by a substantial margin of three times the national average and 50 percent more than the second highest state. Kerala has been showing an alarming trend of even members of entire families opting or being forced to end their lives together. According to the National Crime Records Bureau's report on Accidental Deaths and Suicides in India, 1997, the rate of suicides in Kerala per lakh of population was 28.5 (the highest among states excluding Union territories), while the all India figure was only 10 (Krishnakumar, 2000).

The analysis of suicide by cause, means, and gender also does not reveal anything striking about Kerala *vis-à-vis* other states. The age-wise distribution, however, shows that the proportions of suicides in the categories 'Below 18 years' (5.6 per cent) and '18-30 years' (30.8 per cent) are well below the national average (11.2 per cent and 43.7 per cent respectively). Meanwhile, the proportion of Kerala suicides among people '30-50 years' (39.2 per cent) and '50 years and above' (24.4 per cent) are greater than the national average (32.2 per cent and 12.8 per cent respectively), according to the National Crime Records Bureau statistics. It is tempting to say that since Kerala has a dramatically higher life expectancy and because states with the lowest suicide rate (Jammu Kashmir— 0.5 per lakh, and Bihar—1.5 per lakh) suffer some of the greatest adversity in the country including low life expectancy and high risk of death by violence, that suicide is more likely if one has higher expectations of living longer. This analysis is too crude and general, though it does suggest an avenue for further research (Halliburton, 1998).

Alcohol is a villain in many homes. Women are now more independent in Kerala society and this has brought consequent problems, along with the positive aspects. The old are being neglected and so are their values. A vulgar culture, glorifying the ills of society, pervades the living rooms through the media. This, together with the fragmentation of families has formed a potent combination, disturbing peace within families. Of the total number of suicides in the state, 15 to 20 per cent are group or family suicides (Krishnakumar, 2000). It was also found that a much greater number of suicide attemptees came from nuclear families (79 per cent) rather than joint families (21 per cent) (Halliburton, 1998).

Deepa Annamachaly (cited in Halliburton, 1998) has conducted a study of police records on suicide in the city of Kochi, and found that suicide was more common among forward caste Hindus, when compared to Christians and Muslims and backward caste Hindus, and that suicide was more frequent among those who had high school education than it was among illiterates. This also suggests that those who have higher expectations due to socio-ethnic background and education are more likely to commit suicide.

Ideologies of secularism, modernization and development may be influencing the high rate of suicide. Many, such as the classical sociologist Max Weber, (as cited in Halliburton, 1998) have asserted that the modernist rationalist world view demystifies life, causes it to lose some of its magic, and replaces it with a cold, pragmatic view of the world. More recently, psychologist Louis Sass (as cited in Halliburton, 1998) claims that modernism promotes hyper reflexivity, which leads to psychological disturbance because of excessive internal reflection. It is also suggested that the development of a secular ideology in Kerala—a pragmatically-oriented philosophy that has not expressed a philosophy of the self and its suffering—has aided to increase the standard of living of Keralites, yet somehow allowed more cases of suicide to develop (Halliburton, 1998).

There has also been condemnation of the role of some sections of the media in the increasing rate of suicides. A high level of literacy also meant a large readership for newspapers and magazines. The frustrations of the educated unemployed have probably resulted in a huge audience also for the so-called pulp fiction magazines and television serials. Also, there are indicators that the vivid depictions in the media of the frequent instances of suicides and the methods used by the victims have encouraged a large number of persons to end their lives in a similar manner (Krishnakumar, 2000).

Though further studies are required on this, unknown to society at large, sexual abuse of children is also a reason for psychotic and depressive illnesses in adolescents and youth in Kerala who attempted to kill themselves or had suicidal tendencies, according to Dr. Elizabeth Vadakekara, psychiatrist at the Government General Hospital, Thiruvananthapuram (as cited in Krishnakumar, 2000). The SMHA also identified child abuse as an area of concern. Often parents and teachers are unaware of this problem and fail to recognize telltale signs of sexual abuse in children (Krishnakumar, 2000).

Alcoholism

The alcohol consumption rate in the state has increased manifold and is today one of the highest in the country, according to the Alcohol and Drug Information Centre, India. Kerala stands first in the per capita consumption of alcohol (8.3 litres against the national average of 5.7). Fifteen per cent of the population consumes alcohol. Studies have shown alarming trends in the liquor consumption patterns in the state, such as a substantial increase in the number of "new drinkers", the emergence of women including young ones as a new group of "social-drinkers", and an increase in alcohol related crimes, road accidents, diseases including psychological illnesses and deaths. Most drinkers are in the 21 to 40 age group, the same group where the maximum number of suicides also take place. Depression, together with alcohol or drug use can be lethal (Krishnakumar, 2000).

Drug Abuse

Kerala has also shown an increase in crimes registered under the Narcotic Drugs and Psychotropic Substances Act. The SMHA identified drug addicts as another group at risk for suicidal behaviour. In one of the successful attempts by the SMHA, a rehabilitation centre for drug addicts at Vallakkadavu in Thiruvananthapuram is being run with the participation of the local community. Surprisingly, all the 27 young men who attended the first phase of the de-addiction programme told counsellors that they had attempted to commit suicide at least once, at one stage or the other of drug use (Krishnakumar, 2000).

The Gulf Wife Syndrome

Several thousands of Keralite families are divided in space, half of their members living in Kerala and the other half making money outside. Thousands of women in Kerala spend years separated from their husbands working in Central Asia. There was the plight of the "Gulf Wives" – those women whose husbands are or have been, migrants in Central Asia (Santosh & Malecha, 2000).

Psychologist Syed Mohammed (cited in Santosh & Malecha, 2000) at the psychiatric clinic at Chavakkad, a well-known Gulf Malayalee pocket in Kerala, opines that the symptoms exhibited by young wives are similar to those of women with sailor husbands. Besides loneliness, it calls for sexual adjustment. The common complaints are mild depression, aches, pains and hypochondriac tendencies. According to the Kerala Migration Study, conducted recently by the Centre for Development Studies, these women were hardly equipped to cope with the situation (Santosh & Malecha, 2000).

Stress, Anxiety and Depression

The divorce rate is going up. So are the instances of examination-related mental illnesses. Also, Kerala being a literate society, the pressure on the children to 'excel' in school comes from the family and society and the resulting problems mainly psychological, with tendencies towards suicide, fall on the students and the family members, especially mothers (Saradamoni, 1999). Depression is being trivialized as a psychological problem, and only 5 per cent of the patients in Kerala get treatment (Krishnakumar, 2000).

Schizophrenia

There is a two per thousand prevalence of Schizophrenia in Kerala. The distribution of chronic schizophrenia is equal among both sexes and in the urban and rural areas; the prevalence of the disease is high among divorcees (and more in men divorcees than women divorcees), and more among the less-educated and unemployed; about 90 per cent of the patients seek help under one system of medicine or the other (51.1 per cent in the private sector); 0.6 per cent each still seek faith healing and *manthravadam* or such black magic remedies; and 9.7 per cent do not seek any help at all (Krishnakumar, 2000).

Crime and Violence

The state has the second highest crime rate in India. It is not something, which can be seen as if "it was there always but is being reported more now". Domestic violence is also on the increase in the state (Saradamoni, 1999).

The mental health scenario described above indicates therefore that despite apparent well-being, Kerala society and people are disturbed by various factors. A large section of the people are silent, but that does not mean that they do not wish to change for the better, to feel less competitive, more relaxed and safer (Saradamoni, 1999).

The above observations are not intended as a critique of Kerala's achievement in health, education and social welfare. It is only to bring to notice that every progressive step Kerala has taken has thrown up problems before the state and to stress the need for a serious attempt to understand them in their totality. The paradoxical impact of social programmes and socio-economic development should be taken in the context of the fact that Kerala has the lowest overall death rate in India. This points to considerations that should be taken into account, and set backs that may be encountered, on the road to creating a society that helps provide basic material well-being and opportunities for self-realization to the average citizen.

Towards Mental Health: Kerala's Potential

The vibrant civil society in Kerala has facilitated the emergence and survival of a large number of cultural movements and groups, which do not have direct political affiliation. These groups and the percolation of general awareness to the grass-roots, thanks to the model of development itself, can be tapped to mobilise a people's movement towards mental health in Kerala (Halliburton, 1998).

In fact, the perceived higher rate of psychopathology may relate to the fact that Kerala has a dramatically higher number of mental hospitals than other Indian states: with only four percent of India's population, Kerala has one-third of India's mental hospitals. The proliferation of these institutions plus the dissemination of information about psychology and psychiatry in the popular print and visual media in Kerala, may influence Malayalees to express their suffering in psychological idioms (Halliburton, 1998).

Towards Prevention

A people's movement towards preventive mental health already seems to have begun in Kerala. Local bodies and voluntary agencies have been coming forward in the past few years to try and evolve suitable mental illness prevention strategies. Kerala is one state where the police were forced to start, due to popular pressure, a telephonic suicide prevention counselling centre in a small village (Nooranad in Alappuzha district) because 30 to 50 suicides used to occur there each year. Another new village, Panangad in Kozhikode district has started attracting similar attention (Krishnakumar, 2000).

For the first time an epidemiological field study to provide an official estimate of severe mental morbidity was conducted in 13 out of the 14 districts of the state by the State Mental Health Authority in 1998. Although the study covered only the chronically mental ill, its findings are significant in so far as they point to the dearth of data and facilities for the increasing number of others who require help (Krishnakumar, 2000).

Perhaps for the first time in the country, a people's initiative for suicide prevention was launched at the panchayat level at Ponnani in north Kerala. The aim is to make the four gram panchayats, which witnessed a spurt in suicides in recent years, a 'no-suicide' zone. The Ponnani block panchayat also set up a Centre for Community Mental Health Studies in order to create awareness about depressive illnesses, psychoses, alcohol and drug abuse, and about ways to identify risk groups and prevent incidence of mental illness (Krishnakumar, 2000).

The Centre has identified rapid socio-cultural changes, a rising gap between aspirations and capabilities of individuals, a false impression that a high consumption capability is the symbol of a higher social position, disappearing moral values and disintegration of traditional support systems, among others, as possible special circumstances in Kerala that may be responsible for the high incidence of suicide (Krishnakumar, 2000).

The Centre for Community Mental Health Studies organised a state-level camp with the support of the Planning Board at Tavanur, which called for immediate intervention by the Kerala Government and the local bodies to curb the number of suicides. The 'Ponnani Document' adopted by the camp includes guidelines for the State Government, the local-bodies and NGOs to evolve immediate long-term preventive strategies (Krishnakumar, 2000).

The document suggests that the government and the local bodies establish at least one suicide-prevention centre in each district, continuing education facilities for doctors to identify and treat depression-related mental illnesses, life-skills education for children (incorporating approaches to seek, offer and appreciate crisis support, problem solving and evolving mature views on matters of love and sex), counselling centres in colleges, reorientation of priorities by NGOs to make suicide prevention a major area of their activity, and training for priests, social workers, public men, the police, teachers and others to deal with people in distress. It also calls on the media to be restrained in reporting incidents of suicide, especially in glorifying them and presenting them as a problem-solving method (Krishnakumar, 2000).

Kerala has many challenges before her and history has time and again proven that she has the potential to rise to the occasion.

REFERENCES

Cassinder, R. (1995). Making Kerala model more intelligible. *Economic and Political Weekly, 48,* 3085-3092.

Franke, R. W. & Chasin, B.H. (1999). Is the Kerala model sustainable? Lessons from the past: Prospects for the future. In M.A. Oommen (Ed.), *Rethinking development: Kerala's development experience I* (pp. 118-148). New Delhi: Concept Publishing Company.

Halliburton, M. (1998). Suicide: A paradox of development in Kerala. *Economic and Political Weekly, XXXIII* (36&37), 2341-2345.

Isaac, T.M., & Tharakan, P.K. (1995). Kerala: Towards a new agenda. *Economic and Political Weekly, XXX* (31&32), 1993-2004.

Krishnakumar, R. (2000, April 28). State of despair. *Frontline,* 97-100.

Krishnakumar, R. (2000, November 24) The lure of the brew. *Frontline,* 36-39.

Mathew, G. (1999). Preface. In M.A. Oommen (Ed.), *Rethinking Development: Kerala's development experience I.* (pp.vii-x). New Delhi: Concept Publishing Company.

Oommen, M.A. (1999). Introduction. In M.A. Oommen (Ed.), *Rethinking Development: Kerala's Development Experience I* (pp. xv-xxxiii). New Delhi: Concept Publishing Company.

Santosh, K. & Malecha, R. (2000, July 16). Engulfed in loneliness and fear. *The Hindu Magazine,* pp. I, II.

Saradamoni, K. (1999). Kerala model: Time for rethinking. In M.A. Oommen (Ed.), *Rethinking Development: Kerala's Development Experience I* (pp. 159-174). New Delhi: Concept Publishing Company.

Satchidanandan, K. (1999). Everyday and the avant-garde: The contexts of modernism in Malayalam literature. In M.A. Oommen (Ed.), *Rethinking Development: Kerala's Development Experience I* (pp. 23-35). New Delhi: Concept Publishing Company.

Tharamangalam, J. (1999). The social roots of Kerala's development debacle. In M.A. Oommen (Ed.), *Rethinking Development: Kerala's Development Experience I* (pp. 175-197). New Delhi: Concept Publishing Company.

Tornquist, O. & Tharakan, M. (1996). Democratisation and the radical political project: Case of Kerala. *Economic and Political Weekly, XXXI,* 28, 1847-1858.

Verma, D.M. (2000, December 25). Abuse of medical technology. *The Hindu,* p. 6.

14

"Are Marriages Made in Heaven?" Caste-Based Rule Systems for the Process of Marriage Partner Selection in Specific Caste Groups of Gujarat

RACHANA KULKARNI and SHAGUFA KAPADIA

Introduction

Culture is an overarching framework of learned activities, which conform to the norms and are passed from one generation to another. The normative behaviours of culture become conventions, which its people take for granted (Valsiner & Lawrence, 1997). The cultural rule systems are a part of these conventions and act as guidelines of thought regularizing the social rules, and provide individuals with systems of justification, conduct and explanations of events (Boesch, 1987, cited in Eckensberger, 1995). These rule systems change in their stringency over time and new conventions emerge. Within the boundaries set by the cultural rules, individuals work as active agents to develop a "personal culture", which represents the degree of conformity in a highly stratified culture like India (Valsiner & Lawrence, 1997). Thus, human behaviour is best understood as a dynamic interface between the individual and the cultural context with a focus on how the meanings of the rule systems have been interpreted and keep changing.

Note : We are thankful to Ashlesha Kulkarni for collecting part of the data for this paper as part of her master's thesis.

Marriage in any culture is valued as one of the major milestones to be crossed in adult life. It also symbolizes the legal and social sanction given to a relationship, which generally results in family formation. Conventions about normative marriage patterns differ from culture to culture, including the process of partner selection. In most societies, especially non-western, arranged marriages are a norm (Dube, 1997) whereas in western societies, the process of partner selection is more individually directed.

In India, especially in the Hindu religion, *'Vivaha'* is considered to be one of the most important *'samskara'*. The indissolubility of marriage is a norm clearly stated in key religious texts (Apte, 1978), and an early-arranged marriage within one's own caste group is a norm for girls in India (Gulati, 1995). Girls are the *"izzat"* (prestige) of the natal family and all socialization practices are geared towards preparing them for the future role of a wife (Das, 1982). Thus, marriage for girls in India is not only a future goal, but also an inevitable social requirement.

Menarche plays an important role in the socialisation of a girl because after menarche, the girl is considered "ready" for marriage and child bearing (Dube, 1988). A lot of restrictions are imposed on her mobility (Datar, 1991), essentially to manage her sexuality (Dube, 1997). Now that the girl is no more a child, there is an urgency to get her married or protect her till she is married. Pre-pubertal marriages are prevalent in some parts of India and though the consummation of marriage is delayed, the girl's fate is "sealed" and her virginity, "protected"

'Caste' is another factor, which plays an important role in marriage. The Hindu society has been divided into four *"Varnas"* from the Vedic times, namely *Brahmins*, *Kshatriyas*, *Vaishya* and *Sudra* (Sathe, 1999). The caste system has laid down certain prescriptive and proscriptive rules for the selection of a marriage partner and marriage outside endogamous groups is not allowed.

In most traditional societies the ties of kinship are strong; the strongest are those of the near ones constituting the domestic group, the household and the family (Sinha, 1988). The kin networks mediate marriages by defining the type of spouse, the number of spouses allowed, and which persons are eligible for the match (Chinoy, 1967). With social change, kin and elders of the family have created avenues where the young people of the same caste can meet at social gatherings and fix marriages under their surveillance (Shah, 1988). Parents are allowing their children wider choice (Dave, Dave & Joshi, 1998) along with the matching of horoscope and consent from the parents, which are part of the conventional trend of arranged marriages.

A key factor considered in selecting a marriage partner is the qualities of the partner. A study on international mate preferences (Buss *et al.,* 1990) demonstrated that traditional Asian societies placed more than average value on chastity, as compared to the western sample. In the Indian sample, more than average value was placed on characteristics like desire for home and children, education, intelligence, and health of the partner. Traditionally, in the Indian context, the social identity of the person and the *'samskaras'* inculcated in the person by the family were given most importance in partner selection (Parikh & Garg, 1995).

In contemporary times, parents manifest a flexible attitude and have started considering the likes and dislikes of their children in partner selection. At the same time, children have also expressed the need to marry after consulting their parents and relatives (Shah, 1998; Rao & Rao 1985).

Over the years, changes have gradually seeped into the sacramental convention of marriage and partner selection process. The present study has focused upon the rule systems for the marriage partner selection process in specific caste groups, and attempted to examine how these are being adhered to, or altered in practice, across generations. The marriage partner search and selection process has been conceptualized in three overlapping stages.

Initiation of Search : The initiation of search has rules which dictate when to start the search.

Actual Search : This stage is characterized by the active search which involves further exploration and filtering of specific proposals by the parents.

Final Decision : The final stage is characterized by the decision to accept one proposal and reject others, and the culmination of the process into marriage.

Conceptual Framework of the Study

Figure 14.1 depicts the conceptual framework of the study. It shows the stages of partner selection within the larger socio-cultural context. The process is guided by certain normative rules and involves some key persons within and or outside the family.

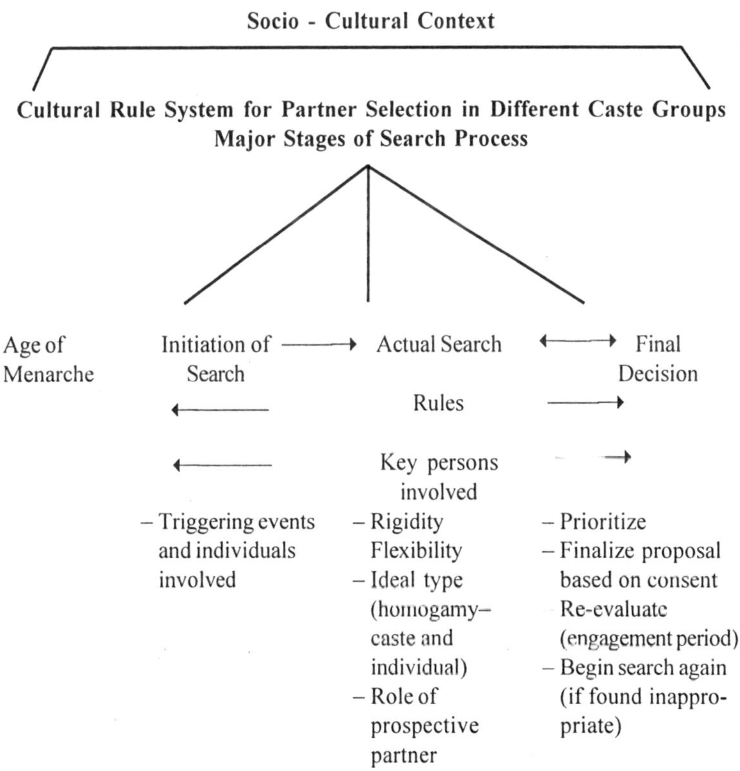

Fig. 14.1 : Socio-cultural dimensions of marriage partner selection

Based on the conceptual framework, the study focused upon the following *research questions* :

1. What are the cultural rule systems in the process of marriage partner selection in specific caste groups of Gujarat?
2. What is the process of marriage partner selection with respect to (a) initiation of search, (b) actual search, and (c) final decision?

METHOD

The study was descriptive—qualitative in nature and employed qualitative methods to answer the research questions.

Sample

The sample of the study constituted 12 dyads of adolescent girls and their mothers, and 12 recently married women (maximum five years) from six caste groups, namely Malis, Vankars, Garasias, and Brahmins, Patels and Brahmabhatts. The Malis, Vankars and the

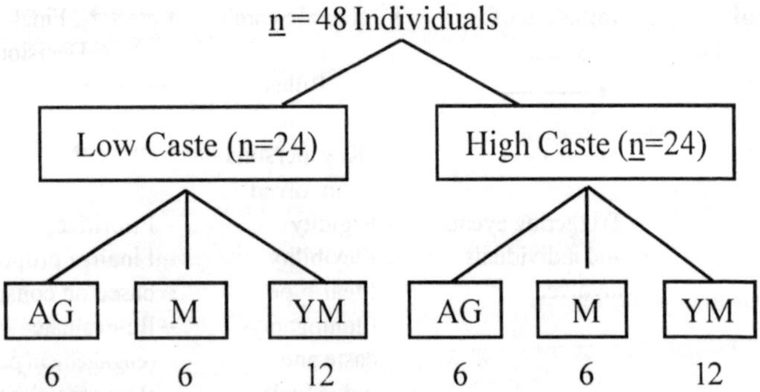

Index : AG = Adolescent Girls (14 - 24 Years)
M = (Their) Mothers (35 - 50 Years)
YM = Young Mothers (18 - 30 Years)

Fig. 14.2 : Sample Design

Garasias belong to the low caste, and Brahmins, Patels and Brahmabhatts belong to the high caste. The sample was selected using the purposive and snowball techniques.

The study used a range of qualitative and participatory research methods like informal group discussions with community women, community mapping and in-depth interviews.

Data Analysis

The entire data set of 48 interviews was disaggregated by caste. As the information obtained was qualitative in nature, qualitative methods of analysis like data matrices, pathways for processes, event-listings and role-ordered matrices (for details see Miles & Huberman, 1994) were employed. Whenever appropriate, frequencies were calculated and presented, along with the qualitative findings.

RESULTS AND INTERPRETATIONS

Section A presents the socio-demographic profile of the informants. The first research question on cultural rule systems is dealt in Section B. Corresponding to the second research question, Section C deals with the process of partner selection.

A. Socio-demographic Profile of the Sample

It was evident from the socio-demographic information that the education levels of the mother-adolescent dyads in the high and low caste groups are different. The mothers and adolescent girls of the high caste have completed or are undergoing secondary school education, whereas in the low caste dyads, all the informants fall in the range of no formal education to secondary school education. This factor is also related to the early age of marriage in the low caste, which is in the range of 10-16 years, in contrast to the high caste sample where the age of marriage ranges between 18 to 22 years.

For the young mothers, all the informants from the low caste groups belonged to the age group of 18-22 years, whereas those from high castes belonged to the age group of 22-28 years, which points to the lower age at marriage in the low castes. Most of the low caste informants were educated up to primary school ($n = 11$) whereas those belonging to the high castes had completed schooling ($n = 7$) and some had completed graduation ($n = 5$).

B. Cultural Rules for Partner Selection: Caste Comparisons

This section gives information about the existing cultural rules for partner selection followed by the informants, and compares the adherence and flexibility between the caste groups. Table 14.1 shows the cultural rules and major differences (between high and low castes) in adherence to rules at each stage of the partner selection process.

The caste differences in rule systems are most prominent in the stage of initiation of search where chronological age and the factors of age at menarche (low caste) and education (high caste) play a determining role. Also, differences between mothers and adolescent girls were seen in the age of initiation of search, which is higher for the girls than for the mothers. The consent and involvement of the adolescent girls and young mothers is more evident in the high caste than in the low caste. For the mothers of the adolescent girls, in the high caste there was very limited scope for individual consent, whereas in low castes, no individual opinion was sought. Interestingly, horoscope matching is a pre-requisite for search in the high castes unlike that in the low castes, where it is considered only for the purpose of deciding the date and time of marriage. The period of engagement is longer in the low castes, and it is essentially used by parents for financial and other preparations for marriage.

Changes in relation to the prescriptive and proscriptive rules for partner selection and some of the rituals related to the same are evident. More flexibility in adherence to cultural rules is seen in high caste groups. The data revealed permissibility of self-selection

Table 14.1 : Major Differences in Rule Systems of High and Low Caste Groups (n = 48)

Stage of Partner Selection Process	Rule Systems: High Caste	Rule Systems: Low Caste
Initiation of Search		
– Age of initiation	– 16 - 19 years	– 10 - 15 years or below 15 years
– Determining event	– Completion of education; at least HSc level	– Onset of menarche (*Nahti–dhoti thai tyare*)
Actual Search		
– Who is involved in search / bringing proposals?	– Relatives, caste based associations	– Relatives, neighbours
– Contact with boy's family	– Can be done directly	– Generally done through mediator only
– Girl's consent	– Formal meeting or "interview" (may occur at boy or girl's place)	– "See" the boy – Not taken for mothers
– Exchange of token money for girl & boy	– After proposal is finalized with agreement of both families ("*aal-mail*" in Patels, "*sakar-nariyal*" in Brahmabhatts)	– When girl is 'liked' by other party (the money "*chanlo*" may be returned, if other party is not interested)
– Take the girl outside her house to see proposals	– Girls may accompany	– Girls can't accompany
– Horoscope matching	– Requirement	– Not compulsory
Final Decision		
– Period of engagement	– Short duration (2 - 6 months)	– Long duration (1 year or more)
– Involvement of girls	– More involvement in entire process	– Relatively less involvement. Parents decide major matters like time of marriage and social/financial transaction
– Girl's departure to the in - laws' house	– Immediately after marriage	– Postponed till girl attains menarche of even 1–2 years after menarche ("*umar layak thay tyare*")
– Dowry	– More evident	– No rule, but it is in the form of social obligations ("*vyavhar*")
– Secrecy before finalizing	– Highly maintained	– Not rigidly maintained

and inter-caste marriages in high castes. Under certain circumstances, families could also share the expenditure for marriage rather than the girl's family alone having to bear all expenses. In the low caste groups, gender differences are evident in matters of hypergamy and meeting of the prospective spouses. The boy may exercise his power and demand a meeting with the girl; he also has the prerogative of expanding the caste- based boundaries in partner selection.

Table 14.2 depicts the involvement of kin in the process of marriage partner selection.

Table 14. 2 : Roles of the Different Persons involved in the Process of Partner Selection in High and Low Caste Groups (n = 48)

Roles	Initiation of Search	Actual Search	Final Decision
Parents	• Decide when to initiate search • Tell relatives to find proposals	• Decide criteria for partner selection (with or without consultation with girl or boy) • Filter proposals	• Negotiate time of marriage • Plan for expenses • Maintain cordial relations with boy's family
Kin networks (close relatives, neighbours, friends, priest)	• Bring proposals	• Mediate between two families • Inquire about families and individuals • Help in arranging meeting • Can mislead the parents by giving false information • Object to a marriage due to vested interests	• Mediate between two families • Advise and give consent • Help parents financially (especially maternal uncle)
Girl/Boy	• Limited role (High Caste)	• Meet or "see" the boy/girl (In case of Adolescent girls and young Mothers) • Decide to accept or reject proposal • Give consent	• Limited role (consent)

As indicated in Table 14.2, not surprisingly, parents play a major role throughout the selection process, while kin networks supplement in terms of bringing proposals and acting as mediators between the two families. At times, some relatives may also play a 'negative' role by preventing the proposal form working out. In some of the informants' own words, "*Fachad mare, ane lagan tuti pan shake, atle ame koi ne keheta nathi, jyar sudhi pacco nirnay na lai le". (They intervene and the marriage can also break up; that is why we do not tell anyone till the final decision is taken.)*

C. Process of Partner Selection

On the basis of information about the rule systems and the normative process of partner selection, as described by the informants, the pathways of the search process were created for both the caste groups (Figures 14.3and 14.4).

As depicted in Figures 14.3 and 14.4, the key aspects differentiating the search process in the high and low caste groups are menarche and education as determining factors for initiation of search, differential use of horoscopes during actual search, the duration of the engagement period and departure of the girl to the in - laws' house. In the low castes, horoscopes are matched mainly to determine the auspicious time of marriage and the age of the prospective bride and groom. In some cases, the horoscope was not matched at all. In the high castes, matching horoscopes is a rule but one that may not be adhered to compulsorily; it depends essentially on the belief of the family. In some castes, the horoscope served as a good excuse to reject proposals. The engagement period is shorter in the high castes, than in the low castes. Engagement can be broken in both the caste groups, if the family or the boy is not found suitable or if there is interference by some relatives, who have vested interests and want to prevent the marriage. The girl is sent to the in-laws' house immediately after marriage in the high castes, whereas in the low caste groups she is sent after one or two years of marriage or after she attains menarche (in case of pre-pubertal marriages, n=2) or reaches the "appropriate" age (17 - 18

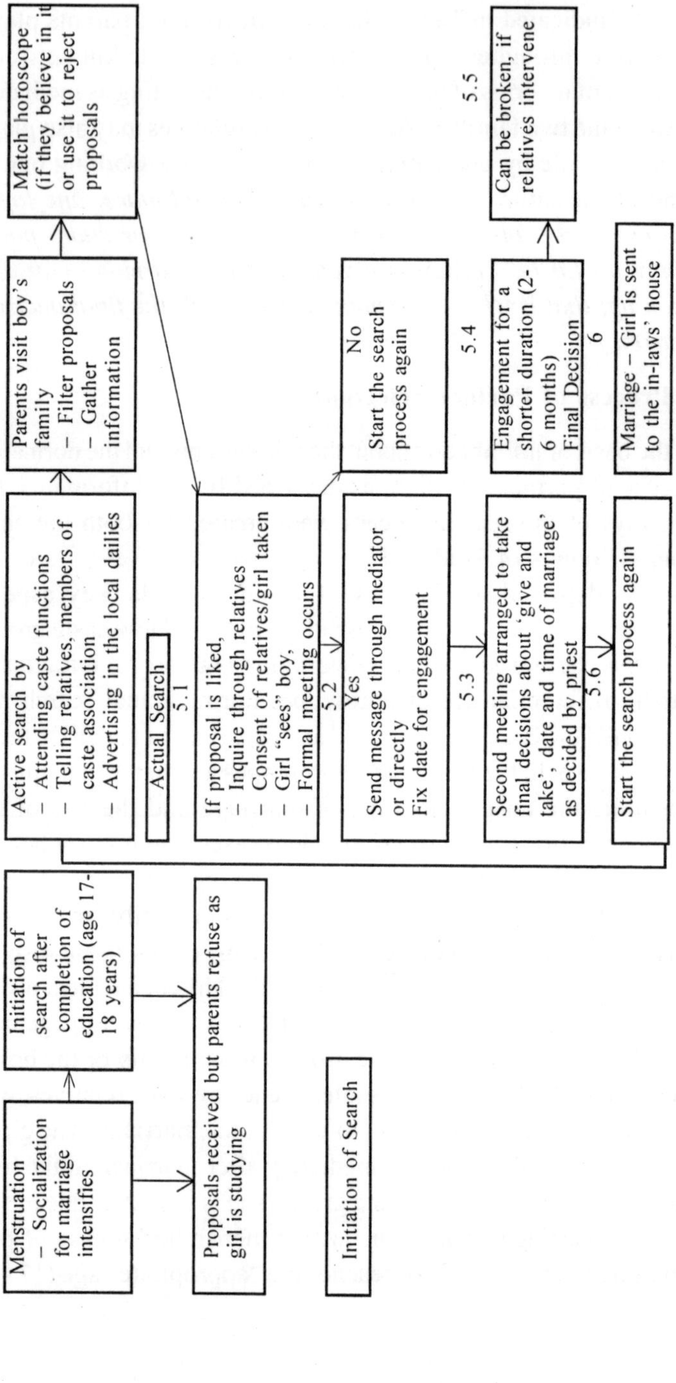

Fig. 14.3 : Pathways in the Process of Partner Selection in High Caste Groups (n = 48)

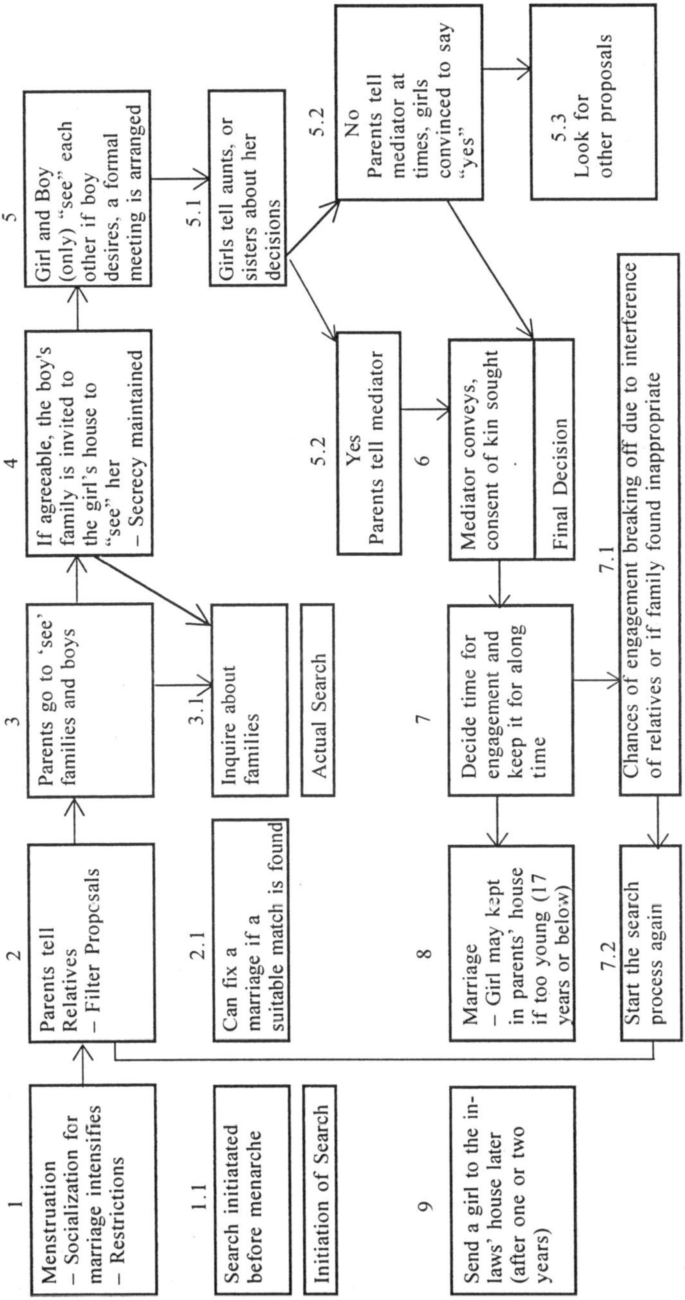

Fig. 14. 4 : Pathways in the Process of Partner Selection in Low Caste Groups (n = 48)

years) "*umar layak thay thare*" *(when she reaches the appropriate age)*. The data reveals that the search process is more or less similar for mothers and adolescent girls, with variation in one or two aspects, for instance, the mothers were not allowed to "see" the boy and their involvement was limited.

Tables 14.3 and 14.4 contain information derived from the search profiles of each of the 48 informants through an event listing. The event listing included the number of proposals considered, rejected and accepted (with reasons for the same) in chronological order for each informant. A summary for the entire sample is presented in Table 14.3.

Table 14. 3 : Comparison of Search Profiles of the High and Low Caste Groups (n = 48)

Dimensions of Search Profiles	High Caste			Low Caste		
	AG	YM	M	AG	YM	M
1 Average age of initiation of search	18	18	16	13	15	12
2 Average number of proposals considered (per informant)	2-3	6-7	3-4	1-2	4-5	1-2
3 Average number of proposals rejected (per informant)	2-3	5-6	1-2	0-1	3-4	0-1
• Average number of proposals rejected by parents	2-3	3	-	3	3	3
• Average number of proposals rejected by self and family	-	4-5	2	-	2-3	2
4 Number of cases where parents alone considered proposals	-	6	3	4	6	6
5 Number of cases where parents fixed the marriage without consulting the girl	-	-	2	3	3	6

Index : AG = Adolescent Girls (14-24 Years), M = (Their) Mothers (35-50 Years)
YM = 'Young' Mothers (18-30 Years),

In the low castes, the girls "see" less number of proposals (one to four proposals for each person) so rejections are also less as compared to the high caste (two to seven proposals for each person). This implies a shorter duration of the partner selection process in the low caste groups. Across the caste groups, parents consider the proposals first and the filtering continues, but in the low caste groups parents may fix the marriage during the search process itself, without consulting the girl ($n = 12$). Also, the absence of the girl's consent is seen more in the mothers' generation across caste groups ($n = 2$ and 6).

Table 14.4 : Factors Considered for Partner Selection in the High and Low Caste Groups (n = 48)

Factors	Local Terms	High Caste			Low Caste		
Characteristics of the Family		YM	M	AG	YM	M	AG
• Nature of the family members	*Ghar na loke no svabhav kevo che;*	4	17	9	9	15	10
• Type and size of family and house	*Ghar ma ketla loki che; sah – kutumb rahe che*	4	–	–	8	–	2
• Urban residence	*Gamada ma nathi rahevu;*	4	–	–	–	1	–
Total			**38**			**45**	
Characteristics of the Individual							
• Nature of the boy (caring, intelligent etc.)	*Chokara no svabhav;*	6	23	14	9	14	15
• Income/Job	*Naukari dhando; shu kamay che?*	8	6	4	6	1	4
• Education	*Bhantar saru che;*	6	3	4	3	1	1
• Age	*umar vadhare no hoy*	–	2	1	–	3	3
• Appearance	*dekhav*	2	–	–	–	2	5
• Less Dowry	*Mangvanu ouchu hatu*	2	–	–	–	–	–
• Nearer to mother's house	*Mummy nu ghar pase pade avu hatu*	1	–	–	–	–	–
• Vices	*Vysan (daru, jugar, pan – padiki)*	1	–	–	2	2	3
• Others (good voice, similar interest)	*Avaj gamyo; shoukh jeva hata*	2	–	–	–	–	–

Note : The frequency total is more than 48 because each category has multiple responses.

Index : AG = Adolescent Girls (14-24 Years), M = (Their) Mothers (35-50 Years), YM = 'Young' Mothers (18-30 Years).

As indicated in Table 14.4, the high and low caste informants give more importance to individual characteristics (*ns*=85 and 74 respectively) as compared to the familial characteristics (*ns*=38 and 45 respectively). Within individual characteristics, informants from both caste groups gave most preference to nature of the individuals, followed by job and education. On the other hand, the mothers gave higher preference to education as well as family background in selection of a partner for their daughters. It is interesting to note that all the adolescent girls said that they would like to have husbands who are more educated/qualified than them.

Discussion and Conclusion

Cultural rules are broad frames of reference, which monitor and set the boundaries for partner selection. In the present study, as expected, adherence to a rule system is prevalent across caste groups. However, flexibility in actual operation is evident more in the high castes. The flexibility of rules is not about changing the existing rules or dissolving them altogether, but it means interpreting 'new' meanings out of the same rules and adapting them in ways that are practically suitable to the present situation.

Continuity and Change in the Process of Partner Selection

Continuity of traditional practices is seen in the Indian society as these practices are found to have functional utility (Sinha, 1988). Some of the rules of partner selection, like caste endogamy, facilitate adjustment to the new family due to the familiarity in the practices, so may be, this rule persists. At the same time, the rigidity with which it is followed is fading as self-selection is being allowed and accepted, more so, if the person is from the same larger caste group. Saraswathi and Pai (1997) also point to marriage alliance across caste boundaries, which are likely to bring about changes in the institution of marriage. Such changes are an indication of the impact of modernization and education, especially in the urban areas.

Across the groups, the kin play a special role in bringing proposals and mediating between two families. One can see change in the present times, especially in the high caste groups, where the involvement of the kin is decreasing (they act only as supporters). The reduced role of kin could be attributed to the nuclearisation of the families, limited social contacts and the orientation of people changing from duty boundedness to more of an obligatory or personal concern orientation (Mishra, 1995).

Hindu parents have a prime religious duty to marry their daughter propitiously (Kakar, 1979). Even today, parents consider their children's, especially daughter's marriage, as one of the prime duties (*dharma*). But one can witness some social change in this respect due to education and the value attached to it by parents. Today, parents from the high castes, low middle-income families, want their daughters to be educated. It also helps in finding a good match. Similarly, in the low castes, girls are allowed to avail some form of vocational courses (like sewing, beauty parlour courses, etc.), which would help them to be independent, if the need arises.

The adherence to the traditional mode of partner selection is accompanied by the realization for the need to let the girl and boy meet before finalizing the alliance. Ironically, as an antithesis to the change in this process, the adolescent girls themselves do not wish to take responsibility for the final decision. Thus a paradox becomes evident in the study.

Perspectives on Marriage in a Cultural Context

In any social context, marriage is a conscious exchange. According to Lonner and Adamopoulos (1997) all human behaviour is based on exchanges comprising love, status, goods, services, etc. Marriage also comprises emotional, social and material exchanges (sending the daughter away, gaining a son-in-law, *vyavhar*, dowry). The tendency would thus be to have a fruitful exchange. The screening of proposals is an important aspect of partner selection wherein the pros and cons of each proposal are weighed and the aim is to choose proposals which would reduce 'risks' in future and anchor on to qualities which have potential for security, for example, education, occupation, technical know-how, nature of the family members.

In the high castes, the girls considered more number of proposals. Some of them did not like the system of being "displayed" to a boy or his family during a formal meeting. In such situations, where the involvement of the individual is more, the psychological impact is likely to be more intense. This is accentuated by the pressure to get married, which often results in compromising one's criteria for the prospective groom, especially on the part of parents.

Overall, one can see more adherence to the rule systems in the low caste groups. The possible explanation for this could be that these groups live in a distinctly different ecological setting wherein the goals of an individual are limited to a great extent by the economic constraints, lack of infrastructure and facilities of education. Moreover, there is a collective tendency of staying together with many close-knit extended families for cost effectiveness. This affects social behaviours as people live in a shared culture of role hierarchy, leading to adherence to rules and intolerance to rule transgressions.

In a cultural context, where there are so many rules to guide and control human behaviour, the self-reflexive quality of the human organisms takes charge (Eckensberger, 1994). They adhere to some rules, which facilitate the achievement of personal goals or have functional value, and which are conducive to social living in future. They also newly interpret some rules, which changes the course of conventions over time. There is always an element of fore thought that guides the decisions of the people. The consequences of one's actions are viewed in terms of the number of problems or positive outcomes one is likely to encounter, when one is part of the larger cultural milieu.

Marriage is thus a convention bound by many other social dynamics within one's sub-cultural group. The continuity of the rule systems is influenced by these dynamics, over and above the prescriptions of the culture. The different processes are regulated to maintain continuity and bring about change, during which culture itself undergoes transformation.

REFERENCES

Apte, U.M . (1978) . *The sacrament of marriage in Hindu society from Vedic period to Dharmashastras* . New Delhi: Ajanta .

Buss, D.M., Abbott, M., *et al.* (1990). International preferences in selecting mates: A study of 37 cultures. *Journal of Cross-Cultural Psychology, 21* (1), 5-47.

Chinoy, E. (1967). *Society: An introduction to sociology* (2nd ed.). New York: Random House.

Das, V. (1982). Reflections on the social caste of adulthood. In S. Kakar (Ed.), *Identity and adulthood.* (pp. 89 -104). New Delhi: Oxford University Press.

Datar, C. (1995). Democratizing the family. *Indian Journal of Social Work, LVI*(3),211-223.

Dave, P., Dave, K. & Joshi, A., (1998, July). *Family responsibilities: An Indian perspective on the changing roles of men and women.* Paper presented at the International Union of the Family Organisation. England: Oxford.

Dube, L. (1988). On the construction of gender: Hindu girls in patrilineal India. In K. Chanana, (Ed.), *Socialization, education and women: Explorations in gender identity* (pp. 167-207). New Delhi: Orient Longman.

Dube, L. (1997). *Women and kinship: Comparative perspectives on gender in South and South-East Asia* . New Delhi: Vistaar.

Eckensberger, L.H. (1994). Development of morality. In W.J. Lonner & R.S. Malpass (Eds.), *Psychology and culture* (pp. 14-19). Boston: Allyn & Bacon.

Eckensberger, L.H. (1995). Activity or action: Two different roads towards an integration of culture into psychology? *Culture & Psychology, Vol.1*, pp.67-80. New Delhi: Sage.

Garg, P.K. & Parikh, I.J. (1995). *Cross roads of culture: A study of transience.* New Delhi : Sage.

Gulati, L. (1995). Women and family in India- continuity and change. *Indian Journal of Social Work, LVI* (3), 133-140.

Kakar, S. (1979). Setting the stage: The traditional Hindu view and psychology of Erik. H. Erikson. In S. Kakar (Ed.), *Identity and adulthood* (pp. 3-12). New Delhi: Oxford University Press.

Lonner, W.J. & Adamopoulos, J. (1997). Culture as antecedent to behavior. In J.W. Berry, Y. H. Poortinga, & J. Pandey (Eds.), *Handbook of cross-cultural psychology: Vol. 1. Theory and method* (pp. 43-84). Boston: Allyn & Bacon.

Miles, M.B. & Huberman, A.M. (1994). *Qualitative data analysis* (2nd ed.). New Delhi: Sage.

Misra, G. (1995). Reflections on continuity and change in the Indian family system. *Trends in Social Science Research, 2(1),* June, 27-30.

Rao, V.V. P. & Rao, B.N. (1985). *Marriage, the family and women in India*. New Delhi: Heritage.

Saraswathi, T. S. & Pai, S. (1997). Socialization in the Indian context. In A. Kao & D. Sinha, (Eds.), *Asian perspectives on psychology* (pp. 81-92). New Delhi: Sage.

Sathe, V. (1999, January 22). Reform Hindu society to stop conversion. *The Times of India,* p. 10.

Shah, A.M. (1998). *The family in India: Critical essays.* Hyderabad: Orient Longman.

Sinha, D. (1988). The family scenario in a developing country and its implications for mental health. The case in India. In P.R. Dasen, J.W. Berry, & Sarotorins, N. (Eds.), *Health and cross-cultural psychology : Towards applications. Vol. 10.* (pp.48-70). New Delhi: Sage.

Valsiner, J. & Lawrence, J.A. (1997). Human development in cultures across lifespan. In J.W. Berry, P.R. Dasen & T.S. Saraswathi (Eds.), *Handbook of cross –cultural psychology. Vol. 2. Basic processes and human development* (pp. 69-106). Boston: Allyn & Bacon.

15

Identification of Probable Antecedent and Process Variables in the Study of Stress in Information Systems Personnel

K.S. RAJESWARI and R.N. ANANTHARAMAN

Introduction

Information Systems Professionals (ISP) or software professionals form the single largest group in Software Engineering, which is an area of constant growth. This group includes programmers, developers, systems analysts and network specialists. The role of software professionals could include programming, system maintenance, project estimation and management, conflict resolution, job allocation, technology and people management apart from continuously training oneself as well. They are expected to adhere to demanding deadlines, innovate applications, enhance competitive position, in the face of continuously changing technologies and methodologies.

In addition, the software professional faces the risk of obsolescence. This obsolescence is not restricted to the realm of skill alone, but permeates the aspect of knowledge and mindset as well. Moreover, the scope of the software professional's job ranges from understanding the expectations of the multi-cultural clientele to managing and running a system at the client's site, which is probably, situated several thousand miles away. Such boundary spanning activities often required of technical professionals lead to the occurrence of role conflict and role ambiguity. The above mentioned work pattern causes stress for the information system personnel. It is the scope of this paper to identify the sources of stress and also explore the factors that buffer or enhance the effects of the stress felt by the individuals.

Review of Literature

To date, little attention has been devoted to occupational stress among ISP. The limited research available is focused on ISP in United States (Ivanecevich *et al* 1983; Weiss, 1983; McGee, 1996; Moore, 2000), Canada (Kaluzniacky, 2000), Singapore (Lim & Teo, 1996, 1999) and Japan (Fujigaki, 1993; Furuyama, 1993). Also, the respondents of these studies were predominantly employed as Information Technology (IT) enablers in various types of organizations.

In combination with employers' expectations and the dynamism of the industry itself, several factors like job environment, personality, self-efficacy and social support contribute to an employee's commitment to the organization and job satisfaction. One particularly important factor is occupational stress. The perception of stress by an individual depends on his efficacy on the job, his personality, perceived sense of control, his relationship with his colleagues and the like. It also depends largely on the person's interaction with the environment—including a person's interaction with computer and its related technologies, which can broadly be termed human computer interaction.

Information Processing Professionals see technology as a pre-requisite for their existence and hence the rate of change of technology has profound effects on them. Men and women who plan, design and monitor these systems experience greater techno-stress in jobs and environments (Glass, 1997). "High performance requirements with high technology can exercise a dangerous influence on the human personality... anyone who is constantly working or playing with computers is at risk" (Brod, 1984 p. 76,). The various health problems unique to computer users can also be a source of pressure. Japanese managers deliberately underestimate software development time—a practice that heaps stress on the backs of those subject to unrealistic expectations—and a practice not unknown in the rest of the world (Glass, 1997). Thus there is considerable reason to believe that ISP is significantly at risk of serious " burnout" (Kaluznaicky, 2000).

Stress models in the studies stated above concentrate on job environment stressors such as perceived workload, work demands, role conflict and role ambiguity, job scope, job pressure and obsolescence. Relationship with others, communication with colleagues and users, demands of the users, career concerns and fairness of rewards have also been identified as stressors in an ongoing study among IT personnel conducted by Sethi *et al.* (1997). The outcome variables in these stress models include job (dis)satisfaction; job induced tension, negative affectivity, work exhaustion and intention to turnover. In the Canadian study (Kaluzniacky, 2000) conducted by University of Winnipeg, role of personality factor and emotional job dependency factors are also being researched.

The core relationship between stressors in the working environment and strains is a well-researched topic. Role ambiguity and role conflict (Fisher & Gitelson, 1983, Jackson & Schuler, 1985), underutilization of skills (Gupta & Beehr, 1979, Kaufman & Beehr, 1986, 1989), role overload (Beehr, 1976), interpersonal conflict (Beehr *et al.* 1996), job future ambiguity (Kaufman & Beehr 1986, 1989), gender discrimination (Sanchez & Brock, 1996) and situational constraints (Jex & Gudanowski, 1992) are some examples of stressors that are related to strain. Uncertainty as a part of process facet has been researched to some extent (Pardine, 1987; O' Driscoll & Beehr, 1994; Beehr, 1987; Fenlason *et al.,* 1997).

Moderators play a very important role in the perception of sources of pressure and the resultant outcome. Studies on personal characteristics as moderators of stress-strain relationship include the much researched Type A behaviour (Ganster, 1987; Cooper & Payne, 1991). Yet the reason pertaining to why Type A behaviour buffers moderation only for certain stress-strain combination and not others is still to be explored (Beehr, 1998). Studies that pertain to locus of control (Bogg & Cooper 1995; Kahn & Byosiere, 1992; Parkes, 1991), efficacy beliefs (Bandura, 1982; Jex & Gudanowski, 1992; Riggs & Knight, 1994; Jex & Bliese, 1999), organizational commitment (Leong *et al.* 1996) and collective efficacy (Riggs & Knight, 1994), as moderators are very few. Jex and Bliese (1999) have identified efficacy, as an important variable whose role in the occupational stress process should be researched further. Social support is a situational moderator that is frequently studied (Beehr, 1995; Kahn & Byosiere, 1992). Work control, as a moderator needs to be explored further. Current research on personal moderators is promising and future research in this is warranted (Beehr, 1998).

Strains themselves can be categorized into physical, psychological and behavioural types (Beehr, 1998). Of these, behavioural strains are in need of further investigation. The study of consequences of stress includes mental health (Parkes, 1991, Bogg & Cooper, 1995; Spector, 1988; Leong et al 1996), job related strain (Mullarkey *et al.* 1997), general strain (Mullarkey *et al.* 1997), absenteeism (Parkes, 1991, Spector 1988), job satisfaction (Mullarkey *et al,* 1997, Riggs & Knight; Bogg & Cooper, 1995, Leong *et al,* 1996), and intention to quit (Leong *et al.* 1996, Jex & Gudanowski, 1992). Stress related symptoms reported by Information Systems managers include feeling restless and unable to concentrate, feeling irritable and tense, feeling tired and having low energy (Weiss, 1983). Information System literature, surveys and anecdotal evidences point out the prevalence of stress and in particular the work exhaustion faced by software professionals (Moore, 2000). The concept of work exhaustion which might result in depersonalization, voluntary turnover or lowered self esteem and job dissatisfaction have been conceptually analyzed in depth (Moore, 2000).

Gaps Identified in the Area of Stress Research in ISP

Stress research in ISP has predominantly followed the cause-effect model. The cause-effect model may not be able to bring out reasons why only certain people in an organization are able to retain high levels of motivation and attain high levels of productivity and creativity consistently or why certain others give excellent output only at times and so on. It is in this niche that role of personality (*e.g.*, 16PF), sex role identity (BSRI), emotional quotient (EQ), efficacy beliefs could play a role which individually and /or collectively cause variations in the way a person responds to stress.

Information Systems Personnel have a need to constantly keep themselves up to date with the latest ideas, innovations and technology, in order to meet the users' expectations, which adds pressure to their work demands (Lim & Teo, 1996). Uncertainties and abstractness are two important properties of technology that influence human behaviour (Mullarkey, 1997). The resultant modification of behaviour when faced with threats from these properties may lead to stress.

In addition, insights from the area of cognitive, affective and behavioural reactions of individuals to technology could be borrowed and incorporated in the area of stress research. Perceived behavioural control encompasses perceptions of resource and technology facilitating conditions, as well as perceptions of ability, or self-efficacy. Research in the area of Information Systems has demonstrated a strong link between self-efficacy and individual reactions to computing technologies, in terms of learning to use computers and computer software (Compeau *et al.* 1999). Hence it is worthwhile to study the role of self-efficacy, more particularly computer self-efficacy (Venkatesh & Morris, 2000) and personal outcome expectancies, as moderators in the study of stress among ISP.

Self-efficacy with respect to information technology use will be an influencing factor in decisions that concern the kind of technology to be adopted, and efficient use of the chosen technology. Certain demographic variables such as education and domain specific knowledge can play a crucial role in determining self-efficacy and hence influence technology acceptance and usage preference (Venkatesh & Morris, 2000).

Yet another important factor that determines preferences, intensity of usage (Venkatesh & Morris, 2000) and associated comfort levels that may have a profound effect on technology resultant stress is prior computer experience. Research also suggests that computer attitudes and anxiety are influenced by prior experiences with computers (Bradley & Russel, 1997; Colley *et al.* 1994; Rozell & Gardner, 2000). Prior computer experience determines the computer attitudes and anxiety. Also research has shown that positive attitudes predispose people towards using computers while negative attitudes contribute to computer avoidance (Rozell & Gardner, 2000). In addition, people who experienced negative attitudes have been found to have lower computer self-efficacy as well (Rozell & Gardner, 2000). Probably, the age at which the exposure to computer occurs in combination with the frequency of exposure determines the intensity of usage and the ease with computers, which may account for the individual variation in personal stress levels.

In particular, software professionals in the development division are involved in developing user-oriented technologies, where the role of client or the end-user is very significant. Clients for software companies are typically global in nature, drawn from various cultures with each culture differing significantly from one another in terms of task approach, orientation and communication and presentation style. Hence every single interaction, with the client beginning from obtaining precise information on user's expectation, system specification, time constraints, existing system infrastructure of the client, depends on the degree of communication of the client in terms of content, clarity and precision. The successful development of the software (technology) largely depends on these interactions. The variations in the cultural approach to task performance, client negotiations and job specifications may be potential antecedents for stress, especially for ISP, who are basically technology users or innovators, with very little exposure to cross-cultural management.

Also, sending software professionals for projects abroad, or body shopping of ISP is a common feature in developing countries, wherein the ISP are sent typically to developed countries of the clients to work on off-shore projects for a certain period of time. This transition is considered a motivating factor that provides overseas opportunities for the ISP by the organizations. This kind of transition from developing countries to developed countries and back to the parent country for short periods of time may result in stress.

Unlike other engineering disciplines, where the number of women is less, there is a considerable presence of women in the Information Systems sector. Research has pointed out that women in countries like Singapore have a need to prove themselves in the male dominated profession (Jick & Mitz, 1985; Martocchio & O'Leary, 1989) and this has placed enormous stress on the female professionals in terms of workload and performance. Hence, female software professionals in Singapore have reported significantly higher mean scores than male software professionals in certain areas such as role ambiguity, job induced tension, dissatisfaction and intention to quit (Lim & Teo, 1999). It would be interesting to study the difference in stress among male and female software professionals in India.

Limitations and Future Research Directions

This paper is an exploratory attempt at conceptually identifying certain technological and environmental antecedents of stress among software professionals. In addition, the paper proposes that research in factors that influence the stress-strain process, especially in technological environment like computer self-efficacy that determines technology acceptance decisions, prior exposure to computers and such related factors be attempted to understand the stress-strain process in a high technology environment.

The factors mentioned in the above discussion are purely speculative in nature and their worthiness have to be established in empirical research. There is also further scope to expand this work using personal variables like autonomy, locus of control, perception of control, need for clarity and achievement motivation of the individual. Longitudinal studies, conducted over a considerable period of time, that involve stress-bursting interventions would be able to provide long-term solutions to the problems of ISP in combating occupational stress.

REFERENCES

Bandura, A. (1982). Self-efficacy mechanism in human agency. *American Psychologist, 37,* 122-147.

Beehr, T.A. (1976). Perceived situational moderators of the relationship between subjective role ambiguity and role strain. *Journal of Applied Psychology, 61*, 35-40.

Beehr, T.A. (1987). The themes of social-psychological stress in work organizations: From roles to goals. In A.W. Riley and S.J. Zacaro (Ed.), *Occupational stress and organizational effectiveness* (pp. 71-102). New York: Praeger Press.

Beehr, T.A., Stacy, B.A., Murray, M.A. & Jex, S.M. (1996). Work stress and coworker support as predictors of individual strain and job performance. Paper presented at the annual meeting of the Academy of Management, Cincinnati, OH.

Beehr, T.A. (1998). An organizational psychology meta-model of occupational stress. In C.L. Cooper (Ed.), *Theories of Organizational Stress* (pp. 6-27). NewYork: Oxford University Press.

Bogg, J. & Cooper, C.L. (1995). Job satisfaction, mental health and occupational stress among senior civil servants. *Human Relations, 48,* 327-341.

Bradley, G. & Russel, G. (1997). Computer experience, school support and computer anxieties. *Educational Psychology, 17,* 267- 284.

Brod, C. (1984). *Technostress.* London: Addisson – Wesly.

Compeau, D.R. & Higgins, C.A. (1995). Computer self-efficacy: Development of a measure and initial test. *MIS Quarterly, 19,* 189-211.

Compeau, D.R. Higgins, C.A. & Huff, S. (1999). Social cognitive theory and individual reactions to computing technology: A longitudinal study. *MIS Quarterly, 23,* 145-158.

Colley, A.M., Gale, M.T. & Harris, T.A. (1994). Effects of gender role identity and experience on computer attitude components. *Journal of Educational Computing Research, 10,* 129-137.

Cooper, C. L. & Payne, R. (1991). *Personality and stress: Individual differences in the stress process.* London: John Wiley & Sons Ltd.

Fenlason, K.J., Johnson, J. & Beehr, T.A. (1997). Social support, stressors and strains: Support for a cognitive model of job stress. In J.I. Sanchez (Chair), *Understanding the role of social support in the process of work stress: The missing links.* Symposium presented at the Annual meeting of the Society for Industrial and Organizational Psychology, Inc., St. Louis, MO.

Fisher, C.D. & Gitelson, R. (1983). A meta-analysis of the correlates of role conflict and ambiguity. *Journal of Applied Psychology, 68,* 320- 333.

Frese, M. (1987). Human-Computer interaction in the office. In C.L. Cooper and I.T.Robertson (Ed.), *International Review of Industrial and Organizational Psychology.* London: Wiley.

Fujigaki,Y. (1993). Stress analysis: A new perspective on peopleware. *American Programmer, 6,* 33-38.

Furuyama, T., Arai, Y. & Lio, K. (1993). Fault generation model and mental stress effect analysis. In *Proceedings of the Second International Conference on Achieving Quality in Software,* Venice, Oct 18-20.

Ganster, D.C. (1987). Type A behavior and occupational stress. In J.M. Ivancevish and D.C. Ganster (Ed.), *Job Stress: From theory to suggestion,* (pp. 61-84). New York: Haworth Press.

Gupta, N. & Beehr, T.A. (1979). Job stress and employee behaviors. *Organizational Behavior and Human Performance, 23,* 373-387.

Glass, R.L. (1997). The ups and downs of programmer stress. *Communications of the ACM, 40,* 17-19.

Ivanecevich, J., Napier, H. & Wetherbe, J. (1983). Occupational stress, attitudes and health problems among information systems professionals, *Communications of the ACM.*

Jackson, S. E. & Schuler, R. S. (1985). A meta-analysis and conceptual critique of research on role ambiguity and role conflict in work settings. *Organizational Behavior and Human Decision Processes, 36,* 16-78.

Jex, S.M & Bliese, P.D. (1999). Efficacy beliefs as a moderator of the impact of work-related stressors: A multi-level study. *Journal of Applied Psychology, 84,* 349-361.

Jex, S.M. & Gudanowski, D.M. (1992). Efficacy beliefs and work stress: An exploratory study. *Journal of Organizational Behavior, 13,* 509-517.

Jex S.M., Beehr, T.A. & Roberts, C.K. (1992). The meaning of stress items to survey respondents. *Journal of Applied Psychology, 77,* 623- 628.

Jick, T.D. & Mitz, L.F. (1985). Sex differences in work stress. *Academy of Management Review, 10,* 408-420.

Kahn, R.L. & Byosiere, P. (1992). Stress in organizations. In M.D. Dunnette (Ed.), *Handbook of industrial and organizational psychology, Vol. 3 (2nd edition)* (pp. 571-650). Palo Alto, CA: Consulting Psychologists Press, Inc.

Kaufman, G.M. & Beehr, T.A. (1986). Interactions between job stressors and social support: Some counterintuitive results. *Journal of Applied Psychology, 71,* 522-526.

Kaufman, G.M. & Beehr, T.A. (1989). Occupational stressors, individual strains, and social supports among police officers. *Human Relations, 42, 18,* 5-197.

Kaluzniacky, E. (2000). Work stress factors among Information Systems professionals in Manitoba. (www.ncf.ca/itwellness/manitoba.html.)

Leong, C.S., Furham, A. & Cooper, C.L. (1996). The moderating effect of organizational commitment on the occupational stress outcome relationship. *Human Relations, 49,* 1345-1363.

Lim, V.K.G. & Teo, T.S.H. (1996). Occupational stress among IT personnel in Singapore. *International Journal of Management, 13,* 456-465.

Lim, V.K.G., & Teo, T.S.H. (1999). Occupational stress and IT personnel in Singapore: Factorial dimensions and differential effects. *International Journal of Information Management, 19,* 277-299.

Martocchio, J.L. & O'Leary, A. M. (1989). Sex differences in occupational stress: A meta-analytic review. *Journal of Applied Psychology, 74,* 495- 501.

McGee, M. K. (1996). Burnout. *Information Week, 569,* 34-40.

Moore, J.L. (2000). One road to turnover: An examination of work exhaustion in technology professionals, *MIS Quarterly, 24,* 141-168.

Mullarkey, S., Jackson, P.R., Wall, T.D., Wilson, J.R. & Taylor, S.M. (1997). The impact of technology characteristics and job control on worker mental health. *Journal of Organizational Behavior, 18,* 471-489.

O' Driscoll, M.P. & Beehr, T.A. (1994). Supervisor behaviors, role stressors and uncertainty as predictors of personal outcomes for subordinates. *Journal of Organizational Behavior, 15,* 141-155.

Pardine, P.A. (1987). Empirical test of a cognitive model of work stress. Paper presented at the annual meeting of the Eastern Psychological Association, April.

Parkes, K.R. (1991). Locus of control as moderator: An explanation for additive *versus* interactive findings in the demand- discretion model of work stress? *British Journal of Psychology, 82,* 291-312.

Riggs, M.L. & Knight, A.K. (1994). The impact of perceived group success-failure on motivational beliefs and attitudes: A causal model. *Journal of Applied Psychology, 79,* 755-766.

Rozell, E.J., & Gardner, W.L. (2000). Cognitive, motivation and affective processes associated with computer-related performance: A path analysis. *Computers in Human Behavior,* ***16***, 199-222.

Sanchez, J .I., & Brock, P. (1996). Outcomes of perceived discrimination among Hispanic employees: Is diversity management a luxury or a necessity? *Academy of Management Journal, 39,* 704-719.

Sethi, V., Meinert, D., Barrier, T., King, R.C. & Sethi, V. (1997). A preliminary examination of stressors in information systems personnel. In *Proceedings of the Conference of Association of Information Systems,* Indianapolis, Aug 15-17.

Spector, P.E. (1988). Development of the work locus of control scale. *Journal of Occupational Psychology, 61,* 335-340.

Spector, P.E. (1998). An organizational psychology meta-model of occupational stress. In C.L. Cooper (Ed.), *Theories of organizational stress* (pp.153-169). New York : Oxford University Press.

Spector, P.E., Dwyer, D.J. & Jex, S.M. (1988). Relation of job stressors to affective, health and performance outcomes: A comparison of multiple data sources. *Journal of Applied Psychology, 73,* 11-19.

Venkatesh, V. & Morris, M. (2000). Why don't men ever stop to ask for directions? Gender, social influence and their role in technology acceptance and usage behavior. *MIS Quarterly, 24,* 115-139.

Weiss, M. (1983). The effects of work stress and social support on information systems managers. *MIS Quarterly, 7,* 29-43.

16

Organizational Culture and its Relationship with Performance and Success

KAILASH B. L. SRIVASTAVA

Introduction

Executives from today's most successful organizations strongly believe and devote significant time and resources toward ensuring that their organizational culture drives performance and produces business results. In today's competitive market place, which is continuously changing in an uncertain environment, it is necessary to focus on culture as a critical lever for success. Managers are relating the success of organizations with the current conceptions of culture. It has become inevitable for organizations to develop and maintain a strong culture for better performance and to compete in a changing business environment.

The concept of culture has entered into organizational literature from anthropological and sociological sources but there are certain conceptual problems related to the study of culture regarding the components and dimensions of culture, and the various assumptions about culture in organizational set-up. Various authors have tried to conceptualize culture as shared qualities, values, and beliefs (Parsons, 1970, Sathe, 1983, Deal & Kennedy, 1982; Deshpande & Webster, 1989; Chatman & Jehn, 1994), meaning structures (Silverman, 1970), myth and rituals (Trice & Bayer, 1983), and social structures (Harris, 1980). Thus, descriptions of culture have focused on a number of concepts such as ideologies, beliefs, the basic philosophy, values and norms and tangible signs (artefacts) of organizational members and their behaviours.

Many authors have proposed a number of dimensions such as a firm orientation to customers, employees, results and achievements, innovation, productivity and costs, and employee orientation to technology and company. Deal and Kennedy (1982) proposed two dimensions—the degree of risk orientation and speed of feedback on actions taken. Kilman, Saxton & Serpa (1985) also proposed two dimensions, which focus on technology and human being, and short to long-term goal. Schein (1985) introduced certain assumptions about the culture, and tried to relate it with the environment, reality, time and space, human nature, and human relationship. Some authors have identified such dimensions as innovation, stability, respect for people, outcome, detail, and team orientation (Chatman & Jehn, 1994; Hofstede, Neuijen, Ohayv & Sanders, 1990; Sackmann, 1992; Deshpande, Farley & Webster, 1993). Thus it can be said that various dimensions proposed by these authors are contingent ones, and relevant for different purposes, and there is a need to explore various dimensions of culture.

Assumptions about the culture in organizational settings are based on managerial perceptions. Two most widely shared assumptions in the literature are that it is homogenous and shared among organizational members, and at the same time leader generated and leader centered. The first assumption may not hold true in complex organizations, and the second one reflects biases in managerial research. Thus, it is necessary to generate empirical based knowledge by examining the structure and dynamics of culture in organizational settings. It can also be said that in any organization, members may have common perceptions, but realistically all members may not do so to the same degree. There may be a dominant culture within the organization, which is shared by a majority of members such as a set of core values, and a sub-culture shared by only a group of members in various departments or units of the same organization, which is reflected in their experiences (Robbins, 1988).

Organizational performance has been related with the type of culture an organization has such as a strong culture or a weak culture. Founders and the policy makers create a culture in the organization where people would be most productive and effective. The leaders and policy makers form a core group to create the cultural values, norms, and the climate needed for success. All the members of the organization try to maintain a strong culture by sharing the core values. It also depends upon the commitment, socialization process, and on the job experiences of the members. Strong and weak cultures have their impact on employee behaviour. If employees accept the core values then they would have greater commitment leading to strong culture. It reflects a very high agreement among the members about what the organization stands for. The culture is transmitted through the process of socialization where employees come to know about its structure, processes, systems, norms, and expected behaviour patterns. Culture is transmitted through stories (narrative events about the founders and success stories), rituals (repetitive sequences of activities expressing the core values), languages, symbols and gestures.

Many authors have established and supported the hypothesis that successful organizations have a strong culture (Deal & Kennedy, 1982; Kilman, Saxton & Serpa, 1985; Ouchi & Price, 1978; Pascale, 1985; Peters & Waterman, 1982; Schein, 1985; Weick, 1985; Deshpande, Farley & Webster, 1993; Chatman & Jehn, 1994). Most of these studies are at the conceptual level, and have not measured either performance or how it is related to culture. Some studies have tried to relate culture with certain organizational outcomes. Jenstor and Bigler (1986) reported a significant relationship between cultural pattern and the pursuit of organizational strategies. Dunn, Norburn, and Birley (1985) found a positive correlation between marketing effectiveness and customer oriented culture. Amsa (1986) showed a definite relationship between loitering behaviour (unauthorized rest breaks) and company beliefs about the desirability of discipline. Some studies have tried to relate culture with the financial performance of a firm (Gordon & DiTomaso, 1992; Taylor & Bowers, 1973). Denison (1984) found that certain traits such as organization of work, emphasis on human resources, decision-making process, and coordination were significantly correlated with company's standardized return on investment. Deshpande, Farley, and Webster (1993) found that higher level of business performance were most closely associated with a market culture, one that emphasizes the values of flexibility and innovation. Marcoulides and Heck (1993) found that organizational culture significantly affects the performance. These studies confirm the notion that the culture of a firm is related to organizational performance and individual success. Research evidences also indicate that variations in cultural values have significant impact on employee turnover and employees' job performance (Sheridan, 1992). Thus it can be said that most admired firms have a strong organizational culture, and a strong culture can facilitate better organizational and individual performance.

The present study examined the strength of organizational culture and its relationship with organizational performance, personal effectiveness, perceived success, comparative success, pay, and promotion. Organizational culture was conceptualized and quantified in terms of widely shared and strongly held values. Organizational performance was measured in terms of financial performance of the firm such as profit after tax, surplus, and sales growth. Personal effectiveness and success were conceptualized in terms of perceived effectiveness and success of the individual on the job. Comparative success was measured in the terms of relative success. It was supplemented by the objective data related with pay, and promotions received by the study respondents. In order to examine the nature of the relationship among these variables and differences in their perception, the following hypotheses were proposed.

H_1 : The organizational culture would be positively related with organizational performance, personal effectiveness, success, pay and promotion.

H_2 : There would be differences in the perception of role incumbents for all the variables across hierarchy.

METHOD

Sample

The sample consisted of hundred and fifty executives (150) drawn from six private sector organizations located in Mumbai (Maharashtra), and Surat (Gujarat). Organizations employing at least 400 people were included in this study. The executives belonged to three different levels of hierarchy (lower, middle and higher). The decision to include only these organizations was guided mainly by approachability and convenience factors. Thus at the best we could adhere to purposive sampling procedure in the selection of the organization, but the selection of executives was done randomly form these organizations.

Measures

The data from executives were collected through a structured interview schedule. Several scales were used to measure various underlying concepts. Some of these measures were specially designed for this study. A total of six variables, namely organizational culture, personal effectiveness, perceived success, comparative success, pay, and promotion were measured.

Organizational culture was measured by using a questionnaire consisting of 30 items. It measured managers' perceptions of how their organizations operate, and the values that drive the behaviour of those working in the organization. It included a number of dimensions such as risk taking, rewards and recognition system, individual initiative, direction, conflict tolerance, communication pattern, and management support.

Personal effectiveness was measured using a nine items questionnaire, and had dimensions such as how effective individuals are in completing the task assigned to them.

Success was measured by adopting Rao's scale (Rao & Pareek, 1986), and consisted of eight items. It measured to what extent employees perceived themselves successful on the job.

Comparative success scale consisted of five items. It measured the extent to which the employees perceive themselves successful compared to others in the organization.

Measures on pay and promotion were also obtained from the respondents. It was then converted in to grades using a five-point scale depending upon the level of pay and number of promotions received.

Results and Discussion

To recapitulate, the objectives of this study were to understand the strength of culture and its relationship with certain dependent variables such as personal effectiveness, perceived success, comparative success, pay, promotion, and organizational performance. The data were analyzed in univariate perspectives and all the variables were treated as a single construct. The pattern of relationship among these variables was examined. ANOVA was computed to examine the differences in the perception of role incumbents among these variables across hierarchy. On the basis of the strength of the culture, organizations were classified into two categories as having a strong culture and a weak culture by ranking the mean score on organizational culture. An objective parameter related to the organizational performance such as profit, sales turnover and reserves were taken for three successive years to find out whether organizational culture was positively related with organizational performance.

Strength of Organizational Culture and its Relationship with Dependent Measures

In order to measure the strength of organizational culture in six private sector organizations, total score on organizational culture was obtained and mean score was calculated ($x = 93$). This mean score was used as a cut-off point to classify organizations into having a strong or a weak culture. On the basis of these results, four organizations were classified as having a strong culture and two organizations as having a weak culture (see Table 16.1).

Table 16.1 : Mean Score on Organizational Culture at different levels of hierarchy

Organization No.	Mean Score	High Level	Middle Level	Low Level
1	113.6	124.60	112.58	102.3
2	98.56	97	100.30	98.40
3	88.65	101.330	85.30	79.34
4	98.57	102	96.34	97.39
5	88.27	93	88.39	83.42
6	95.78	98	94.36	95.40

From the table 16.1 we observe that mean score of two organizations having a weak organizational culture was less than the average mean score of organizational culture taken together for all organizations and four organizations had above average score. The data were also analyzed to find out the difference across hierarchy for organizational culture, which showed that perception of organizational culture was comparatively better among higher level executives compared to lower and middle level executives, except in one organization where middle and lower level executives had scored better on culture compared to higher level executives. The results showed that the top management was more committed in accepting the core values and this may be due to reward and recognition achieved.

The results of the inter-correlation among these variables showed that organizational culture had a positive relationship with personal effectiveness, perceived success, comparative success, pay, and promotion (see Table 16.2).

These results suggest that a strong organizational culture would result in better performance of employees and employees would be more productive, and successful on the job. A set of core values adopted by the employees in such organizations can make a difference in their perception about themselves and their success in careers. Personal effectiveness was also positively related with individual success, comparative success, pay, and promotion. It means that a better performing employee perceives himself more successful compared to others at his level. He is being rewarded monetarily through a better pay packet, and also gets an opportunity to grow up in the hierarchy. Similarly a positive relationship of perceived individual success with pay and promotion suggests that a successful career is associated with reward, advancement, and recognition at the work place.

Table 16.2 : Mean, SD, and Inter-correlations among Variables

Variables	Mean	SD	Organizational Culture	Perceived effectiveness	Perceived success	Comparative success	Pay	Promotion
Organizational culture	93	11.18	-	.30**	.33**	.31**	.43**	.47**
Perceived effectiveness	34.9	2.3	-	-	.30**	.17*	.34**	.43**
Perceived success	30.1	4.2	-	-	-	.23**	.40**	.57**
Comparative success	16.9	5.6	-	-	-	-	.43**	.55**
Pay	3.69	3.9	-	-	-	-	-	.51**
Promotion	.21	2.4	-	-	-	-	-	-

Degrees of Freedom = 148, Significance Level * = .05 ** = .01.

Thus, it can be said that organizational culture has its impact on individual effectiveness and success. Sheridan's (1992) results supplement these findings that depending upon the strength of culture in the organization performance varies, and a strong culture is positively related with better employee performance. Strong leaders, a sense of sharedness, and intensity create strong cultures. People in such organizations share the same core values and show their commitment towards these core values. Organizations propagate these values through orientation programmes, word to mouth, and day-to-day work habits. Organizations also give promotion, raises, recognition and other form of rewards, such as profit sharing, stock ownership etc., to those who adhere to these core values.

Differences in Perception Across Hierarchy for all Variables

In order to find out the difference in perception among the role incumbents across hierarchy, F-statistic was used. The results are presented in Table 16.3.

Table 16.3 : ANOVA Differences in Perception of the Role Incumbents across Hierarchy

A. Organizational Culture					
Source	**S S**	**DF**	**MS**	**F**	**P**
Between groups	15511.5	2	7755.58		
Within groups	2910.96	147	19.8	39.16	.01
Total	18422.2	149			
B. Perceived Effectiveness					
Between groups	109.93	2	54.96		
Within groups	80.77	147	.54	100	.01
Total	191.7	149			
C. Perceived Success					
Between groups	1058.54	2	529.27		
Within groups	4067.2	147	27.66	19.13	.01
Total	5125.74	149			
D. Comparative Success					
Between groups	459.06	2	229.53		
Within groups	7110.67	147	48.37	4.74	.01
Total	7569.73	149			
E. Pay					
Between groups	103.0	2	51.5		
Within groups	2311.32	147	1.57	32.72	.01
Total	2414.32	149			

F. Promotion					
Between groups	20.84	2	10.42	13.51	.01
Within groups	113.3	147	.77		
Total	134.14	149			

It was found that perception of organizational culture at higher, middle and lower level executives differed significantly. These results are also supported by average mean score on organizational culture at different levels of hierarchy. Similarly, results also showed that there were significant differences in the perception of employees at different levels for perceived effectiveness, perceived success, pay and promotion. Thus, it can be said that a person at a higher level in the organizational hierarchy experiences being more effective and successful compared to those who are below in the hierarchy as he gets better monetary reward and recognition. These differences in the perception stem from the fact that sharing a set of core values is more dominant in the people working at the higher levels in the hierarchy, and there is a strong commitment among them. There is a need to propagate these core values down the line so that people working at middle and lower levels in the organizational hierarchy also share them, and have strong commitment toward these values. Organizations should also follow such a policy of reward and recognition so that members across the hierarchy get the benefit and it would encourage them to share the core values more intensely.

Culture and Organizational Performance

Comparative organizational performance for three successive years (1995-96, 1996-97 & 1997-98) was used to find out whether companies with strong cultures were consistently performing better. The financial performances of the firms were analyzed in terms of sales, reserves and profit after tax. These three parameters were used to measure the firm's performance. The results showed that those organizations that had a strong culture, there had been a considerable increase in the sales, reserves and surplus, and profit after tax compared to those organizations that had a weak culture, as there was no significant increase in sales, reserve, surplus, and profit after tax. These results further support the notion that a strong organizational culture is predictive of financial performance in subsequent years. Thus it can be said that both the hypotheses which were proposed were true as organizational culture was positively related with organizational performance, personal effectiveness, individual success, pay and promotion. There were significant differences in the perception of role incumbents for all these variables across the hierarchy, which confirms our second hypothesis. Companies with strong culture can be characterized as highly dynamic and fast growing. They have also adapted themselves with changing economic environment in order to remain competitive. Organizations should try to adopt policies and systems, which can facilitate the development of a strong culture.

Conclusion

On the basis of these results it can be said that organizational culture may be an important predictor of employees' job performance, success, and organizational performance. Organizations having a strong culture had better financial performance, and people also shared a set of core values created and nurtured by its leaders. Perception of culture across hierarchy varied significantly and this should be taken care of by the top management in order to make sure that everyone in the organization irrespective of their position in the hierarchy shares those core values and has commitment. Organizations should also try to develop and maintain a strong culture by following certain practices such as recognition and promotion of individuals who perform their job well. There is a need to develop an appropriate culture, which can produce consistently positive results, and is also shared by the organizational members.

REFERENCES

Amsa, P. (1986). Organizational culture and work group behaviour: An empirical study. *Journal of Management Studies, 23,* 347-362.

Chatman, J.A. & Jehn, K.A. (1994). Assessing the relationship between industry characteristics and organizational culture: How different can you be? *Academy of Management Journal, 31,* 522-553.

Deal, T. & Kennedy, A. (1982). *Corporate cultures: The rites and rituals of corporate life.* Reading Mass: Addison- Wesley.

Denison, D.R. (1984). Bring corporate culture to the bottom line. *Organizational Dynamics, 13,* 5-22.

Deshpande, R. & Webster, F.E. (1989). Organizational culture and marketing: Defining research agenda. *Journal of Marketing, 53,* 3-15.

Despande, R., Farley, J.U. & Webster, Jr. F.E. (1993). Corporate culture, customer orientation, and innovativeness in Japanese firms: A quadred analysis. *Journal of Marketing, 57,* 23-37.

Dunn, M.G., Norburn, D. & Birley, S. (1985). Corporate culture. *International Journal of Advertising, 4,* 65-73.

Gordon, G. & DiTomaso, N. (1992). Predicting corporate performance from organizational culture, *Journal of Management Studies, 29,* 783-793.

Haris, L. (1980). Analysis of a paradoxical logic: A case study. *Family Process, 19,* 19-33.

Hofstede, G., Neuijen, B., Ohayv, D. & Sanders, G. (1990). Measuring organizational culture: A qualitative and quantitative study across twenty cases. *Administrative Science Quarterly, 35,* 286-316.

Jenstor, P.V. & Bigler, W.R.J. (1986). *Organizational culture in different strategic contexts: A study in the banking industry.* Paper presented at the Conference on Strategies for Financial Institution, London.

Kilman, R.H., Saxton, M. J. & Serpa, R. (1985). Introduction: Five key issues in understanding and changing culture. In R.H. Kilman, M.J. Saxton, R. Serpa & Associates (Eds.), *Gaining control of the corporate culture.* (pp. 1-16). San Fransisco: Jossey Bass.

Marcoulides, G. A. & Heck, R.H. (1993). Organizational culture and performance: Proposing and testing a model. *Organizational Science, 4,* 209-224.

Ouchi, W. & Price, R. (1978). Hierarchies, class and theory Z: A new perspective on organizational development. *Organizational Dynamics, 7,* 25-44.

Parsons, T. (1970). Culture and social systems revisited. In S.A. Tyler (Ed.), *Cognitive anthropology.* (pp. 61-89). New York: Holt Rinehart & Winston.

Pascale, R. (1985). The paradox of 'corporate culture': Reconciling ourselves to socialization. *California Management Review, 27,* 26-41.

Peters, T. & Waterman, R. H. (1982). *In search of excellence.* New York: Harper & Row.

Rao, T.V. & Pareek, U. (1986). *Behaviour processes in organizations: Concepts and cases.* Oxford University Press: New Delhi.

Robbins, S. P. (1988). *Organizational behaviour.* New Delhi: Prentice-Hall of India.

Sackman, S.A. (1992). Cultures and sub-cultures: An analysis of organizational knowledge. *Administrative Science Quarterly, 37,* 140-161.

Safford, G. S. (1988). Culture traits, strength and organizational performance: Moving beyond strong cultures. *Academy of Management Review, 13,* 546-558.

Sathe, V. (1983). Implications of corporate culture: A manager's guide to action. *Organizational Dynamics, 12,* 5-23.

Schein, E. H. (1985). *Organizational culture and leadership.* San Fransisco: Jossey Bass.

Sheridan, J. E. (1992). Organizational culture and employee retention. *Academy of Management Journal, 29,* 1036-1056.

Silverman, D. (1970). *The theory of organizations: A sociological framework.* London: Heinemann.

Taylor, J. & Bowers, D. (1973). *The survey of organizations.* Englewood Cliffs: NJ Simon & Schuster.

Trice, H.M. & Bayer, J. M. (1983). Using six organizational rites to change culture. In R. H. Kilmann, M. J. Saxton, R. Serpa, & Associates (Eds.), *Gaining control of the corporate culture.* (pp. 759-769). San Fransisco: Jossey Bass.

Weick, K. (1985). The significance of corporate culture. In P. Frost, L. Moore, M.Louis, C. Lundberg & J. Martin (Eds.), *Organizational culture.* (pp. 381-390). Beverley Hills, Calgary: Sage.

Notes on Contributors

T.S. Saraswathi is Professor in the Department of Human Development and Family Studies at M.S. University of Baroda. She has published widely on child development and related fields. Her major publications include *Developmental psychology in India: An annotated bibliography; Human development and family studies: An agenda for research and policy* (co-edited with B.Kaur); *Capturing complexities: A methodological study of women, households and development* (co-edited with an international team); *The handbook of cross-cultural psychology, 2nd ed.* (co-edited with an international team); and *Culture, socialization, and human development: Theory, research and applications in India* (edited).

Bhargavi V. Davar is a freelance researcher based in Pune and is presently on a Homi Bhabha fellowship to study community mental health in India. She has been actively involved with women's groups in creating a context of discussion and research on women and mental health in India. Bhargavi's research concerns include the social and political bases of mental health sciences, especially as it relates to gender, culture and mental illness. Her major publications include *Psychoanalysis as a human science: Beyond foundationalism* (co-authored), *Mental health of Indian women: A feminist agenda,* and *Mental health from a gender perspective* (edited), all published by Sage. Founder of the Bapu Trust, Bhargavi is also the editor of *Aaina,* a newsletter pertaining to mental health advocacy issues.

Ajit K. Mohanty is Professor of Psychology at Utkal

University, and has been the Coordinator of the Centre of Advanced Study in Psychology in the same university. He received his doctoral degree from University of Alberta, Canada where he was a Killam Scholarship awardee. He was also a recipient of the Fulbright Post-doctoral Fellowship at the University of Wisconsin, Madison. His major area of research concern is psycholinguistics including multilingualism, language acquisition and reading development. In addition to publication of papers in national and international journals, he has authored the book *Bilingualism in a multilingual society* and edited the volume *Perspectives on indigenous psychology.* He has been President and Convener of the National Academy of Psychology (India).

Jyoti Verma is Professor of Psychology at Patna University. Recipient of gold medals from Banaras Hindu University and Patna University, Dr. Verma has been Indian Council of Social Sciences Doctoral Fellow at A. N. Sinha Institute of Social Studies, Patna and was awarded the Young Scientist Group's Award by the Indian Science Congress Association. She was also awarded the USA Government Fulbright Post-Doctoral Fellowship in Psychology and visited Paris under the Indo-French Social Scientists' Exchange Programme and later at the invitation of the Maison des Sciences de L'homme, Paris. Dr. Verma was also selected for conducting a research on Indian Diaspora in France in October-November, 2000 by the French Ministry of Research & Higher Education. She has collaborated in a number of international research projects with European and American Universities. Dr. Verma has published around 40 papers and is Consulting Editor of a couple of international journals. Her research interests include cross-cultural psychology, psychological well being, Indian traditional thought and community development concerns.

Manas Kumar Mandal is presently an Associate Professor in the Department of Humanities & Social Sciences, Indian Institute of Technology, Kharagpur. He received his M.A. and Ph.D. degrees from Calcutta University and worked in Banaras Hindu University as a lecturer. His areas of specialization are social and clinical psychology. Dr. Mandal has over 60 international and 10 national publications and three books to his credit. Dr. Mandal was awarded University Gold medal, Young Scientist award, Career award, Fulbright fellowship (USA), Shastri fellowship (Canada), NSERC fellowship (Canada). He was also a visiting professor in Kyushu University, Japan.

Mithilesh Singh is currently Lecturer of Psychology at S.B.P.G. College at Badlapur, U.P. She has done her Master's from Banaras Hindu University, Varanasi and the major area of her research interest is experimental social psychology.

Sonali Bhatt-Marwaha is a Ph.D. research scholar in the Department of Psychology and parapsychology, Andhra University. She holds M.A. and M.Phil degrees from SNDT Women's University, Mumbai. Her current research interests are in the interface between philosophy, religion and psychology.

Mamata Verma is Senior Lecturer at the Department of Psychology, Gulab Devi Girls Post-graduate College, Ballia, Uttar Pradesh. She obtained her M.A. in Psychology from Mahatma Gandhi Kashi Vidyapeeth, Varanasi, and Ph.D. from the Department of Pediatrics, Institute of Medical Sciences, Banaras Hindu University. She is interested in the study of cognitive development of children, and is currently trying to examine the relative contribution of ontogenetic and socio-cultural factors to the development of cognitive functions. She has contributed some significant articles to journals in this area.

S.K. Upadhyay is Reader in the Department of Pediatrics, Institute of Medical Sciences, Banaras Hindu University. She obtained her M.A. and Ph.D. in Psychology from Banaras Hindu University. She is interested in studying the effect of environmental and nutritional factors on cognitive development of children. She has been associated in a number of research projects in this area and has published several papers in professional journals and edited volumes. Currently she is trying to apply psychological principles to the treatment of developmental problems of children.

R.C. Mishra is Professor of Psychology at Banaras Hindu University. A D. Phil. from Allahabad University, he has been Post-doctoral Research Fellow, Shastri Research Fellow and Visiting Professor at Queen's University, Canada. He has also been Visiting Professor at University of Geneva and Jean Piaget Archives, Switzerland. His principal interest is in cultural influence on human development, and he has contributed numerous articles to national and international journals, in the fields of cognition, acculturation, schooling, and cross-cultural studies and chapters to edited volumes including the *Handbook of Cross-Cultural Psychology* and *Handbook of Culture and Psychology.* He is the author of *Ecology, Acculturation and Psychological Adaptation: A Study of Adivasis in Bihar* (1996) and co-editor of *Psychology in Human and Social Development: Lessons from Diverse Cultures* (in press).

Aparna Vajpayee is U.G.C. Project Fellow at the Department of Psychology, Banaras Hindu University. She obtained her M.A. from Banaras Hindu University, Varanasi and Ph.D. from Chaudhary Charan Singh University, Meerut. She is interested in the study of psychological development of children of disadvantaged and weaker sections of the Indian society, and has done significant work with respect to intervention for their cognitive development. Her interests also include the study of physical and mental health problems of women of tribal communities. She has contributed several articles to edited volumes and research journals in the fields of cognition, health and community development.

George Kurian is presently with the Thapar Institute of Engineering and Technology's School of Management and Social Sciences, at Patiala. He acquired his M.A. from the University of Calicut and Ph.D in cognitive psychology from IIT, Kanpur working on language and thought in ontogeny and psychopathology. As a research officer at the Institute for Yoga and Consciousness, Visakhapatnam, during the late eighties, he concentrated on the study of the microgenetic approach to consciousness and laterality effects in cognitive control mechanisms and biorhythms. Presently he is working on a DST sponsored research programme on the time course in cognitive processing involved in Stroop-like effects and colour categorization and memory. His publications include referred commentaries and research reports in the *Behavioural and Brain Sciences, Journal of Neurolinguistics, Perceptual and Motor Skills, Psychological Studies,* to name a few. His contribution *Microgenesis of consciousness* is included in the Springer Series in Neuropsychology-Cognitive Microgenesis (Ed. Robert E. Hanlon) and published by Springer-Verlag.

Urmi Nanda Biswas is presently Reader in Psychology, M.S. University of Baroda, Vadodara. She holds a Doctoral degree in Psychology from Allahabad University in the area of Social and Organizational Psychology. She has published over two dozen research papers including monographs and book chapters in the area of social and organizational psychology. She has recently completed a major research project on Adolescent Sexuality sponsored by Population Council, New York along with Prof. C. N. Daftuar. Her research interests include work stress, women entrepreneurship, and poverty and social mobility. Prior to her career in teaching she was involved in a voluntary organisation in Ganjam, Orissa, engaged in education and livelihood programmes.

C. N. Daftuar, the only D.Litt. in Organizational Behaviour in India is presently Professor of Psychology, M.S. University of Baroda, Vadodara. His current research and intervention interest is in the area of Stress and Trauma. He has been a National Associate of UGC and was involved as visiting faculty/scientist to national and foreign institutes such as University of Technology, Loughborough, UK; Applied Psychology Unit, University of Cambridge, UK; Railway Staff College, Vadodara; Institute of Public Enterprises, Hyderabad; IIT, Kanpu;, Academy of HRD, etc. Besides publishing three books and over seventy research articles in reputed research journals, he has constructed more than a dozen psychological and behavioural tools including HRD and Training related instruments. He has edited research journals like, *Behaviourometric,* ASHRAM Newsletter and has been associated with several other Indian journals. He has founded Association of Stress Research and Management (ASHRAM) and Council of Behavioural Research. He is also interested in social service and has helped victims of Latur earthquake by counselling.

Abhilasha Srivastava is currently working for her D.Phil degree *on Low-income working women: Coping with Socio-economic Stressors and Quality of Family Life* at G.B.Pant Social Sciences Institute, Allahabad. She obtained her M.A. degree from Allahabad University and M.Phil from Indian Institute of Technology, Bombay, specializing in Planning and Development. She has taught psychology at Rajghat Besant School, Varanasi and has published a number of research papers and creative writings in journals and edited volumes.

Sadhana Natu, presently at Modern College, Pune has been teaching Psychology for the past 13 years at the graduate and post-graduate levels. Her doctoral research was on gender roles of young males. Her areas of interest include gender and psychology, women and mental health, youth issues, and mental health advocacy and has been associated with NGOs working on these issues. She is also associated with Bapu Trust, a Pune-based organization working for mental health advocacy.

Nalini Bikkina is an M. Phil in Psychology from Andhra University. Her areas of research interest include psychology applied to national development and endogenous development. She was the recipient of the *Durganand Sinha Memorial Research Presentation Award* (2000) for her paper titled *Kerala Model of Development: Some Socio-Psychological Fall-outs and Implications for Mental Health.*

Rachana Kulkarni is a doctoral candidate and UGC-Junior Research Fellow at the Department of Human Development and Family Studies, M. S. University of Baroda. She was awarded the 'Dr. Pramila Phatak Post-Graduate Research Fellowship for excellence in research' for her Masters' degree at the Department. Presently, she is working on her research on socio-cognitive frameworks and moral judgments within parent-adolescent relationships in Indian families.

Shagufa Kapadia is presently Reader in the Department of Human Development and Family Studies, M. S. University of Baroda. Her research interests include gender and cross-cultural perspectives in human development, specifically identity, self and social and moral reasoning in adolescence. Currently she is involved in an Indo-German collaborative cross-cultural project related to cultural rules for marriage partner selection.

K. S. Rajeswari is presently working for her doctoral degree in the Department of Humanities and Social Sciences, IIT, Madras.

R.N. Anantharaman is presently Professor of Psychology in the Department of Humanities and Social Sciences, Indian Institute of Technology, Madras.

Kailash B. L. Srivastava is currently Assistant Professor at Indian Institute of Technology, Kharagpur. He completed his master's degree in psychology from Gorakhpur University and Ph.D. from Indian Institute of Technology, Kanpur specializing in Organizational Behaviour and Personnel Management. He has teaching and research experience of about 10 years in various institutions like BITS, Pilani; T.A. Pai Management Institute, Manipal. He is currently engaged in research and consultancy in strategic HRD, performance management, industrial relations. He has published a number of papers in national and international journals, and has guided M.Tech and Ph.D students in the area of HRD.

INDEX